A Guide for the Idealist

A Guide for the Idealist is a must for young professionals seeking to put their idealism to work. Speaking to urban and regional planners and those in related fields, the book provides tools for the reader to make good choices, practice effectively, and find meaning in planning work. Built around concepts of idealism and realism, the book takes on the gap between the expectations and the constraints of practice. How to make an impact? How to decide when to compromise and when to fight for a core value?

The book advises on career "launching" issues: doubt, decision-making, assessing types of work and work settings, and career planning. Then it explains *principled adaptability* as professional style. Subsequent chapters address early-practice issues: being right, avoiding wrong, navigating managers, organizations and teams, working with mentors, and understanding the career journey. Underpinning these dimensions is a call for planners to reflect on what they are doing as they are doing it. The advice provided is based on the experience of a planning professor who has also practiced planning throughout his career. The book includes personal anecdotes from the author and other planners about how they launched and managed their careers, and discussion/reflection questions for the reader to consider.

Richard Willson is a professor in the Department of Urban and Regional Planning at Cal Poly Pomona, California. His scholarship is in planning theory, professional development, and transportation planning. Richard Willson holds a Ph.D. in urban planning from the University of California, Los Angeles, and is a Fellow of the American Institute of Certified Planners.

A GUIDE FOR THE IDEALIST

Launching and Navigating Your Planning Career

RICHARD WILLSON

Routledge
Taylor & Francis Group

NEW YORK AND LONDON

First published 2018
by Routledge
711 Third Avenue, New York, NY 10017

and by Routledge
2 Park Square, Milton Park, Abingdon, Oxon, OX14 4RN

Routledge is an imprint of the Taylor & Francis Group, an informa business

Library of Congress Cataloging-in-Publication Data
Names: Willson, Richard W., author.
Title: A guide for the idealist launching and navigating your planning
   career / Richard Willson.
Description: New York : Routledge, 2017. | Includes bibliographical
   references.
Identifiers: LCCN 2017015003 | ISBN 9781138085855 (hardback) |
   ISBN 9781138085879 (pbk.)
Subjects: LCSH: Planning—Vocational guidance. | Personality and
   occupation.
Classification: LCC HD87.5 .W55 2017 | DDC 307.1/2023—dc23
LC record available at https://lccn.loc.gov/2017015003

ISBN: 978-1-138-08585-5 (hbk)
ISBN: 978-1-138-08587-9 (pbk)
ISBN: 978-1-315-11119-3 (ebk)

Typeset in Bembo and Gill Sans
by Apex CoVantage, LLC

Cover art: Hot Wheels, 2010, Oil on canvas, by Richard Willson

To my mentor, Paul Niebanck

Contents

Figures

Tables

Boxes

Acknowledgments

This book is a collective project. It reflects insights I have gained from teaching and mentoring students over the last three decades. I am grateful to them for sharing their journey with me. Cal Poly Pomona has provided me the professional home for this work, supporting my natural inclination toward experiential learning. My experiences as planning practitioner and researcher have shaped these insights in ways that recognize the interplay of theory and practice in urban and regional planning.

Most of my research career has been devoted to transportation planning. Issues of theory and pedagogy also percolated over this time. The arc of the research is from solving transportation and land use problems, to thinking about how planners solve problems, and here, to enhancing planners' personal effectiveness. My interest and involvement in mentoring grew throughout this transition. This book is an expression of this evolution.

I have benefited from generous professional and academic mentors, including Frankie Banerjee, Ed Cornies, Peter Gordon, Margarita McCoy, Jean Monteith, Paul Niebanck, Donald Shoup, and Martin Wachs.

I am thankful for the assistance provided by former students who commented on drafts while I searched for themes and approach. They include alumni of the Department of Urban and Regional Planning: Brian Bulaya, Madai Castillo, Maryanne Cronin, Thanya Espericueta, Doug Feremenga, Hisano Hamada, Emily Hoyt, Eve Moir, and Patrick Prescott. Olivia Offutt served ably as a research assistant on the project. Commenters from other professional fields include Josh Boxer, Maya Efrati, Karen Febey, Pat Moore, and Keith Rohman.

I am indebted to my academic colleagues, who provided sage advice and/or generously commented on draft chapters, including Dina Abdulkarim, Howell Baum, Linda Dalton, Hollie Lund, Paul Niebanck, Samina Raja, Leone Sandercock, and Martin Wachs.

Thank you to professional colleagues in planning and publishing who advised me along the way, including Ed Cornies, Camille Fink, Samantha Gonzaga, Terri O'Connor, Marina Primorac, and Miguel Vazquez. I am grateful to Bobbie Albrecht, who provided an opportunity to gain feedback through blog postings on these topics on the American Planning Association website.

The book includes anecdotes that tell personal stories about planning and related fields. Thank you to text box writers Arianna Allahyar, Brian Bulaya, Andrea Burnside, Jaime Engbrecht, Doug Feremenga, Aiden Irish, Carlos Jiménez, Terri O'Connor, Mandy Park, Patrick Prescott, Keith Rohman, Miguel Vazquez, Karen Watkins, Al Zelinka, and three anonymous writers.

My wife, Robin Scherr, gave me invaluable insights and suggestions from her urban planning experience, along with strong support for the project. I would not be the person I am without her. My children, Maya Scherr-Willson and Jenna Millican, provided counsel and writing advice along the way. I acknowledge my late parents, William Anthes Willson and Jean Stokes McLean, from whom I gained commitments to curiosity, reason, and beauty.

The book's insights have been influenced by years of study with Rabbi Mordechai Finley. It reflects his commitment to clear thinking. And among writers, Jiddu Krishnamurti, Leonard Cohen, and Avivah Gottlieb Zornberg have introduced me to lyrical, poetic interpretation of the human condition.

Lastly, I am grateful to Routledge for their interest and enthusiasm for the project, and especially to Editors Kathryn Schell and Nicole Solano, as well as Editorial Assistant Krystal LaDuc.

Chapter 1

Introduction

A Guide for the Idealist's Path

Understand and speak,
practice human courage.

"Okay, fine."

That's what a longtime colleague said to me when I shared my vision for change. It was his friendly way of reminding me that a personal planning vision is only the beginning. The *path* to achieving the vision matters. It is one of discovery, personal and professional growth, and meaningful work. This book is a guide to put vision in action.

I see planning's mission as bringing repair to the world. Our concerns run the gamut, from fair administration of zoning rules to tackling global issues such as climate change or inequality. We recognize the interconnectedness of natural and human systems, and we seek to increase livability, reduce suffering, and regenerate the natural environment. Future-oriented, our commitment is to the public good.

As with many idealistic fields, planning practice is a worthwhile challenge. The world is not waiting for us to change it. Entrenched interests, ideological differences, prejudices, and ignorance may rule the day. Moreover, because change doesn't happen all at once, planning reform is a process, not a project with an end date. There's no future plateau where everything is settled. Planning has long time frames for implementation, ethical dilemmas, warring stakeholders, and red tape. Facing these obstacles unprepared can be deflating, or worse, disillusioning. It's a tragedy for the profession when a planner gives up out of frustration or cynicism. In the pages that follow, I explain a planning style called *principled adaptability* that cultivates creativity and resiliency. It leads planners to seize opportunities, practice effectively, and find meaning in their work.

The planner's journey has two aspects. The first aspect is the work itself. The following chapters offer methods for making good choices about experiences, jobs, and professional effectiveness. An intention to "do good" plays out in a dynamic environment with many influences and reactions. Planners do not control the enterprise, but we have influence. Change is a dynamic process. A short-run effort may produce a later win that can't be anticipated, such as when a community organizing effort produces a new community leader. Furthermore, the world evolves as planning work unfolds. Planners need a long-term view of their impact.

The second aspect of the planner's journey is growing as a person of character. I use this term to refer to a bundle of personal attributes that determine how we respond to situations and circumstances. Planners need reliability, grit, courage, empathy, integrity, honesty, clarity about values, and good work habits. For example, developing empathy makes planners better listeners who are able to understand community narratives. Planning's demand for ethical reasoning also enlarges the individual. What is the good? Do the ends justify the means? How does context influence what is right? Developing listening and ethical reasoning abilities engages the whole person, not just the planner's professional identity, and has benefits beyond professional work.

Today's Planners

The primary audience for the book is those starting out in planning and allied idealistic professions, although there are insights for all planners. In my experience, each generation of planners brings different strengths and weaknesses to the profession. My thinking is guided by the qualities I see among those starting in the field, which gives me cause for optimism. As with every generation, new planners seek meaningful work in the public interest. But rather than instinctively seeking a 'Planner 1' position in a local jurisdiction, they think broadly and creatively about the settings for their work. These new planners understand the regulatory function of planning, but they are also entrepreneurial in seeking a broader range of ways to make change. Livability, equity, and sustainability drive their vision.

This new generation of planners is skilled in networking and collaborating in a diverse workplace across race, ethnicity, religion, gender, sexual orientation, ability, and class. They engage networks in new ways to solve problems, find jobs, and support one another. Many are as likely to write an app as they are a plan, using advanced research and analysis capabilities. Resilient out of necessity, they face the economic challenges of a recovering job market and student loan debt. Some are the first in their family to attend college; others return to planning school with family responsibilities.

Appendix A summarizes research on the characteristics of the generation that is entering the planning profession. Despite media accounts of differences among generational groupings, properly controlled studies show that they are more alike than they are different. This book, therefore, is written for all planners, regardless of age.

How Do Idealism and Realism Meet in Planning?

The overarching theme of the book is engaging idealism and realism in planning practice. This stems from the utopian roots of planning (idealism) and the fact that our work is embedded in political, economic, and natural systems (realism).

Idealism has two common meanings: (1) to live by a high standard of behavior and (2) to form and pursue noble principles.[1] Both meanings apply to planners—standards of behavior are defined in the American Institute of Certified Planners (AICP) Code of Ethics, as are aspirational principles such as justice, sustainability, a long-term perspective, and recognizing the interrelatedness of things. In short, we are a reform-oriented profession.[2]

Planning's idealistic origins lie in reform movements related to healthy and safe housing, social justice, and blight removal, as well as utopian thinking. Those planners imagined a better future and wanted to make change. When I survey my students, most self-identify as idealists. Planning's critique of the status quo, its sense of possibility, and its desire for change are the roots of planners' passion. Idealism provides the orientation, purpose, and inspiration. It is what gets the planner out of bed in the morning. Of course, idealists could spend too much time living in their heads, imagining what could be rather than seeing what is, or being naïve about their worth.

Having said that, some planners are more naturally attuned to a practical approach to solving immediate problems. We might call them realists. *Realism* is commonly taken to mean the attitude or practice of accepting a situation as it is and being prepared to deal with it accordingly.[3] Planning demands realism because we hope that our ideas are implemented. Planning work isn't just imagining better cities, but rather seeking to improve real ones. That means realism about history, economics, the physical and social sciences, social relationships, power relationships, and feasibility of implementation. Realism can check an impractical or naïve vision born of idealism.

Planning's role in the democratic state reinforces the need for realism. For the most part, we are advisors to decision-makers, not the decision-maker. Planners rarely have the opportunity to do "clean sheet" planning with broad implementation power. Moreover, the objects of our work have a physical reality, as found in buildings, infrastructure, and environment conditions, and a human reality, as seen in social relations, communities, and conflict. Realism demands that we see things as they are.

The realist recognizes that planning occurs in a complex system of political, economic, and physical checks and balances. In engaging competing interests, possible improvement is often incremental, not systemic. Realism might suggest that perfect is the enemy of the good in a particular instance, meaning that holding out for the ideal solution could impede incremental actions that would move things in the right direction. Realism prefers the messiness of the democratic process to one where an idealist is in charge. Realists also ask: how does the idealist know his or her vision is correct? They are concerned about accountability, unanticipated impacts, and human self-interest.

Planning practice requires an *engagement* of idealism and realism. Effective planners deftly navigate this space—they can hold both concepts simultaneously and choose between them as circumstances warrant. For example, one of my mentors had a strong commitment to justice and fairness but was not naive about the dark side of human nature. She was able to hold idealism and realism simultaneously while resolving a specific issue. This is a form of pragmatism— using reason and logic to solve problems in specific instances, without being beholden to theory—but I think it is more than that.[4] A pragmatic approach produces incremental gains that lead to more systematic change. It lets planners realize that they did some good at the end of each day. My mentor didn't give up any of her idealism in dealing with the world as it is. *A Guide for the Idealist* provides tools to engage idealism and realism, and explains the principled adaptability planning style as a way forward.

Planning Compared to Other Professions

Planning theorist John Friedmann defines planning thusly: "planning . . . links scientific and technical knowledge to actions in the public domain. . . . Planning is not wholly concerned with either knowing or acting but rather serves as the link" (Friedmann, 1987, p. 38). This is planning's strength and a reason why idealism and realism are engaged in practice. As mentioned, the public domain is a complex stew of politics, different visions, and uncertainty about the efficacy of solutions.

Being the link between knowledge and action rather than *either* a source of expertise *or* a political facilitator means that we have a complicated task in establishing professional legitimacy as compared to narrowly defined professions. Indeed, planning's idealism/realism dimension differs significantly from its related professions. The three examples that follow illustrate the differences:

- **Urban geographers** generate knowledge about spatial relationships in cities and regions. Their spatial analyses inform research papers and government studies, so the quality of knowledge generated is paramount (realism). The work may be used to propose change, but geographers don't carry the proposal through the political process. That's what planners do.
- **Civil engineers** make change by applying technical knowledge to solve physical problems in the urban environment—roads, transit systems, water and sewer, power, etc. Quantitative determinations and standards show the best approach. Cost-effectiveness drives their work—designing infrastructure and other solutions that meet straightforward criteria of innovation, design quality, and cost (realism). Planners, on the other hand, address complex, messy questions about whether an infrastructure facility supports social aims.
- **Architects** make change by designing buildings. Functionality (realism) and beauty (idealism) motivates them. Although they have values about aesthetics and sustainability, private clients drive day-to-day work (realism). In contrast, planners ensure that buildings support the broader community from design, economic, and social standpoints.

Many professions have relatively clear-cut relationships with clients, but planning is a complex enterprise involving idealism and realism. The ability to hold two seemingly contradictory concepts without negating one or the other is a sign of intellectual maturity. Although the realism perspective naturally flows from the physical and social sciences, the source of an individual's idealism is not clear to me. Some planners are idealistic from the beginning, others do not feel particularly idealistic, and still others develop idealism later in their careers. The inspiring and effective planners I've known and studied reconcile idealism and realism, which makes them adaptive, resilient, and wise. Even though "idealist" is in the title of the book, I don't claim that an idealist temperament is required of the nascent planner.

Throughout the book, boxes provide personal anecdotes that relate to each chapter. They provide relatable stories that amplify the points being discussed. These are the stories of my planning career and those of other planning practitioners, providing insights on career paths and experiences. Box 1.1 discusses how my idealism grew slowly over my career.

Box 1.1 I'm Not Feeling It

Do you feel idealistic? If not, is planning wrong for you? Not at all—take the long view on this issue. For me, idealism didn't drive my decision to become a planner. I was a 17-year-old high school student who had decided against pursuing a music career as an oboist and needed to pick a new college major on short notice. I selected planning out of self-interest. Cities intrigued me. I enjoyed thinking about how patterns of land development, systems of infrastructure, and industry develop and function. As a child, my sister and I rode bikes around our neighborhood and made maps. Growing up in Windsor, Ontario, an automotive town located across the border from Detroit, Michigan, the economy was on display in the rail yards, river ferries, iron-ore lake freighters, and the factories and suppliers. The city was like a production machine.

My friend's big brother was a planner for the city, so I knew that the planning profession existed, but I didn't know much about the work of planners. Although planning interested me, I just wanted an interesting job that provided a middle-class lifestyle without working on an assembly line. My friend who chose that path boasted of "25 years and out," a promise of retirement at age 43.

I had no change agenda. My initial career steps were opportunistic—I just wanted a planning job. Idealism emerged slowly as I moved from establishing myself as a professional, for my own gain, to understanding planning challenges and wanting to do something about them. Idealism required agency on my part—and it grew as my career developed. Other planners have told me that their idealism emerged only after they gained positions that offered a measure of freedom and autonomy, which occurred later in their careers. Over time, my sense of the gap between "what is" and "what could be" grew, as did my sense of "what should be." My idealism was born in this realization and has grown over my career. If planning is your interest but not your vocation, give it some time. You might find yourself thinking differently in the future.

Motivation

It is one thing for idealist planners to have a vision for their planning career, but without motivation we may have deep thoughts in coffee shops but little impact on the world. Like idealism, motivation is mysterious. Why is it different from person to person? Is a person born with it, or is it something that develops? Although both factors play a role, the good news is that motivation can be cultivated, and it can grow with age and experience. When planners find internal motivation, of course, they won't have to force themselves to do anything. They'll naturally want to do it.

Motivation differs from self-discipline. My self-discipline is so-so; my motivation is strong. Take physical exercise, for example. If self-discipline is what gets a person to do something they would rather avoid, like working out on a weight machine, then motivation is fostered when an activity, like playing a sport they love, serves them in a fundamental way. People who find "their" sport enjoy practicing it throughout their lives. Those who force themselves to exercise purely for health reasons may have trouble keeping it up. The inspired planners I know overcame resistance to their path, found meaning in their planning practice, and are motivated to do good. If planners discover their fundamental purpose and core values, they won't need much self-discipline.

The following are starting points for possible motivation issues. The reader may wish to reflect for a moment to see if any of these apply.

- Planners who are motivated (theoretically) but have poor self-discipline. They want to achieve meaningful work, but it is difficult to get organized. They can be distracted, may not attend to long-term goals, and lack follow-through. Said bluntly, they don't walk their talk.
- Planners who haven't found their core purpose in planning, and where that purpose is required for motivation to flourish.
- Planners whose current job doesn't not line up with their motivation. If they are community organizers at heart, they may be unmotivated by working at the zoning counter. They can overcome this with self-discipline, but who would want to?
- Planners who know their purpose but are reluctant to express it. Acknowledging a purpose carries a responsibility to perform. They may also be concerned about deficiencies in skills or their ability to function in the complex administrative and political setting of planning. One response is

to turn away from the obligation. This turning away can come in the form of resistance of one kind or another. They are scared.

- Planners who like to keep their options open and avoid commitments. This need for flexibility can produce an unsatisfying career over time. They don't stay in one job long enough to really give it a chance. This may be protection against the pain of failure.

There are practical ways of addressing all of the motivation issues listed above. I don't have magic words on how to discover motivation, but reflecting on the bullet points is a start. Some may need to get organized, whereas others need to find the type of planning that excites them. It can be as small as finding the right type of organization or the right mentor. The beginning planner shouldn't worry *too much* about motivation. The book and its processes suggest ways to explore it. Also, planners may consider relying on process and schedules when motivation is lacking. In other words, "fake it until you make it." This may sound phony, but it can help planners push past periods of low motivation that would otherwise derail them.

Another perspective on motivation is that it is there all along, but that forms of resistance are blocking it. Steven Pressfield (2002) describes types of resistance in his book *The War of Art*. The book is about creative endeavors, but I have seen each of the resistances in my planning work. Here are some of his examples:

- Fear of the unknown, or fear of change.
- Grandiose fantasies. Rather than focus on the work, planners focus on a glorious, hoped-for outcome, a distraction from the immediate steps that can be taken.
- Rationalization—reasons for avoiding the work out of fear of failing at the planner's calling.
- Procrastination. Putting things off devalues the precise moment in which the planner is living.

If Pressfield is right, people don't have to *force* their way to find motivation or purpose. Instead, they can outsmart resistance—for example, seeing fear as perhaps pointing toward something that will make them stretch and grow. Once they identify resistance, the solution is to create habits of thought and action that allow an inner purpose to emerge. This will support effective action.

Motivation isn't a constant—a professional's motivation changes throughout his or her career. A frustrating job may sap motivation, and then an inspiring one will reignite it. That spark can be as small as a particular planning issue or a single interaction with a planning constituent. Motivation is commonly regarded as necessary at the beginning of a planner's career when there are pressures to prove competence and make a living. That is certainly true for some, but other people's motivation grows as they age. Otherwise, we wouldn't have presidential candidates in their seventies, who want to pursue their limited remaining number of opportunities with gusto. Box 1.2 describes my path to motivation.

Why Take My Word for It?

My perspective is based on experience as an urban planning practitioner, teacher, and scholar. Initially, I was a public agency planner in Canada and the U.S., but I've spent the last 30 years in roles as professor and chair in the Department of Urban and Regional Planning and interim dean in the College of Environmental Design at Cal Poly Pomona. In addition, I have a small consulting practice that has provided transportation planning solutions to public agencies and developers for 25 years. My planning research and practice focuses on reforming transportation and land use for livability, sustainability, and social equity. I've written books on reforming parking requirements and managing parking for smart growth. I also work on climate change, planning theory, leadership, and pedagogy.

Experiences outside of professional work also shape my perspective. Being married for 30 years taught me about love, understanding, and commitment. Raising two children introduced me to new kinds of love and grounded me.

I'm a distance runner. Competing in marathons taught me about effort, the mind/body connection, and trying hard. While running, I've worked out vexing questions, clarified my thinking, and gained new ideas. Racing taught me the equanimity and fraternity of competition. It also taught me resiliency in adapting to changing conditions over the course of a race and in dealing with disappointment.

As a hobby, I paint urban landscape scenes in oil in the *plein air* painting style—working outdoors in the varying conditions of light, weather, and passersby. Painting in public is a form of performance art, and it develops observation skills that are useful in planning. Like running, it offers no guarantee of results but gives expression to aesthetic inclinations that aren't realized in technical planning tasks.

I embrace change and eschew it. After growing up and starting my professional life in Canada, I moved to Los Angeles and haven't moved since. Being

Box 1.2 The Path of Motivation

In my teenage years, I sought to get by without extending myself. I recall how slowly time passed at boring jobs with punch clocks. Dissatisfaction with those experiences provided the motivation to find work that relied on my intellect, was interesting, and didn't trade physical labor for a paycheck. I went to college at a time when many of my friends began working on the automobile assembly line, for big wages. They had new cars and girlfriends; I hitchhiked and was single. One friend had a Chrysler Cordoba, metallic blue with a white vinyl top. After a night out, we piled into the car with some friends, and one of them said, "Is this your dad's car?" He turned slowly, and said, "No, it's mine." That may have been the greatest moment in his life.

Survival dominated my thoughts in undergraduate planning school. My fellow students were high achievers. I struggled to keep up, finding motivation in competition. I feared the future, though, feeling unready for professional responsibility. That was the only time in my life I bought lottery tickets. Up to this point, my motivation was based on survival. I started my planning practice career and began to find my footing.

In my mid-twenties I moved to Los Angeles to pursue a Master's degree in planning. Suddenly, I was smarter, funnier, and more attractive. It was the same "me," but the move changed everything. I chose to reinvent myself, and that changed everything. The ponytail, big 1980s glasses, and punk rock dance moves were just an external manifestation. I wanted to be at the top of my class. I wanted to win. Wanting to win is an important motivation, but obviously not the only one. As I learned more about urban and regional planning, a new, altruistic motivation emerged—to improve planning and public policy. The manifestation of this was to bring economic rationality to transportation planning decisions.

My first job in Los Angeles placed me in an agency that had resources and clout. The salary was so good that I felt I was stealing money. My motivation was to influence public policy for efficiency and sustainability. After a few years of working at what I considered to be a dream job, the organization's charismatic leader was ousted by the city council, and the agency adopted a more defensive posture. At that point my motivation flagged—I wanted out. I considered retooling and pursuing an MFA in painting.

In the midst of this uncertainty, an assistant professor position was posted at California State Polytechnic University (Cal Poly) Pomona. Being a professor had not occurred to me, but I chased the opportunity, armed with practice experience and a couple of publications. To my surprise, I got the job. That started a new motivation chapter—to obtain a Ph.D. and succeed as a teacher and researcher. As this story attests, my motivation shifted from survival, to personal gain, to making contributions to planning policy and research, and most recently, to teaching and mentoring. The arc of my story is from survival to service.

rooted in two cultures helps me understand how differently people perceive the same phenomenon or idea, such as expectations about the role of government. Experiences outside of a planner's home culture help them negotiate the diverse environment of work.

My insights reflect what I have learned from experiences, successes and failures, and people—my parents, wife, children, students, colleagues, alumni, managers, consulting clients, mentors, gurus, and religious teachers. Mentors have been pivotal in my life, but only since I realized that they existed. They have supported me, prodded me, challenged me, and listened to me. Seldom did they provide direct advice. Most often, they helped me come to good questions to answer myself.

But that's me; this book is for the new generation of planners. I want them to achieve their dreams and to do the meaningful work of repair in the world.

The Benefits of Reflection

In my experience, reflection makes people wise. In the forthcoming chapters, there are invitations for readers to pause and consider the values, purposes, and strategies for launching their career and practicing their profession. Planners have a commitment to thinking things through instead of making random choices or selecting the first thing that comes along. In short, planners believe in reason. We've all heard ironic stories about the plumber whose own house has leaky pipes. To heed that warning, planners should use *planning* to guide their careers.

Upcoming chapters describe ways of thinking about choices. All of those processes benefit from reflection. Many people already reflect on life's choices, but for readers who are interested in ways to reflect, Appendix B describes deliberative methods, such as journaling, talking and listening, and using diagnostics of interest and work style. The private journal may be unfathomable to some, the stuff of tea-drinking English poets from a bygone era. But reflection can also work in a non-deliberative way, in activities that open the door for insights. Non-deliberative methods include physical activity, meditation, art-making, and joining a group on a similar journey.

I use reflective writing to understand the world, find my purpose, and make choices. It helps me figure things out, and on the occasion when I read something I wrote years ago, I can assess the clarity of my thinking. I'll never read many of the entries, but the process of writing them has value.

Young planners are busy building a life. The idea of pausing to reflect may seem like a poor use of time to those facing the challenges of building careers, relationships, and their futures. Reflection can be disruptive if it brings up an uncomfortable realization or makes apparent the need for change. I get it; I didn't reflect much when I was young.

I'm pushing reflection because I've benefited from it. It put me on a path toward a meaningful life, and it has helped me recover from disappointments. I came to it late in the game, but it is worth starting early. A stop for coffee provides an opportunity to jot a note on a cell phone in 30 seconds. I see a regular practice of reflection as a commitment to freedom and an act of courage. Of course, reflection also helps answer practical questions such as:

- Should I work for a public agency or consulting firm?
- How do I know when I should leave a job?
- How can I deal with city council members who don't appreciate planning?
- What should I do when the city manager asks me to overlook environmental problems for a favored developer?

Map of the Book

A Guide for the Idealist is organized around opportunities and challenges on the journey of a planning professional. Along the way, I offer elements of my story and the insights of colleagues and young planners. The first portion of the book is about early-career choices, the "launching" part. For most of us, the first degree or first job won't likely be the only choices, so this section also speaks to those re-launching their careers. Chapter 2 addresses doubt—the "am I good enough?" question and ways of dealing with it. Next, Chapter 3 presents methods for deliberating and making choices, outlining a process that considers feelings, rational thought, and the soul. Chapter 4 considers questions about the type of planning work that is a good fit for the planner, such as modeling, policy, or organizing, while Chapter 5 helps idealist planners select a work setting that supports their goals, growth, and effectiveness. Chapter 6, titled "Career Plans Are Useless," discusses the challenges with the traditional five-year career plan and suggests better ways to navigate a career path.

The methods of planning studied in school may be quite different from those experienced in the planner's first decade of practice, so navigating the period requires growth and insight. The second half of the book is about succeeding in that phase. Chapter 7 describes a model for effective practice based on the idealism–realism continuum. It advances the idea of *principled adaptability* as the path to effective practice and contrasts it with planning styles that lead to "burnout" or "checkout" responses. Chapter 8, called "Being Right," addresses an early career challenge for idealist planners. It provides techniques for mediating the difference between what the idealist planner thinks is right and what happens.

Being idealistic generates ethical challenges. For example, how does a planner decide if it is permissible to lie or mislead for a higher end? Chapter 9, entitled "Avoiding Wrong," provides ways of thinking about and resolving ethical dilemmas. Of course, the work of reform is never done alone—as planning work is done with others and within organizations. Chapter 10, entitled "Navigating Managers, Organizations, and Teams," provides ideas on productively engaging with managers, organizations, and team members. The vital process of attracting and benefiting from mentors is addressed in Chapter 11. Chapter 12 concludes the book with a discussion of the 'hero' narrative that planning idealists may hold, providing takeaway points for effective planning practice. Lastly, the Appendices include a research summary on generational differences and suggestions on methods for reflecting.

And Now to You: Using the Book

Each chapter includes a conclusion where I speak in a more direct tone to you, the reader. As you read the main body of each chapter, consider whether the examples and instances apply and fit your experience and perspective. In each chapter conclusion, I will speak more conversationally, as if we talking in my office. You decide whether it is over tea or coffee.

My hope is that this book will help you enhance your professional competence, which in my view includes resilience. In physical terms, resilience is "a quality in objects to hold or recover their shape." As planners, for example, we seek to increase the resilience of natural systems to regenerate themselves when disrupted. In planning practice terms, I take this to mean an ability to respond to a decision that disappoints. Planners' resiliency means their work is not thrown off by unanticipated events or disappointment. Resilient planners think clearly, make good choices, and adapt to changing conditions.

There are many ways to use this book. Read the chapters in sequence or go directly to the one that grabs your attention. Underline key sentences, journal about the ideas, or consider the discussion prompts at the end of each chapter alone or with fellow planners. Go for a walk, throw the book in the air, or give it to someone who needs it—do whatever is necessary. When finished reading it, you'll know more about yourself, and you'll be better able to chart a course to a meaningful planning career. Use reflection to support good decisions about your career and the way you practice planning.

Think of my advice as a voice from your future. I was once you, a young planner, and now I am older and have seen the arc of my planning career. I have had the pleasure of watching my students' careers develop and my work bring positive change to planning. There are mysteries in the process of personal and professional development—you are on a path whose ultimate destination you cannot yet see. In my early planning career, I didn't have a clue what awaited me. The experiences you amass over the coming decades will create something meaningful—something later, something you can't imagine now. What I know now, with certainty, is that a reflective, well-considered planning career pays benefits in satisfaction and empowerment later in life. It helps you grow as a person of character and bring repair to the world.

Discussion/Reflection Questions for Chapter 1

Each chapter concludes with discussion/reflection questions. I know what some readers are thinking: "Oh boy, now he's giving us homework." You may have done all the reflecting you want in reading the chapter, but these questions may be useful in synthesizing your thoughts and reactions. You may prefer to read the book through and go back to the questions later. If you make notes, you can compare your thinking now and when you have completed the book, and then again later in your career. If you are in a discussion group, your fellow group members may reveal a wide variety of thoughts on idealism and motivation in the planning field.

1. How do you define the mission of planning?
2. Are you an idealist? How would you define the term? Where does your idealism originate from? How do you decide how to reconcile your idealism and realism?
3. Consider planning and a related profession. How does idealism appear in each profession? What is the implication of that idealism for planning practice?
4. What motivates your work? Has that changed over time, and if so, what have been the stages of motivation?

Notes

1. We are using the common definition of *idealism*. In philosophy, idealism has another meaning, which is that reality can only be known through activities of the mind. It emphasizes how human ideas shape society.
2. The AICP Code of Ethics can be viewed at www.planning.org/ethics/ethicscode. htm.
3. The philosophical understanding of realism contends that objects have a real existence that is not reducible to a universal mind or perceiving agent.
4. The philosophical understanding of pragmatism is that an ideology or proposition is true if it works satisfactorily, that the meaning of a proposition is to be found in the practical consequences of accepting it, and that unpractical ideas are to be rejected.

References

Friedmann, J. (1987). *Planning in the public domain: From knowledge to action.* Princeton, NJ: Princeton University Press.
Pressfield, S. (2002). *The war of art: Break through your blocks and win the inner creative battles.* New York, NY: Black Irish Entertainment, LLC.

Part I

LAUNCHING

Chapter 2

Am I Good Enough?

You ask me why, the Ginko leaf curled
so tightly against the harsh Atlantic wind.

Am I good enough? For the job? For graduate school? For the promotion? For the leadership role? To write this book? For some people, the answer is "of course I am." They believe they can achieve any goal if they fully apply themselves to it. After all, *someone* has to do the job—and the confident person likes his or her odds.

Extraordinary skills and character provide the confidence to start challenging tasks and carry them out with poise. They help a planner push through difficult times. My mentoring experience suggests that doubt is the more common condition, whether it is justified or not. That's how I am wired; many talented people have similar feelings.

Research on personality types suggests many human experiences of doubt, so I'm not suggesting a universal perspective. Rather, this chapter explains the helpful and disabling functions of doubt, using a framework that compares job performance and doubt. It encourages readers to examine the ways in which doubt functions, for good and for bad, in their professional life. Then, I suggest ways of managing doubt so planners reach their fullest potential.

Doubt and Performance

To a planner who is troubled by the "good enough" question, my blunt response is this: *maybe not*. A planner could fail despite good intentions and effort, but there's only one way to find out. Failure is embarrassing, but there are many rewards for those who risk the effort. The good news is that because planning practice is so broad, there are lots of ways of doing it. Not being 'good enough' for one type or level of planning leaves many other choices.

It is useful to compare level of doubt with performance. Table 2.1 frames this relationship. The rows array three levels of doubt: minimal, realistic, and excessive. Planners can assess their level of doubt using the self-reflection methods in Appendix B and by getting input from trusted mentors. This is not a simple assessment, because doubt varies across work types and settings. Planners may be confident in a staff meeting but unsure of themselves when doing quantitative analysis.

Low and high performance levels are shown in the columns of Table 2.1. Two categories keep things simple, but obviously performance exists along a continuum and depends on the task. Compared to doubt, ratings of performance should come from others—teachers, supervisors, employees, and clients, and other external sources. Useful sources include job reviews, grades in school, feedback from clients and co-workers, job offers, etc. A realistic view of performance can be obtained by consulting these sources.

Doubt and performance combine in different ways. Figure 2.1 visually arrays the six combinations of doubt and performance. The planner can assess which ellipse best describes the current situation. Two of the six cells are discussed here to highlight the distinctions. For example, if planners with minimal doubt consult trusted sources who say that they are not performing well, then

Table 2.1 What to do about variations in doubt and performance

	Evidence of low performance	*Evidence of high performance*
Minimal doubt	Seek a realistic assessment of performance. Strive for improvement and adjust goals and work setting.	Be tolerant of people who are working to improve. Learn to work in teams.
Realistic doubt	Use doubt to identify areas for improvement.	This is the sweet spot—use doubt to stay on track.
Excess doubt	Get a realistic assessment of your potential and adjust goals.	Develop mental tricks to outsmart doubt. Accept affirmations. Get mad that less-talented, doubt-free people may surpass you.

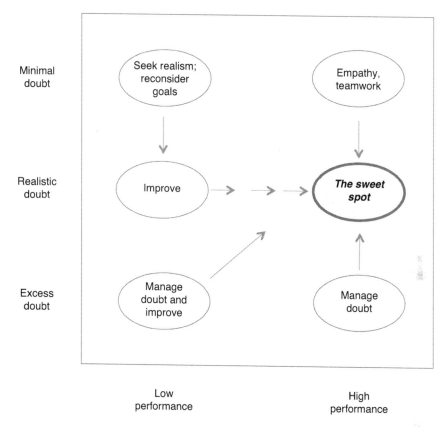

Figure 2.1 What to do about doubt and performance

they may be ignoring weaknesses and should seek better job/skill/motivation matches. A realistic assessment, as painful as that may be, allows them to take action before the outside world does. They can avoid being blindsided, by being fired for disappointing a consulting client or not passing the public agency probation period. Planners attract the loyalty and support of their supervisors if they take ownership of weaknesses and make improvements.

An alternative combination is excess doubt/high performance. Some talented planners undervalue their abilities or work habits. They hold themselves back with "am I good enough?" questions. They may not recognize their competence in basic areas such as reliability, precision, tact, following instructions, or working independently and on teams. Instead, they may focus on a minor limitation such as a weakness in design or geographic information system (GIS) skills, despite the fact that teams can be structured to address team-member weaknesses. Excessive doubt can color their view of performance where they excel. In that case, planners should manage or outsmart doubt.

Supervisors may take advantage of excess doubt/high-performance employees. They may think, "thank you very much—stay doubting!" and take credit for the planners' hard work. Meanwhile, less-talented people pass them on the organization ladder. This perspective may also keep planners from asking for a raise when they deserve one.

High performance carries with it a responsibility to work hard. In that respect, unwarranted doubt can be an abdication of responsibility to the profession. It is worth taking some time to reflect on Table 2.1, as each cell calls for a different response. Doubt is a pivotal issue in some planners' careers, so we explore it further using a lens of narcissism to shed light on this tricky concept.

The Narcissism of Minimal Doubt

Narcissism is characterized by selfishness, a grandiose view of one's own talent, and a craving for admiration.[1] Clearly, lacking doubt without any reference to performance can be an expression of narcissism, sometimes called grandiose narcissism. If planners never consider their weaknesses or ability to perform, they ignore the natural distribution of talent. Most people aren't good at everything. Being overconfident leads to errors and failures that undermine long-term success. Such planners may take on more than they should in work scope and then disappoint clients, customers, and collaborators. Others may be impatient with those who don't work the same way, or as quickly, as they do. Blind to the advantages of other ways of doing things, they may be less likely to follow good advice.

Minimal doubt may be the consequence of narrowly defining competency around strengths, or by assessing performance more favorably than is justified. Idealist planners may be good at some things, such as brainstorming, but not at recognizing a weakness such as follow-through. They may have a logical mind, but they cannot perceive intangibles. If they focus only on strengths, they avoid challenges or feeling fallible and miss out on opportunities to grow. For example, a GIS expert might feel infallible about mapping and data analysis work products but be fearful of making presentations. By steering away from weaknesses, the doubt-avoider maintains a positive self-image but loses out on opportunities for growth.

Contemporary culture emphasizes personal affirmation, which is good for self-esteem but means that some planners don't realistically assess their inadequacies. When she was young, my daughter received a participation trophy for being on a swim team even though she never won a race. Was this undeserved? Aren't trophies for those who win? I asked her about this a decade after she received it, and her view was that the trophy was a confirmation of teamwork. This perspective is valid, but excess affirmation can generate unrealistic self-assessments and a sense of entitlement. Doting parents, success in athletics, teachers who inflate grades, or attendance at elite schools may produce planners with a sense of entitlement, and they may underperform and squander opportunities.

Life has a way of catching up with those who lack realistic doubt. Although they can work for their parent's company, use political connections to land a public agency job, or parlay relationships with non-profit board members, poor performance eventually catches up with them. The best way to avoid such a situation is to realistically assess strengths and weaknesses, welcome challenging experiences, and actively seek feedback. Because *excess* doubt is more common, the rest of the chapter will deal with that issue.

The Narcissism of Excess Doubt

It may seem that narcissism and doubt are oxymoronic, but there can be narcissism in excess doubt, sometimes termed "insecure narcissism." The doubter does not boast of his or her talents, but the doubter's worries reveal an underlying narrative of specialness associated with perceived deficiencies. This self-absorption puts a twist on boastfulness—boastfulness of woe. The narcissist doubter places himself or herself at the heart of the matter, acting as the judge of competency.

Because planning deals with messy problems and incorporates science, social science, design arts, and politics, it is difficult to judge success. There are few unambiguous markers of achievement. The long view suggests that it is not for planners alone to decide if they are good enough. The planning profession provides feedback on performance all the time, through professors, selection committees, supervisors, clients, employees, and decision-makers. Planners should seek this feedback, take it in, and decide what to make of it.

It is normal to ask questions about competence at the beginning of a planning career, but it isn't a good idea to spend too much time on "am I good enough?" Instead, planners should focus on realistically assessing weaknesses and doing something about them. More time should be spent on finding ways to play an effective role in the planning issues that really matter. "Am I good enough?" can be a distraction that competes with staying on task, encourages procrastination, and derails the work. If things have fallen apart in their past, doubters may overcompensate for that in trying to guarantee success. For example, an earnest effort to improve a planner's qualifications by getting an extra degree could create the inadvertent impression that a person is a "professional student" who doesn't have a clear direction. Moving forward requires a degree of focus and a commitment to improve.

Recently, a student of mine missed a deadline for a research project. He emailed me explaining that his computer crashed, saying he understood that the excuse sounded flimsy, and he suggested I give him an F in the class. He had done good work in the past and was a person of good character. I was willing to give him an extension. But instead of waiting for me to decide, he pre-decided. It's a sign of good character to take responsibility for a misstep—this student's intention was honorable—but he chose to punish himself. Of course, he may also have wanted release from the stress of delivering the product. Instead, I gave him an extension, and he finished his work and graduated. The moral of the story is to face up to mistakes or failures, but let the world decide the consequences. In this case, it would have been better to explain the situation and ask me if there were any options for dealing with it. In stressful moments, planners can cultivate a practice of asking questions instead of filling in the answer to avoid the anxiety of the moment.

An individual planner doesn't have perfect knowledge to assess his or her own worth—a weakness may not be serious, or it may not matter for a given task, or it may be that in combination with others, he or she is effective. If poor writing is a problem, for example, planners can develop a game plan for improvement, identify ways of tracking common errors, and get editing help.

Planners may also be blind to their strengths. For example, some take their competency for granted. Competency means being able to understand a problem or assignment, marshal resources, think clearly, write effectively, be reliable and trustworthy, work in a team, work without excessive guidance, and be a person of good character. That's what employers want. Instead, doubters may focus on a minor dimension that is missing.

Excess doubt shouldn't lead planners to withdraw from challenges that can be mastered. They have to do the work, every day, but they won't win every day. Planning occurs in a complex administrative and political framework, which suggests a perspective that is more accepting of setback and human frailty. Staff recommendations are sometimes rejected, consulting proposals are not selected, and grant applications are turned down. The idealist doesn't have to win every time to show up and do the work. Box 2.1 provides an example from my life.

Box 2.1 I Don't Run to Win

I run one marathon each year and have done so for the last 20 years. Each time I run, there is a risk of the embarrassment of not finishing due to injury or bad race strategy. My friends know about the race, so any possible failure isn't private. Moreover, I have never won a marathon, or won my age group in one. I will *never* win my age group. Naturally, I have fantasies about a miraculous race that I win in record time and have the opportunity to represent my country in the Olympics, but neither of these dreams has happened come true—yet.

Why do something when you don't expect to win? I run marathons because the experience speaks to a fundamental part of my being. It isn't a rational calculation—when I look back, my decision to start running is mysterious. Twenty years ago, two runner friends were visiting my house and talking about their running exploits. I couldn't participate in the conversation. The next day I got up early and ran six miles, and I've been running ever since. The reason for my first run may seem petty—I didn't like being excluded from a conversation. But of course, that's not why I continued. I had found an athletic activity that fit me. This kind of alignment is easily understood when one picks a hobby. Can this idea of finding an alignment also apply to the idealist planner's professional work?

When in a race, I'm not discouraged about not winning, and I still want to do my best. I respect the runners who beat me, knowing that they did so because they have more natural ability, were more dedicated or trained smarter, or simply had a good day. I enjoy being part of a community of people who value effort. Waiting at the starting line with 25,000 other people making a commitment with an unknown outcome is inspiring.

Running is part of my identity—I want to do it my entire life, even though I am not good enough to win. This experience expanded my understanding of success so that it is broader than winning. For me, success is creating a meaningful life of trying. Having said that, I have not yet learned how to bring this equanimity to urban planning. In my planning work, I always want to "win"—meaning successfully resolving the planning issue at hand—and I am upset when I fail. Maybe some day I will be able to apply my running lessons to my professional work.

Only a naïve person expects win after win, without suffering, failure, or loss. Iris Murdoch calls the better approach a "selfless respect for reality" (Murdoch, 1970, p. 93). There are reasons why neighborhoods, cities, and regions have problems. Economic interests, for example, may benefit from the status quo and resist change. Finding a brilliant solution to a problem is not enough. It has to be put into practice, which involves politics and at least some disgruntled parties. The more planners understand this reality—that there are conditions independent of them—the better they can avoid being disillusioned or angry that change hasn't occurred as hoped. Of course this is easier to say than do, but it provides a perspective for understanding effectiveness.

Managing Doubt

Doubt can be managed if planners understand how it functions and are able to observe it and outsmart it. What is its source? Some people describe it as a "bird" that perches on their shoulder and whispers critical comments that undermine confidence (e.g., "you're not good enough" or "you're a fraud"). This is disabling for creative planning work in which there is subjectivity about the quality and success of outcomes. It is tempting to blame this 'bird' on a critical parent, teacher, or other tormentor from childhood, but doing that stands in the way of evolving as a person. A person may have faced withering criticism in the past, but diminishing its role over time supports personal and professional growth.

Of course, it is hard to just "get over it." A helpful practice is to distinguish between valid and invalid criticism. Valid criticism is reality-based, calm, and true. It is actionable. This is the case on both professional and personal levels. Receiving valid criticism from a person of good will is not disabling. It helps planners move forward and improve. Box 2.2 provides an example from my role as academic department chair.

Invalid criticism is another matter. It could stem from jealousy about a person's talents, or from resentment about background or position, or simply be an abuse of power. It may have little to do with the person being criticized but more about the person delivering it. Invalid criticism can stem from a bad manager and/or organizational culture. Invalid criticism should be shrugged off.

Of course, it is not easy to distinguish between valid and invalid criticism— that requires reflection and objectivity. Planners may consult with mentors and trusted friends, and use reflection. Table 2.2 suggests responses to different combinations of doubt and criticism validity. The rows array levels of doubt while the columns distinguish between invalid and valid criticism. For people with excess doubt, invalid criticism can be disabling. In that case, they shouldn't listen! They should avoid the source of the criticism. On the other hand, people with minimal doubt may not let valid criticism register and thereby miss a chance to improve. It is useful to spend some time pondering and reflecting

Box 2.2 Valid Criticism Does Not Generate Doubt

Recently, a Planning Accreditation Board (PAB) review team visited my academic department to study it and make a recommendation as to whether the programs should be reaccredited. The process involves an extensive self-study report and many days of meetings with students, alumni, employers, and the like. The team considers 54 accreditation criteria. This was an anxious time for me, because a poor review could result in the loss of accreditation and undermine the value of the degree for current and former students. As department chair, it is my job to keep the program accredited.

The team's report was positive, but there were some criticisms. It may seem surprising, but I had a good feeling about the criticisms. They were true, made of good will, and actionable. I agreed with them. I was delighted that the review team saw the reality of the program, with its strengths and weaknesses. As a result, I welcomed the criticism with a feeling of equanimity. This example is criticism at the institutional level. It is similar at the personal level. Criticism is not debilitating if it is true.

When people tell me they think I made a misstep or offended them, I listen, ask for details (like the police report without emotion or interpretation), and mourn my own failures. Naturally, I have a sense of embarrassment and an instinct to defend myself. I try to hold off that initial defensive reaction so I can learn something. Lowering defense barriers helps me assess whether the criticism is valid. Of course, I struggle against a tendency to self-justify, so sometimes learning the lesson takes time, with missteps and hurt feelings along the way. If the criticism is valid, though, I want to make amends and work on avoiding it in the future. Taken this way, criticism is an opportunity for growth, not something that undermines confidence.

Table 2.2 Responding to doubt and criticism

	Invalid criticism	*Valid criticism*
Minimal doubt	No worries, you probably didn't take it seriously anyway.	Take it seriously, resist any tendency to self-justify.
Realistic doubt	Consider its validity—source, evidence, and recognition of context.	Ask for actionable details, make changes.
Excess doubt	Don't listen!	Ask the criticizer to be specific, consider it, and make a step-by-step plan for improvement. Don't glorify it.

on this table. Reflective planners can consider how often their situation falls within which of the cells. Which criticisms are they most likely to trust? Whose criticism should they trust?

Perhaps the most difficult criticism to metabolize is that which comes from within—self-criticism. Many of us, myself included, have an internal judge who makes ruling after ruling about our competency without a fair trial or a defense attorney. I have a daily, internal running dialogue about my deficiencies.

One way planners can reimagine this internal "judge" is to consider themselves the convener of the many voices within, as a president might assemble a cabinet to advise on a major decision. There is a secretary of justice, a secretary of reason, a secretary of fun, a secretary of procrastination, and a secretary of doubt—to name a few. People reflecting can imagine that they are the president who decides which voice to heed in each situation. They are "the decider." Then, they oversee the debate. They allow all the voices to speak, including the secretary of doubt. As they realize that it is nearly impossible to censor this secretary, and others, they realize that the choice is theirs whether or not to act on the recommendations of all these "secretaries."

Religious traditions provide insights on the issue of doubt. Some assert that there is a destructive "formation" built into the self—a part of each person that is resistant to growth and wants to keep things as they are. This destructive formation cannot be banished, but it can be observed and outsmarted. For example, when the "good enough" question arises, the planner might say "hello, voice of doubt" rather than jump to "I'm not up to the challenge." Seeing the voice of doubt from a broader, more objective vantage point allows for clearer thinking.

Excess doubt can also spring from a self-image based on formative decisions that a person made at a young age, such as "I'm a fraud." These internal catchphrases are not apparent early in life because they are invisible structures of personality required for self-preservation, but as we mature, these catchphrases often become restrictive. Once self-limiting catch phrases are named, we can decide their role. Personal reflection can reveal these catchphrases, as can feedback from supportive mentors and friends.

Doubt is also fueled by the false images created in the competitive nature of the working and educational worlds. We don't advertise our weaknesses. The person with the great profile on a job website might have a phobia about numbers. A simple disabler of doubt is to be realistic about the competition. Recently, one of my students applied to a highly regarded Master's program. She reviewed the profiles of the program's current students. Each of them had impeccable academic credentials, meaningful community service, professional experience, and a commitment to the good. Each student branded himself or herself in a unique and appealing way. The impression was of an impossible standard of achievement. This student did not let doubt influence her decision to apply though, and she was later admitted with a generous scholarship.

Reversing the "am I good enough?" question can be empowering. Know that *someone* has to be admitted to the academic program, *someone* has to get the job, *someone* has to make the presentation, and so on. A planner can see themself as that person. Everyone has flaws, weaknesses, and things that make them nervous. A given planner's weaknesses may be different from those around them; they know their own very well but they don't know others' weaknesses. Moreover, that planner doesn't know what the admission committee, city manager, or non-profit human resources (HR) office is looking for—one person's authenticity might be preferred over someone else's perfect academic record.

The 'C' student sometimes achieves the most success. She or he can't do it alone and so collaborates in school and in practice. The 'A' student may be able to do everything alone but sometimes fails in practice because he or she doesn't know how to collaborate. If there is vision and will, but certain skills are lacking, organizing a team that covers all the bases can solve the problem.

In a given job search, one particular strength might be needed to shore up a weakness among an organization's staff. A former student shared that she was surprised to learn that she was chosen for the job even though her experience was lacking. The reason given by the director was that they were seeking a collaborator, not another leader.

Social media worsens the excess doubt problem. It allows us to portray ourselves in the most flattering way—adventurous, happy, successful, and popular. A meta-message from these portrayals is: "Why try? There are more talented, more accomplished people than you" and "Works of the highest quality have already been created, so don't bother." It takes strong will to avoid falling into a stupor of inaction when we see only the best version of other people without knowing the situation in terms of context and history.

Box 2.3 provides an example of false worries based on inadequate information. It involved a situation where I wanted to take a shortcut in my Ph.D. program and feared my commitment to learning would be questioned.

As mentioned previously, excess doubt can justify not trying hard. It lets us off the hook. Seeking to avoid the pain of rejection, or perhaps worse, being ignored, planners may withhold their full effort. But not trying hard is a lousy

---

Box 2.3 Unfounded Concerns

When I began my Ph.D. studies, I was worried that I would not have enough time to complete it properly—I was already working full-time as an associate professor and I had a family. The task ahead felt enormous. I felt sheepish approaching my advisors to ask if I could skip certain classes based on my teaching experience, worrying that they would doubt my seriousness. My time pressures, however, compelled me to ask.

My reluctance to ask for help was based on an inadequate understanding of the situation. When I asked for a course exemption, I didn't know the context for the request, that there was concern about the time to completion for Ph.D. students—the average of seven years was far too long. Faculty members were frustrated by the slow pace of many Ph.D. students. So when I made my request, the reaction was positive. I didn't look like an unserious student, but rather a motivated, directed person who wanted to move through the program in a timely manner. My request was supported. If I hadn't asked, I would have learned more in the extra courses I would have taken, but my research progress would have been slower. I got started on my dissertation in my first quarter of study and finished in three years. My initial worry was based on insufficient information. I couldn't know until I asked.

---

path, so rather than settle for mediocrity, planners should try and try again and be willing to be brokenhearted if the opportunity doesn't work out. The idea that failure is a natural and required part of growth has gained popularity in the culture. This is good. Trying and failing is a legitimate path to personal development.

Turning Doubt Around

Doubt provides critical information because it points toward our aspirations. If we didn't have an aspiration for improving the world through planning, then we wouldn't feel doubt about whether we are up to the task. In this way, feeling doubt may simply indicate that a planner is shooting high. Realistic doubt helps idealist planners improve by motivating them to enhance their planning skills, address weaknesses, and seek others' help.

Of course, planners may try as hard as they can and get nowhere. The world may say "no, that wasn't good enough." How can planners know? If they are locked out of a desired type of work for an extended period, a reassessment is required. Talent is not equally distributed, and there are different types of talent. If planners' assessments of their strengths are not realistic, they can refine work goals in the direction of their talents. If they want to be a community organizer but struggle to work with people, they may be ignoring gifts as a technical analyst whose work supports social justice. The motivation is the same; the manner in which it is realized is different. Alternatively, planners may have the ability to succeed in an area of work but have been in environments that didn't allow success, or the position does not support that type of work. Or, they just graduated at a time when jobs were not available.

Be Attentive to Help and Signposts

I don't want to give the impression that a planner should decide the "good enough" question on his or her own. That's not true. People—supervisors, co-workers, professors, clients, and peers—and signs along the way will indicate potential if a planner is on the lookout for them and listens to them. Planners can also use the reflection techniques provided in Appendix B.

Some planners don't believe they are good enough until a person whom they respect tells them so, or until honors or external awards come. Most of us dream of being recognized, but a surprising number of people have trouble receiving a message that they *are* good enough.

If a planner was raised to be humble, she or he might discount or miss the positive messages. Growing up in Canada, I learned a social value for modesty. Taken too far, this would limit my progress. Box 2.4 provides a story of showing up when invited. Planners should be open to praise and direction from others, especially if the affirmation they receive is for something different from their own perception of their strengths. Because objective assessments about strengths and weakness can come from mentors, Chapter 11 explains how to acquire and benefit from them.

Compete and Collaborate

Of course, managing doubt and overcoming resistance is not all that is required. The world is a busy place, full of ideas, claims, and proposals, and it may not have time for a planner's ideas. Sometimes we have to fight our way in. Planners need to compete for influence on planning questions. Although some planners compete for money or status, others compete for what they need to do their job—a position that provides access to power, a platform for advocating

---

Box 2.4 Being Invited

I didn't visit my professors for course or career advice as an undergraduate planning student. In hindsight, that was foolish, but I simply didn't realize that I should do that. Professors seemed somewhat dangerous and remote. I did fine in school, but looking back, I wonder how much more I could have learned if I had reached out to my professors for feedback and advice.

When I enrolled in a Master's degree program, my introductory economics and statistics professor was loud and demonstrative, with a funny and sarcastic sense of humor. I was intimidated by him. Per my usual practice, I didn't sit in the front row. He let me know he was aware of me, but I kept my place and did not talk with him after class. Mid-semester, he asked me to come see him in his office. My first thought was that I was in trouble, had done something wrong, and that he was angry with me. When I arrived, he handed me my midterm with a twinkle in his eye and said "not bad" to my grade of 95 out of 100. He invited me to participate in research with him. I jumped at the chance.

We undertook research on the predictors of light rail transit patronage and used that model to critique rail development plans in Los Angeles. The invitation brought me into the transportation planning field, which was my first professional job, post-graduation. It led to a research collaboration that produced a co-authored journal article and a book chapter publication, which later helped me land an academic job without yet having a Ph.D. That invitation shaped my career in a profound way.

I have only pondered this recently, but I realize now that that event was the defining moment in my professional life. Lots of challenges and help came later, but I am struck by how unaware I was of the importance of that moment back then. I had no sense of where my professional life would lead. Thank goodness I showed up. I cannot know this for certain, but if I hadn't come to his office when invited, I suspect he wouldn't have asked me twice.

---

for change, respect from allied professions, funding resources, and/or simply presenting a convincing argument to elected officials.

Part of competing is self-marketing. Planners market themselves and create a brand appropriate to their career level. What are they good at? What evidence is there to demonstrate it? They can develop a "skills" section in their resumes that states their strongest qualities. Their brand is a unique combination of skills, abilities, and qualities, some learned and others traits they were born with. Then, planners select methods that are most appropriate to communicate the brand, including networking at conferences, informational interviews with professionals, online work portfolios, and social media. Obviously, doing this is an affront to self-doubt, which may assert its presence during the process. But developing a brand is worthwhile, and in the process, planners may see others' self-marketing more realistically.

As mentioned previously, collaboration is also critical in overcoming doubt. By collaborating, planners learn that everyone has strengths and weaknesses. Well-functioning teams produce better results than do individuals on their own. Instead of avoiding collaboration out of fear that a weakness will be exposed, if planners on a team are transparent about their strengths and weaknesses, then the team can organize itself for the highest effectiveness. Being on an effective team is another way to prove excessive doubt wrong.

And Now to You: Effort Without a Guarantee of Results

I contend that you have a responsibility to the world to develop your gifts to serve others. If you never doubt, seek humility and compassion so that competency does not live alone in an "army of one." If you are a doubter like me, manage it. Deal with feelings of not being up to the task—mourn any lost vision—and get on with it.

I don't accept the answer of metaphorically going home and leading a quiet life. Getting on with it means adjusting, recalibrating, and learning. Engage the "not good enough" question—wrestle with it, fight it, subject it to rational analysis, outsmart it, and trick it. Manage it so you can make good on your professional and life goals. Do so and you will be empowered to create the good. Continued, consistent effort can disable excess doubt.

Doubt is sometimes overcome in pivotal experiences. In my career, I recall when my boss went on vacation during the week of a critical development negotiation. She turned it over to me. I was initially aghast and very nervous, but it was an opportunity for me to be the lead negotiator for my group, and it gave me a doubt-dispelling experience I would not have otherwise had. Box 2.5 is a similar account, of a consultant who had to run a meeting before he thought he was ready because his boss was ill. He rose to the occasion, and that experience propelled him forward.

Managing doubt, overcoming resistance, hard work, creating a brand, and collaborating will bring effectiveness and success. It steers you away from "all-or-nothing" thinking where partial gains are ignored. Be specific about weaknesses and challenging situations—don't generalize. When facing challenges, seek the "police report" version of events (i.e., facts about situations without

Box 2.5 A Pivotal Moment in Overcoming Doubt
By Douglas Feremenga, Ph.D. AICP CEP, Environmental Planning Manager, Transportation Corridor Agencies, Irvine, California

While pursing my undergraduate degree in planning at the University of Zimbabwe, I landed an internship that turned into my first job after graduation. My job with the International Chartered Quantity Surveyors and Consultants Company based in Harare, Zimbabwe was to forecast construction costs and manage projects. Knowledge of analysis, appraisal, construction law, and construction technology were necessary, but I also needed communication and interpersonal skills, leadership, management, and computer literacy. Simply put, this is planning!

My clients included public institutions, private developers, and international development agencies. I worked on projects across sub-Saharan Africa. I was young and loved traveling—I was living the life! As a quick study, I gained my boss's trust, my peers' respect, and my clients' confidence. This was earned slowly, over time. There were times of self-doubt, though. "Maybe I need to stick to traditional planning," I often thought, but I enjoyed what I was doing, and so I pressed on.

My company chaired project design and construction meetings. During my first year, I attended meetings with my boss. Towards the end of the second year, my boss was ill, and I attended a hospital-construction kick-off meeting unsupervised. The hour-long drive to the meeting was filled with self-doubt: "Am I in over my head?" I felt ill-equipped to fill my boss's shoes. He was firm, but just. His meetings were efficient, but thorough. Surely, I wasn't ready—I wished I had chaired just one more meeting with him. I was diving into the deep end with no life jacket—it was sink or swim.

When I arrived, I knew I was with consummate professionals. They exuded experience, and I felt small. I was still assessing how to kick off this meeting when an architect remarked, "I guess we are waiting for the Quantity Surveyors to arrive and start the meeting." That was my cue—"Oh, the Quantity Surveyor is here," I responded. "Ladies and gentlemen, let's get started." I looked like a schoolboy but commanded their attention.

I ran the meeting with an efficiency that made my boss proud. In that pivotal moment, I catapulted myself to a new level. I worked on more projects and my responsibilities increased. I didn't mind the workload; I was right where I wanted to be—learning and growing as a professional.

Growing up in a country with limited resources, I felt that I needed to be one step ahead, one level above my peers, to be competitive. I loved my job, but I was yearning for more. I left my job and my home in Zimbabwe to pursue a Master's degree in planning in the United States. It was an emotional decision and quite an adventure in itself, but I was ready. Goodbye building economics and hello environmental design. That began my sustainability and environmental planning career—indeed, I had found my calling. And it started with being ready.

emotional interpretation). Lastly, don't jump to conclusions without evidence and don't catastrophize.

Realizing and defining your purpose and finding the right workplace also helps manage doubt. To assist in that process, Chapters 4 and 5 offer ways of figuring out the type of planning work and the organizational setting that best serve you.

The payoff to addressing doubt is substantial. Get this right and you will move forward with a balance of confidence and humility.

Discussion/Reflection Questions for Chapter 2

1. How does doubt operate in your internal self-assessments? Does it help you improve or hold you back? What does your doubt say about your aspirations?
2. Reflect on someone you know well. Can you perceive how doubt works in her or his life? Has she or he learned things about managing doubt that can benefit you?
3. Conduct a self-inventory of your planning skills and knowledge. Where do you have doubt and where do you have confidence? Would others agree with your assessment? What plans could you put into place to improve in those areas where your doubt is justified?
4. How does doubt function when planning teams work together in school or work settings? Should doubt be discussed explicitly by team members?

Note

1. Clinical definitions of *narcissism* can be found in American Psychiatric Association. (2013). *Diagnostic and statistical manual of mental disorders* (5th ed.). Arlington, VA: American Psychiatric Publishing.

Reference

Murdoch, I. (1970). *The sovereignty of good*. London, UK: Routledge.

Chapter 3

Making Choices

Go forth
from everything you know.

Launching and advancing a planning career requires making wise choices about education and work. There are so many opportunities in planning—work setting, type of planning, and place—that launching is an exciting and potentially overwhelming time in a planner's career. This mandate for choosing occurs at the same time that young planners are making decisions about personal relationships, affiliations, and family. Compared to other life stages, then, the "launching" stage calls for frequent decisions. Wise choices are achieved with a realistic understanding of the world, solid reasoning, and self-knowledge.

This chapter suggests processes that strengthen the planner's decision-making capability. It describes types of career choices, proposes a three-part decision-making approach, and concludes with ideas about how to make good choices. In addition to charting the planner's career, solid decision-making supports choices made *within* the planning practice, such as making a recommendation on a plan amendment.

Decision-making is like a muscle. It can be developed and improved over time. Conversely, it can be overtaxed and fail. Effective planners develop this capacity over the course of their careers. If planners are reflective about their decisions, there will be few situations where hasty "by my gut" or "just go for it" choices are made that turn out to be ill-advised. In contrast with hasty decisions, another issue is *not* making decisions when they are needed, or avoiding situations that require decisions. A lack of confidence in decision-making can explain procrastination and avoidance.

A solid decision-making process accounts for the fact that decisions are made in a fluid, unpredictable world. No one knows how paths not taken would have turned out. Decisions can't be undone. This is decision-making under uncertainty, the same thing that planners face in practice. Fortunately, there is room for starting over at the beginning of a planning career. Although frequently jumping from job to job early on may raise eyebrows in human resource departments, no one expects beginning planners to have their career choices completely figured out.

In making choices, some say trust your feelings. Others say don't trust your feelings. What are the roles of feeling, anyway? And how do feelings fit with rational thought and the deeper, non-verbal murmurings of your soul? This chapter explores these three elements—feelings, rational thought, and soul—in the reasoning process.

Choices Faced by Planners

We'll start by discussing the types of choices planners make. For example, planners decide *whether* to pursue opportunities. There may also be decisions about taking a new job, relocating, or pursuing a Master's or Ph.D. As well, planners face decisions *in* their work—how to handle a tricky political situation, work with staff in other departments, or interact with a supervisor with whom they disagree.

Deciding Whether to Pursue an Opportunity

Exploring opportunities is one of the most exciting aspects of launching a planning career—considering new work environments, new professional colleagues, applying newfound knowledge, and relocations to new communities. Whatever challenges decision-making poses, they are well compensated for by the thrill of new experiences.

Of course, decisions may create anxiety. For some planners, it raises the "am I good enough?" question discussed in Chapter 2. Some avoid pursuing opportunities because they feel obligated to accept the job if it comes through, or worry that they won't make a good decision. Young planners should recognize that expressing interest in a position is not a commitment to take it. This also applies to pursuing multiple opportunities at once. There is no commitment to an organization until they make a formal offer.

To manage potential anxiety, planners can map out all possible outcomes and consider them objectively. A friend or mentor can look at the list to see if there are any blind spots. The following provides a case where it became evident that there were no bad outcomes. A planner wanted to pursue a job in another country that would require learning a new language and culture and leaving friends and family behind (Box 6.4 provides the details). In this case, possible outcomes to pursuing the opportunity included the following:

- *No job offer.* We all want to win every time, but that is not possible. There is social embarrassment in rejection, but the upside is what that planner learns in the process of pursuing the opportunity.
- *Job offer—planner declines it.* That's not a problem either—it just wasn't the right one, once all the information was in. An applicant is not obligated to say yes by pursuing an opportunity because the full details of the work, salary, and management arrangements are not available until the offer is made.
- *Job offer—planner accepts it but doesn't like the job/the people/the city.* No problem, the planner should stick it out for a year or two, and then pursue other opportunities. She has had an experience that adds professional credibility and has likely acquired new skills and knowledge.
- *Job offer—planner accepts it and then fails.* The planner is let go and returns home with no job and a disrupted life. Although no one wants this outcome, the benefits of the experience can turn into long-term strengths, such as cultural awareness or personal empathy. Taking on such an adventure may be looked upon favorably by future employers, as it demonstrates initiative and a desire to learn.
- *Job offer—planner accepts it and loves it for a few years, and then is drawn to another opportunity.* The planner had a meaningful learning and cultural experience that was on the path to an unknown destination.
- *Job offer—planner accepts it and loves it, and stays forever.* The planner was *that person* all along and found her way. This outcome is self-actualization—finding purpose and identity in a new culture.

This "mostly no bad outcome" story is age- and circumstance-dependent. At the beginning of a planner's career, if there are no family obligations, experimentation is a great way to learn. Of course, professional consequences aren't the only factors to consider—a long-distance move affects family and personal relationships. A good strategy is to assess the professional and personal consequences separately in order to weigh them objectively.

For people further along in their careers, trying something that doesn't work out could have consequences. Human resource departments, with computer-aided resume assessment devices, may have a bias towards traditional career progressions. If planners are always seeking new opportunities, their employers may treat them differently by not giving good assignments because they question their long-term commitment to the organization. The degree of that downside is dependent on the employer's organizational culture—some expect loyalty and others embrace the growth of their employees, even if it means they leave. The point of this story is to suggest that planners get all the possible scenarios on paper and assess them objectively in terms of reward and risk.

Deciding on an Offer

Another example of choosing is deciding about job offers. This deliberative process involves reflection, consultations with family and advisors, research about benefits and downsides, and having the patience to allow the right answer to come clear. Although the employer may be in a rush for a commitment, it's the planner's own process and decision. At stake is whether to accept the offer as is, negotiate a different job title, job description, salary, or other benefits, and whether to give the current employer a chance to counter with a promotion or salary increase. Box 3.1 provides an account of a tough decision that I faced, where it took some time for the right answer to become clear.

Time is an important dimension because the right decision does not emerge in a neat time frame. It's natural to want to escape unsettled situations—to get them resolved quickly, even if wrongly, "to get out of this terrible angst." In the next section, I outline how feelings, rational thoughts, and the murmurs of the soul can be considered. It takes awhile to consider all of them. Play for time if necessary. An acceptable stalling technique is to tell the employer that another visit is necessary to more fully assess the job, the community, and opportunities for spouses and life partners. But eventually the decision must be made.

Box 3.1 A Tough Job Decision

When my children were grown, I thought that I should try something different, get a new job, and live in a new place. My spouse was willing. So I went on the job market and received an offer from a well-regarded university on the other side of the country. It seemed that my desire was fulfilled and that taking this opportunity was a no-brainer. But when the offer was made, I was full of uncertainty.

There were some problems with the new job, but nothing that could not be overcome if it really was my work. The salary was disappointing, and I focused on that. One of my mentors laughed at me when I mentioned my concern about the salary. He said, "If this job is your work, the money issue is a trifle, a distraction, a minor insult that you can work around." He was right.

After hearing that, I returned to the core question: is this job my work? I castigated myself for being scared—of change and that I wouldn't succeed in the new environment. As discussed in Chapter 2, I wondered if I was good enough. I had accomplished much in facing down my fears—generally "going for it" each time. Going for it is important, or else your fears will rule you, but it could also be wrong to *always* do that which scares you. If you do, then your fears rule you. Some people are wired to feel shame if they don't face every challenge.

I had extended phone calls with my mentor discussing the issue. I was emotional—on reflection, more emotional than warranted. That was a hint that something was up. There were other values or desires that weren't part of my rational thought or feelings—and they were seeking recognition.

I went back and forth on the question, driving my spouse and my friends crazy. In one phone call, my mentor said, "I already know what you are going to do," and I said, "Please, please tell me to relieve me of this confusion." Of course, he wouldn't. It was my decision to make, not his.

After weeks of struggle, one day, out of the blue, these words came to me: "I'm not done here [with my existing job] yet." And it was as simple as that. I wasn't done with my job, the students whom I loved, my house, my friends, my community, and my Los Angeles. I heard a murmur from my soul that whispered "not yet." Once that came to me, I was clear. All the other issues fell away. I turned down the offer. I didn't know what awaited me in staying at my job, and I sometimes wonder who I would be now if I had taken the job. I think it was the right decision, but I'll never know for sure. All I know is that I *finally* got to the decision in that moment.

Making a Difficult Work Choice

Junior planners are usually the *recipients* of the decisions of their immediate supervisors and those up the line, rather than making the decisions themselves. But the frequency of difficult decisions increases as planners advance up the management ladder, so it is advisable to develop these decision-making processes early. Ideally, good supervisors involve their planners in decision-making processes and give them responsibility to decide commensurate with their level in the organization.

Let's say a planner is writing a staff report on a conditional use permit for a request to supply less parking than the code requires. In this scenario, assume that the planner has information that suggests that the requirement is indeed excessive. The planner is inclined to recommend approval of the request and presents his or her evidence and rationale to the supervisor. The supervisor understands the logic but reminds the planner that the community groups are sure to oppose this action because they fear that residents of the new building will park in their neighborhood. The planner counters that residential parking permit districts can manage that problem. The supervisor replies, "Sure, but there isn't one in effect now, and the community will oppose creating one to keep pressure for project denial." Based solely on technical merits, the variance should be approved. The planner must decide how to balance the logical answer with community sentiment, taking into account the need for housing and the politics of the district.

Planners face these deliberative choices every day. Having a well-developed decision-making capability helps avoid the extremes—denying the proposal out of hand because it doesn't comply with the code or recommending a level of parking reduction that creates a political backlash that stops the project. In allowing for conditional use permits, planning law recognizes that codes don't always fit the situation and that a deliberative process is beneficial. This requires creativity—and decisions.

Another type of decision is when planners are asked to do something unethical by a public official, consultant, or community organizer. Planners may be asked to bend the rules for a favored developer, or adjust model outputs to help a client compete for a grant. Working at a non-profit organization, planners could be asked to bill hours to a project that has available grant funding even though the actual work performed was on another project. As community organizers, planners could be tempted to fudge the numbers on a grant proposal so that funding for the organization's good work can continue. These situations come frequently for those in the business of making change, and they demand quick resolution.

Decisions on whether to say no to an unethical request and bear the consequences (if any) with employers, supporters, and others are emotional and tumultuous. They require planners to balance competing ethical imperatives, such as a rule-based approach (termed deontic, such as always telling the truth) versus an outcome-based approach (termed teleological, such as lying for a good reason, e.g., a reply to an intending murderer about the location of your children). Complex ethical choices involve both procedural and outcome considerations. The point is to develop the capacity to make choices that serve deeper aims and to use a deliberate, reflective process to arrive at the best decision. Each decision requires a unique balance between outcome and process criteria. These issues are further addressed in Chapter 9, which considers how planners avoid missteps in decisions or actions.

Components of Decisions: Feelings, Rational Thought, and Soul

Having reviewed the types of decisions that idealist planners make, we now turn to a process for making decisions. Decision making may be thought of as an instinctive, relatively quick process. My examination of my own processes and my study of philosophical and wisdom traditions suggests that decisions are more complex. My starting point for decision-making is that planners are in the business of promoting reason in decision-making. But if reason is conceived of as only narrow technical rationality—as when the data support the decision—then it may be deficient. I understand reason as including a broader basis than ends/means concordance.

The following presents three components of decisions: feelings, rational thought, and the soul. They are named separately and sequentially simply to describe them—in practice, all three may be considered simultaneously. The more planners are able to recognize and consider these three elements, the more robust their decisions will be.

Feelings

Let's start with feelings. I contend that contemporary society elevates feelings beyond their appropriate role in decision making. Often, people are exhorted to "go with their gut." But "gut" is often undefined—does this mean feelings, intuition, or something related to indigestion? If it is feelings, which is often the case, they provide essential information, but I assert that they shouldn't dominate decisions. Feelings can point to fundamental values that should be heeded or, conversely, they can be false guides. Being dominated by fear, for example, may prevent planners from taking on doable challenges. Or, planners may allow anger with a nasty colleague to propel them out of an organization that otherwise provides an opportunity to grow. Feelings tend to be fast—not deliberative. They rush us to action. There is no existence without feelings, but feelings should take their place with rational thought and listening for deeper urgings. *Too much* reliance on feelings can lead to impulsive decisions.

People talk about their feelings as if they are sacred and true. Feelings are often related to the part of people that has a goal of self-preservation of the current version of "them." Feelings do not necessarily point to a higher purpose that might be different from what planners are currently doing. Proof that feelings should not drive decisions is often evident when two people are angry with one another. Are they thinking straight and considering the bigger picture? Probably not. Feelings may say "extend the conflict" until one person wins, whereas the calmer rational mind knows that isn't a good idea.

I'm not against feelings. Joy, love, and companionship are wonderful feelings. But other feelings, such as excessive fear and hatred, do not serve idealist planners, and they should not be the only guide to decisions.

Rational Thought

Rational thought is the realm of analysis, evidence, pros and cons, salary comparisons, risk assessment, decision trees, and the like. Even though it is systematic, it occurs in an environment that is uncertain and dynamic. Many tend to think of rational thought as a given capability rather than a skill to cultivate, but it can be cultivated. In fact, planners have extra training in this area because the basis of the planning process is rationality. Information and clear thinking are essential to making good choices, so we can employ our planning skills to assess if the means (what we are about to decide to do) are in alignment with our desired ends (our goals). For example, if I said my goal was to run a marathon in under 3 hours but I did not train for the race, you would say I was irrational. Those means do not support the goal.

Box 3.2 provides an account of a planner's criteria for selecting a job as he relaunches his career on completing his Master's degree. There are three elements: financial feasibility, potential for advancement, and proximity to friends and family. The first and third criteria are straightforward and measureable, but the second one is probabilistic based on research on the prospective organization.

Let's say the planner in Box 3.2 has a job offer. He will want to find out the specifics of salary, working conditions, supervisory arrangements, likely work assignments, and so on. Although not part of his three main criteria, he

---

Box 3.2 Jack of All Trades, Intended Master of Many
By Brian Bulaya, Champaign, Illinois

After completing an undergraduate professional degree in Urban and Regional Planning, I immediately began a Master's degree with an emphasis in International and Community Development, and Entrepreneurship. Now that I am almost finished with this degree, I face conflicting career paths.

I aspire towards a pluralistic career—one that combines my skills and passions in a variety of sectors. At the moment, I am a community builder, entrepreneur, and budding development practitioner. In addition to my graduate studies, I managed and directed an interdisciplinary placemaking group, CitiSpace.

My decision-making process is based on three main criteria: financial feasibility, potential for upward mobility, and proximity to friends and family. With regard to financial feasibility, I first analyze opportunities based on pay, benefits, cost of living, and city amenities. Second, I consider the potential for expedited career advancement and upward mobility. When thinking about this, I ask myself this question: which career opportunity might help me accomplish my 10-year goals sooner? I seek mentorship, promotion, and opportunities to travel and lead teams. Lastly, I crave time with friends and family. I moved out of my parents' home at the age of 16 to pursue higher education, and since then, each choice has taken me farther from the people I care about most. Now that I am 24, I want a job that will allow more contact with them.

Once I graduate, I plan to transition from local urban planning to international development consulting in Washington, D.C. I want to learn the intricacies of operations, logistics, and project management, and advance my technical skills so that I can launch my own firm. I have interests in working in Africa and my home country, the Democratic Republic of Congo. The questions I ask myself are: (1) Given the current state of politics and foreign affairs in America, is this the best time to pursue the development realm? (2) Should I advance my skills in city planning or federal government offices, and then transition into development?

I funnel all of my career decisions through the three criteria for decisions outlined above. In today's entrepreneurial and dynamic environment, I feel that planners must diversify their skill sets and not simply self-select into one career box. Expertise in one field makes the planner an authoritative figure within a specialized niche, but that niche may disappear or become obsolete. My instinct is to maintain a variety of interests, explore each one of them, and not lock myself into just one.

---

will likely seek information on other aspects, such as the organizational culture, the reputation of the organization in the profession, and the general prospects of that sector of planning. No one can predict the future, but it is prudent for the planner to think through possible scenarios for how the job will turn out. Chapter 6 provides more suggestions on how to do this.

Objectivity is key in collecting needed information internal and external to the organization. In other words, if a planner has already decided he or she wants to take the job, he or she may only recognize positive information and discount or ignore negative information. Planners should assess conditions as they really are rather than project an idealized version to justify a decision that has already been made.

Once a planner has collected information about the choice and its context, many tools can help organize thoughts and the evidence at hand. The simplest method is to assemble a list of pros and cons associated with a decision. The pros and cons may be personal *and* related to the planner's mission. Normally, we think of an option with lots of cons as being undesirable, but the risk of a simple list is that the pros and cons are of differing importance. Summing the pros and cons on each side could be misleading, because a single pro or con may trump all of the rest. It would be more analytical to assign weights to the pros and cons, but they may feel like an artificial use of numbers in a decision that should be made more holisitically.

The other way of using a pro and con analysis is seeing it as a learning tool for the process of deciding. In other words, a planner might compile pros and cons that clearly suggest a course of action but then realize "that's not what I want!" That is because the planner realizes that another decision factor, usually a value rather than a fact, has been lurking in the back of his or her mind. It bursts into consciousness and says "wait!" Therefore, the reaction to the pro and con list can be used to probe for other unexpressed values and concerns.

The other aspect of decision-making is that the outcomes have different consequences and probabilities. A decision tree displays all the possibilities so they can be examined in the light of day. I use decision trees to sort through alternative paths with different probabilities and desirability.

Figure 3.1 shows a decision tree for a question that my graduate students face. They have the option of taking a two-and-a-half-day comprehensive exam or writing a thesis as their culminating experience. The exam has a preparatory study class, with the exam offered in the following semester. The thesis takes two semesters at minimum. Both include an oral examination.

The decision tree in Figure 3.1 has three symbols—the square represents a decision point—thesis or comprehensive examination. Paths then follow to circles, which are uncertainty nodes, where different outcomes are possible. Triangles represent terminal nodes, in this case graduation or failure to

Time...

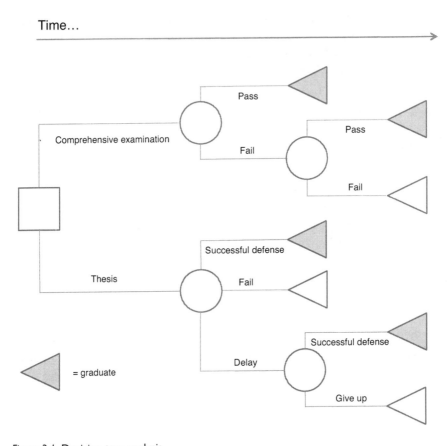

Figure 3.1 Decision tree analysis

graduate in a certain period of time. The terminal nodes of graduating with the degree are shaded. Students assess the value of these terminal nodes— obviously graduating has more value than not graduating, but there may be other distinctions. For example, a student who wants a thesis to provide evidence of research and writing ability may value that option over the comprehensive exam. A student who seeks the challenge of performing under pressure may value the comprehensive exam more highly. And of course, time is also a factor. Finishing the thesis in a year is a more desirable outcome than experiencing a research delay and finishing a year later. Students who don't finish in their final year in the Master's program often have difficulty carving out the time to complete the thesis after they leave school, posing a significant risk. In this scenario, the comprehensive examination can be retaken once, so time delay enters in the scenarios as well.

An estimation process determines the probability of each path. For example, what is the probability that a student will pass the comprehensive exam? That assessment can rely on past exam pass-rates, along with a self-assessment of how the student performs on comprehensive tests in a time-limited format. For the thesis, the assessment is the probability of completing and defending a thesis in the desired time frame. That assessment has to do with the student's time availability, access to data on the research topic, and self-discipline to keep tasks moving. Probabilities summing to 1.0 are assigned to all branches emerging from an uncertainty node.

When I introduce this exercise, many students initially say they want to do a thesis. The key probability is the chance of completing the thesis in the shorter time period. Students often underestimate delays in problem definition, data collection, and analysis. When that is considered, the higher probability of passing the comprehensive examination in the shorter time period may compensate for a higher value being assigned to writing a thesis. When they undergo this step-by-step analytical way of looking at the choice, some students switch to the comprehensive exam. As with all other methods, the decision tree doesn't tell you what to do. Rather, it helps unpack your thinking, identify key variables, and clarify your values and predictions, and ultimately leads to a better decision.

Soul

As with feelings, rational thought alone is inadequate because it doesn't answer critical questions of purpose or meaning. In the example of a person wanting to run a marathon, we would normally say that the goal is a good one because it leads to fitness and accomplishment. But goals can be misguided. For example, what if the reason for the training was to ignore legitimate demands for time from a spouse or children? A seemingly rational goal is more complex when considered in context. Rational thought is good at clarifying mean/ends relationships and following cause and effect, but it is not enough to provide the only guidance on ends. Rational thought taken too far has the opposite effect of overreliance on feelings. It can lead to logical decisions without clear purpose. It can also lead to analysis paralysis, where nothing is decided because one more piece of information is always needed.

Thus far, we have discussed feelings and rational thought, neither of which, I contend, is sufficient on its own. What of the third element, the "non-verbal murmurings of the soul"? This is based on the notion that each person has a purpose, perhaps unknown, that is not available to conventional linguistic expression. I refer to this as the soul, a deep, pre-verbal part of a person's essence. For a religious person, the soul may be understood as a part of the human that has a resonance with the divine. If the person is secular, then the soul may be thought of as the deepest reservoir of meaning. If the idea of soul doesn't fit a person's conception, then perhaps it can be thought of as a purpose. With any of these understandings of soul or purpose, we can't say what the soul knows, but we may sense it in art, music, and interpersonal intimacy. That's why it murmurs, rather than expressing clear feelings or logical statements.

What does a soul know that you cannot express in feelings or rational thought? This knowing can take the form of yearnings, where a planner is drawn to something, someone, or an organization, but doesn't know exactly why. It is the feeling we get when something is just or beautiful. Box 6.4 describes a planner falling in love with Scandinavia and then developing a game plan to work there based on that impulse.

The soul element of decision-making is active when a planner senses an alignment and rightness in the situation or opportunity. We may notice that soul purpose when we observe synchronicity in events, where things just seem to work out and there is a feeling of "rightness." Our soul also might murmur its unease with a course of action with a vague feeling that escapes clear expression. Being aware that we are not just feelings and rational thought is the first step in engaging this dimension. Accepting mystery is another—not everything a person chooses or wants makes rational sense. Soul hints at purpose.

Acknowledging soul in decision-making means giving it time and cultivating quiet so that we can hear its echoes. We may do this at work while dreaming or in fantasies that arise when we awake. The soul doesn't speak directly and can't compete with the cacophony of feelings and logical arguments. Many practices create the kind of quiet when the soul can murmur, such as making art or music, walking in nature, running, sailing, meditating, practicing yoga, etc. As discussed in Appendix B, these activities quiet our minds to create an empty space, the "room" into which deeper purpose can make itself known.

I see life as a journey. If we are attentive to the murmurings of our soul, we will grow throughout our lives, finding deeper meaning in our work, family, and community. When we become older, there is satisfaction in knowing that we have found an alignment between our personal and professional life and our soul.

Good decisions involve a three-part system of feelings, rational thought, and soul. Just acknowledging the presence of these factors improves decisions.

Giving each element its proper due, in sharp contrast to a snap judgment or a "follow your gut" approach, takes a skilled will. The process requires time, internal dialogue, and reflection. It benefits from dialogues with people who can identify blind spots or points of resistance. It may seem complicated and a lot of effort, but consider this: perhaps a planner's greatest capability in bringing repair to the world is bringing good decision-making to public processes.

Slow Down and Speed Up

Each decision an idealist planner makes may require its own pace. Some decisions should be made quickly and decisively, whereas others require extended deliberation. In many instances, I have benefited from slowing down my decision-making so I can consider feelings, rational analysis, and soul. This three-part method also helps me address doubt, as discussed in Chapter 2. Managing doubt is a prerequisite to making good choices. Is doubt a normal concern about leaving friends and family, such as occurs when we leave a comfortable work environment? If that's all it is, we might ignore it. Or is the doubt a whisper from our soul that something is amiss? How can a person tell? A given situation could call for us to face down our fears about growing and trying new things, or on the other hand, help us to recognize subtle, non-verbal messages that say the decision isn't right.

If we decide against an opportunity, an internal critic (or a real person) might criticize that action as a failure of nerve. If the right answer was to decline the opportunity, we shouldn't pay much attention to the critic.

And Now to You: Courage and Authenticity

The advice to slow down and deliberate is useful for most decision-makers, especially the impulsive ones. Yet in some situations, I am *too* deliberative and do not decide on a timely basis. If this describes you, temper your vacillation and choose more decisively. Not choosing is choosing the status quo, which might not be the best thing.

Taking a further step, there *are* times when we should proceed when rational analysis suggests that the cause is lost, the challenge too great, and the risk too high. History is replete with stories of people who decided to move ahead against the odds, even though they felt their inner resources were insufficient. This chapter's suggestions for deliberative decision-making, therefore, should be taken in the context of recognizing the essential role of courage in positive social change. Sometimes we should just commit.

If you are lost in the woods, what should you do? Some people panic, drain their resources, and run in circles. Others sit down where they are and reconnoiter. They may not know where they are going, but they can recognize the path they came on and avoid repeating that. Moving calmly into an unknown future is fine; backsliding and returning the way you came may not be.

Good decision-making can sustain itself in a headwind. One headwind is self-doubt, as discussed in Chapter 2. Another is weak employment conditions that derail otherwise sensible career decisions. A third is expectations, of two types. Your choices may be constrained by what others think you should do—parents, professors, mentors, friends, and supervisors. What they want for you might be right, but only if it's also right for you. Or you may be constrained by your own expectations—for example, that you should be planner director within a decade. These headwinds can knock you off course. Certainly consider input from others, but the best decisions are made out of your authentic self, in freedom.

Choosing produces experience, engagement with the world, and learning. We grow as a people in the experiences we have. Choices may feel weighty at the time, but if you are early in your career, it's fine to make a choice that doesn't work out—it adds to your experience. You are an influential person in a very large system. As my friend Paul Niebanck says, "find a way through that doesn't compromise your integrity and that enlarges your life."

Discussion/Reflection Questions for Chapter 3

1. Reflect on a recent decision you made. How did you decide? How much was the decision shaped by feelings, rational thought, and soul? In reflection, did you deliberate an appropriate amount?
2. Make a list of the top five decisions you expect to make in the next decade. Does the form of decision influence how you should think about it? If so, how; if not, why not?
3. Use the decision tree process to analyze a choice you are currently facing. How do you assess the value of different outcomes and their probability?

Chapter 4

What Is My Work?

Learn your purpose,
and take it to work.

Being productive and finding meaning in professional work is accomplished if the work is aligned with the planner's core purpose. By core purpose, I mean something akin to a personal mission statement—the best use of a planner's idealism, motivation, and talents in professional life. A planner's work must correspond to real needs, of course, so core purpose must intersect with the world's need.

To know their core purpose, planners need self-knowledge. This is gained in a lifelong process of experiencing, reflecting, and discovering. Self-knowledge relies on reflective practices, as discussed in Appendix B. Moreover, because people are dynamic, knowing a purpose is not a one-time event but a continuous practice. The more we know ourselves, the more effectively we can align our planning work with our core purpose.

This chapter provides a framework for considering the types of planning work available, going beyond simple classifications such as land use planner to the variety of ways that a land use planner effectuates change. This chapter is paired with Chapter 5, which addresses different types of organizations within which idealist planners may work. If this choosing seems daunting, consider the alternative—in earlier times, parents, an elder, or a teacher assigned people work, even if it did not suit them. Seen in that light, the opportunity of choice is a privilege.

Types of Planning Work

More than in some professions, acquiring an education in urban and regional planning is just the first step in planners choosing their work. While drawing on the same core identity, the specializations in transportation planning, community development, environmental planning, land use and zoning, and urban design offer different paths. Some subfields of planning are technocratic, others are creative, and still others are political. Although planners may change the focus of their work many times in a career, its important to select a fruitful area for their career launch.

Even when planners know that they want to work in housing, for instance, there are choices about the form of planning practice. A planner could be a housing developer, work on zoning reform that supports housing development, create housing master plans, or generate housing finance solutions. Unfortunately, beginning planners often lack information about the nature of day-to-day work in the different subfields.

The chapter does not provide an inventory of planning work types. It assumes that the reader has an initial idea of the planning subject matter that is of interest. There are useful resources for considering planning subfields, such as *Insider's Guide to Careers in Urban Planning* (2009) and *Becoming an Urban Planner* (2010). Of course, planning subject matter is not the only factor—planning occurs at multinational, federal, state, regional, and local levels, and it occurs in the public, private, and non-profit sectors. Drawing on those resources and others, and organizing the work according to focus, Table 4.1 describes three common types of planning work by their general focus. Planners should consider a wide range of options and narrow down their near-term targets.

The line between planning and allied professions is indistinct. Planning work overlaps with architecture, biology, climatology, community organizing, economics, ecosystem management, engineering, finance, geography, landscape architecture, law, politics, public health, social work, and many other professions. Table 4.2 describes a range of related work that may be considered as planning. These allied professions may use similar methods of problem-solving, analysis, collaboration, organizing, advocating, and the like. Indeed, recognizing these similarities and forming a bridge with them can strengthen the planner's effectiveness.

Table 4.1 Types of planning work

People and Equity	Place and Environment	Systems and Efficiency
• Advocacy planning • Code writing and implementation • Community engagement and empowerment • Community development • Education • Equity planning/ social justice • Housing planning and policy • Planning education • Public health and active communities • Research • Social services	• Climate change planning • Code writing and implementation • Community planning • Disaster response planning • Environmental and natural resources planning • Campus planning and facilities management • Hazard and resiliency planning • Historic preservation planning • Neighborhood, district, and community design • Placemaking/restorative spaces • Planning education • Research • Sustainability/green communities planning and land conservation • Sustainable energy	• Community planning • Economic development planning • Infrastructure planning • Land use planning, law, and code enforcement • Planning education • Research • Spatial planning, including geographic information systems • Transportation planning • Zoning administration and subdivision regulation

Table 4.2 Types of planning-related work

People and Equity	Place and Environment	Systems and Efficiency
• Affordable housing development • Anti-poverty activism • Corporate responsibility advisor • Education reform • Immigrant rights organizing • Labor advocacy • Legislative advisor • Public health advocacy • Public interest law • Research • Social work	• Architectural design • Climate change analysis • Conservation/ecologists/ biologists • Corporate responsibility advisor • Eco-entrepreneurship • Environmental activism • Environmental law • Forest/fisheries management • Campus design and sustainability • Landscape architecture • Parks and recreation • Land stewardship • Legislative advisor • Public interest law • Real estate development • Renewable energy developers • Research	• Job creation/ retention • Redevelopment • Infrastructure engineering • Public administration • Public utility law and regulation • Renewable energy • Research • Software/data visualization/ cartography • Water conservation • Workforce development

This brief review of planning subfields, as described above, is just a start. Beginning planners should focus on selecting their first area of planning practice. I say first, because it will likely change over time. My career, for instance, has addressed land use planning, transportation planning, climate change planning, and planning education. The process for deciding on a subfield should involve internship experiences, shadowing professionals, informational interviews with experts, professional conference attendance, course selections, and discussions with professors. The reflection processes outlined in Appendix B may be useful in this decision.

Follow Your Bliss?

The planner may be thinking at this point, "This can't be that hard—I'll just *follow my bliss* and everything will unfold as it should." This idea was articulated by Joseph Campbell (1968), who combined modern psychology with comparative mythology in the book *A Hero With a Thousand Faces*. He wrote about a process of being called to a purpose, experiencing trials and successes, and a return. Although planners are not mythological heroes, some planners experience something like a "call" to planning in their desire to bring reform and repair to the world. This is evidenced in planning's utopian and social reform roots. Certainly, planners do experience trials along the way, successes and failures, and some are held as models, such as Cleveland advocacy planner Norman Krumholtz.

Campbell also said, "My general formula for my students is 'Follow your bliss.' Find where it is, and don't be afraid to follow it" (Campbell and Moyers, 1988, p. 120). He suggests that openness to a path brings opportunities and synchronicities that a person should follow. This call to have faith, to begin along a path without a clear destination, is inspiring to me and consistent with my experience.

My planning career was launched in difficult economic times, so I would have been skeptical of Campbell at that time. I was trying to get started, to get a job, and to survive economically. I did not *follow my bliss* at the beginning of my career. Maybe I missed something by not having that point of view, but at the time it would have seemed a luxury I could not afford.

As my career progressed and I achieved a foothold in the profession, the "follow your bliss idea" made more sense. I paid attention to how I was feeling about things at each step of the way and actively sought the best use of my abilities. I pursued opportunities that were aligned with my perception of my core purpose.

A cautionary note is that bliss is much more, and much deeper, than doing what we like or what makes us feel good. Planners can't *follow their bliss* unless they have insight. The term *bliss* may give the impression that work should be fun and effortless, but that is not necessarily the case. As one mentor said to me, "maybe Campbell should have said, *follow your work, or follow your blisters."* That rings truer. There is no progress without work, without putting in the effort. And a series of experiences that doesn't feel like bliss could lead to a job that does, as described in Box 6.3, the story of one planner's journey to a dream job.

A second issue with *following your bliss* is to expect perfection before committing. Yes, planners should be true to their core purpose, but they shouldn't stay on the sidelines because a perfect opportunity is not available. A flawed job may lie on a path to a good one. Sometimes, when I've made a suggestion about a work opportunity, a student has said, "that organization doesn't fit my values" or "I wouldn't live in that community." If these reasons are cited too often, those planners won't make the contribution they want. Picky people may overlook opportunities.

Box 4.1 is an account by a non-planner seeking work supporting immigrant and refugee rights. The writer was unable to move directly into the area of work she wanted after a cross-country move, but she decided to make the investment in engaging with her new community by working in the related social justice area of homelessness. She is using this experience to set up a shift into her first preference, immigrant and refugee rights.

Reinterpreting Campbell's quote as *follow your work* puts the idealist in play, even in an imperfect work setting—to meet people, gain experience, and have opportunities to reflect on those experiences. It is possible to be too

---

Box 4.1 The Social Reformer's Path
By Mandy Park, Assistant to the Executive Director, Building Changes, Seattle, Washington

I recently moved to Seattle from the Northeast in search of professional opportunity. I had enjoyed getting to know and working in the distinct rural, agricultural community of Vermont. Despite New England being a homogeneous area, I found networks through which I could link my graduate degree in Intercultural Service, Leadership and Management to my work. Although my interest was working with immigrant and refugee communities and creating more equitable systems, I took on roles that focused on distantly related content and held multiple jobs simultaneously to piece together a full income—often the practice in Vermont. My expectation moving to Seattle was that I would find a single role where I could directly apply my knowledge and skills in a more diverse community.

Once in Seattle, it was just a couple months of informational interviews, job applications, conversations with friends, and personal reflection before I was confronted with a frustrating reality: my original expectations were not going

Box 4.1 (continued)

to be met. I had envisioned myself working as an ally, supporting immigrants, refugees, and equitable processes by managing outreach, advocacy, and education strategies. What became clear was that the ally role in Vermont is markedly different than it is in Seattle. I learned this most clearly when applying for positions with the Seattle Office of Refugee and Immigrant Affairs. I was told by a friend and colleague, "They're looking for someone from within the community. They can do their own work."

The lesson was one I knew well, but one that I needed to revisit: I am not a savior. I do not have a unique capacity beyond those already doing the work. My experiences and observations are important, but they do not stand alone as broadly applicable credentials for "expertise." I can join the movement, but I will not define it. I can have the greatest impact by listening first and then identifying my role second.

I had worked through this lesson thoughtfully and slowly in Vermont—and before that in the Peace Corps. I want my input and influence to be inclusive, well-informed, stakeholder-led, and cautious of unintended consequences. This requires intentional observation and prudent reflection. What is the need as defined by the community who needs it? What work and conditions are ongoing, and what is the history of successes, challenges, and leadership that has shaped them? Where can my specific strengths deliver impact? How can I join the efforts unique to this context without perpetuating the disparity and disproportionality I seek to dismantle? With these questions unanswered, I could not define my ideal role until Seattle and I became better acquainted.

However painstaking, taking time to research, observe, hear, and engage with the community I seek to impact is a critical step towards finding the "right" work. With a passion for supporting immigrant and refugee communities, it was difficult to not have a position doing this work directly. But taking time to understand the locally specific, bigger picture means seeing points of access. It means understanding the implications of my input so that I can find opportunities that are in line with my values. For these, I'm willing to give adequate pause.

Now, as an assistant to the Executive Director of a non-profit working to end homelessness in three Washington counties, I contribute to efforts that positively impact my community. My role does not directly engage me with immigration and refugee resettlement, nor does it offer the application of skills I ultimately seek, but it does provide important links. I am learning about people, systems, politics, best practices, cultures, strengths, challenges, and opportunities unique to Seattle. Working for a well-positioned non-profit sets me up to make cross-sector professional connections. Working with homelessness educates me about this complex issue. With this experience, I am laying the groundwork for making more informed, more positively impactful contributions. With patience, I know it will lead me to the work I want most.

preoccupied with self-actualization. Some school experiences and mentors teach young people to live their dream and to be critical—two admirable things—but in combination those views can go too far.

A third issue with the idea of bliss is that the planner may be serving a false purpose instead of a core purpose. Elements of a false purpose could include:

- *Expectations created by others, such as parents, mentors, teachers, and the like.* Maybe the planner's parents thought he would be a community organizer, but that does not ring true. Perhaps a teacher saw a minor talent and pushed the person to pursue it, ignoring a greater talent. A planner may have an uneasy feeling in following a direction that he or she doesn't fully claim. Or, those around them may expect them to stay the same, even if they want to change.

- *Being able to do something better than the average person.* This does *not* necessarily mean that a planner should do that thing. If good at facilitating tension-filled meetings, a planner will be rewarded for that. But if that causes stress-related health problems, this work may be at odds with a greater purpose. If a planner is a skilled data analyst, there will be rewards in working with geographic information systems or spreadsheets. For some, this work provides an orderly world where a natural inclination to detail and precision is realized. For others, such a work life lacks human interaction.

- *Allowing the natural progression of advancement to lead a planner into an area of work outside of her or his core purpose.* For example, suppose a planner excels at the technical aspects of planning, but in moving up the management level, finds that it is a bad fit. Many planning directors long for the days when they could sketch a design or research a problem.

Part of the process of finding purpose is to identify natural affinities and tendencies. How does the planner process information? How does the planner encounter the world? More specifically, I mean personality dimensions such as extroversion (people-oriented) or introversion (to live in one's head). In addition, there are differences in how people see the world and process information, such as an intuitive approach or empirical, data-driven basis for processing information. There are also distinctions in preferred decision-making processes, such as those who rely on logical thinking or those who rely on emotional information. Finally, some planners prefer a methodical approach whereas others prize spontaneity and flexibility.

Different personality dimensions were identified by psychologist Carl Jung (1981) and are reflected in the Myers-Briggs personality assessment and related tools. People have different ways of perceiving and acting, and self-knowledge about instincts and preferences is helpful. Appendix B provides more discussion about using these techniques as a way of reflecting on purpose. As an aside, understanding more about personality types is a great way to improve a planner's ability to function in teams, manage people, and generally get along in the profession.

A personality assessment may suggest that a planner has a natural tendency for a certain role in planning. Let's say the planner has characteristics that suggest a *mediator* personality type. That type of person is intuitive and good at understanding other people's thoughts. Such an assessment may suggest that she or he should pursue planning work that involves mediation, such as consensus-building at the grassroots community level. The catch is that the planner has to make sure to be good at it too and have the tools to be effective in that work. Such a planner must be assertive in a tense community situation to create the environment for mediation. Similarly, if a planner's type indicates potential as an executive, like a planning director, then the planner also needs the emotional intelligence to go along with a natural tendency to lead.

As discussed here, finding one's core purpose is not easy. Because most people evolve, no one has to figure out their path once and for all. Idealist planners can work on this on the fly. Things are much easier, though, when work decisions can be judged against a provisional definition of the planner's core purpose. All the planner needs to ask is: "Does job opportunity 'A' lead to or take me away from it?" "Does decision 'B' at work advance me in realizing my work?" Considering that basic alignment simplifies decisions.

Sorting out Purpose by Values

What is the technology for finding core purpose and aligning professional activities in support of that? The first step is to gain experiences in a variety of work environments. As planners work in different settings, they can listen to their thoughts and the images that bubble up from their unconscious mind. We may silence discordant thoughts or unconscious voices, however, if what they suggest requires inconvenient changes. Box 4.2 provides an example from my life.

Idealist planners can understand more about their core purpose by considering it in terms of fundamental values. For example, those working in social

---

Box 4.2 Feeling Unease at the Art Gallery

One of my hobbies is landscape painting. I have painted on and off throughout my life. Before I painted regularly, I often felt mildly depressed when I visited art galleries, but I didn't know why. Something was amiss. My legs would get heavy after a few minutes. For starters, viewing so many paintings without studying them carefully seemed to disrespect the work. But on further reflection, I realized there was another issue: the sense that I was spending my time in ways that were out of line with my core purpose. After many decades of reflection, I think my purpose is reaching others through the arts and writing, but I did not have the realization at that time. I often wrote off the sensation as being tired or having a bad day, but I realize that a deeper calling was asserting itself, demanding attention. Awareness of the mismatch between how I spent my time and my purpose brought sadness. Reflecting on this unease and discussing it with others moved it from an implicit concern that I vaguely sensed to one I could identify and consider. I may have pushed away this awareness because acting on it would be inconvenient and make me vulnerable to failure. Landscape painting isn't exactly the hottest thing in the art market. It is always true, however, that I had agency, the authority, to decide what to do about that emergent sense of purpose. And, of course, allowing yearnings expression doesn't give them veto power over your rational choice.

---

planning are motivated by helping people, an expression of a value of love. Environmental planners may be motivated by care of nature, but they are also driven by truth—using science to understand how natural systems function and developing plans to regenerate natural systems.

I believe there are four fundamental values around which a core purpose is organized: love, justice, truth, and beauty. Table 4.3 illustrates the implications of these values by showing the types of work and example jobs associated with each value. The reader might have a different set of fundamental values, but even so, the table illustrates that types of planning work serve different values. Planners may wish to consider and articulate their own value system and whether they have a different interpretation of how values translate to work.

As a thought exercise, consider that all of these four values play some role in motivating professional activity. One or two prominent ones may overlap in a given area of planning work. For example, being a zoning administrator may represent a commitment to fair process (justice), a desire to avoid discriminatory

Table 4.3 Values, types of work, and jobs

Value	Type of planning work	Example jobs
Love	People work: enhancing human capital thorough community development, social service planning, consensus building	Community organizer, facilitator, planning educator, social services planner
Justice	Equity work: fair administrative process, affordable housing, environmental remediation in low- income communities, fairness in public expenditures	Regulator, affordable housing developer, environmental justice advocate, economic developer, social planner
Truth	Science/social science work: environment and systems, and efficiency work: modeling, environmental impact analysis, land use regulation	Regional transportation modeler, environmental impact analyst, climate change planner, researcher, zoning planner
Beauty	Placemaking work: design, design guidelines and review, public art, urban/ nature interface	Urban designer, campus planner, public art administrator, form-based code writer, park planner

practices in zoning (justice), an effort to orderly separate land uses to avoid externalities (truth), and an aspiration for good urban design (beauty).

Truth was the strongest motivating value for me at the beginning of my career—I wanted to produce plans, academic research, and consulting products to improve transportation decision-making. I sought to advance evidence-based public policy. My theory was that good information improves decision-making. As I matured, I learned that good information isn't the only consideration. I became sensitive to the processes of politics and power, and I developed skills to navigate those realms.

Obviously, when planners decide on "their work" doesn't mean that they can impose that view on others. It's not completely for the planner to decide. We return to the notion that planners should seek the intersection of their core purpose and the world's needs. A basic orientation to service will naturally lead them to find out about these needs.

Sorting Out Systems of Change: Grassroots Advocacy Versus Working Inside Big Systems

In addition to figuring out the basic values and subject matter of work, planners benefit by thinking about *how* they will bring about the changes they seek. There are many options, ranging from the grassroots, one person or one community at a time, to working for national governments or international agencies on laws, agreements, tax policy, and other levers of change. Each path has advantages and disadvantages.

Another question to ponder is whether to work for the community as a whole or an underserved group in a community. Some idealist planners think that they *must* work at the grassroots level for an underserved group to be legitimate. That is not the case. Reforms made at international and national levels can have profound benefits for those in need, especially if those reforms are made from within the responsible agencies. For example, there is a broad and systemic impact on transportation equity when a federal transportation bill requires transit project funding applicants to consider impacts on low-income populations.

Let's say an environmental planner seeks to reduce greenhouse gas emissions and is considering the type of work to pursue. Grassroots work is well-suited to those who want a tangible connection to the people, communities, and/or natural systems served. If planners can't stand being behind a desk all day, or bore quickly at meetings, they may love hands-on, grassroots implementation. Grassroots work keeps them grounded and connected to the complexity of the situation. It is very satisfying. Working locally, they can introduce new methods and technologies, generate knowledge and interest in new techniques, build organizational capacity to implement, and so on. They get to speak their truth most of the time. The downside of this approach is less ability to scale-up reform because the work has to happen over and over again in every community.

At the other end of the spectrum, environmental planners could work on a carbon trading scheme at the national or international level. The work is in the realms of economics and law, far from the individuals affected by the scheme. These planners conduct technical analysis, draft agreements and legislation, and set up mechanisms for implementation. They spend lots of time at their desk and participating in meetings. They make compromises in forging agreements among stakeholders. Sometimes, the process seems to go on forever. What they get in return is the power of leverage. A properly functioning carbon trading mechanism has a global or national effect, reducing carbon emissions more broadly than community-by-community implementation can.

Because land use regulation is a local government responsibility in the United States, a career in land use planning is usually practiced at the local level. But even then, there are choices—big city or small town, a mature community or one that has greenfield development.

My research and professional work seeks to use land and resources better by reforming parking requirements and managing parking resources. I have worked locally, community-by-community, to change resident and business perceptions and support reform. This is laborious work because each community undergoes its own process of understanding the issue. Yet I've learned a great deal through the direct feedback that local action produces. The other scale of action is the realm of national law and tax policy. If the intervention is land taxation reform, for example, then *every* community experiences change as landowners reassess their use of land. For example, levying property taxes on land alone—rather than the land and the buildings on the land—creates an economic disincentive for low-intensity uses such as surface parking lots. Because taxes on that land would be the same as if a large building was on it, this would induce property owners to more intensively use scarce land. Such a systemic reform may improve land use efficiency more than working on zoning requirements, community-by-community.

Community-level work is often necessary to produce the "proof on the ground" that a concept works. Only then can national or international action take place. This is what happened in the climate change area, as communities, states, and multistate regions took action while waiting for national and international agreements. Both types of work are necessary. The question for planners is, which work setting is the best fit? Of course, there are options in the middle that balance policy and action. The best way to determine the right place is to seek internships and initial job experiences in a variety of environments so planners can gauge their performance and happiness in each one.

Sorting out Methods of Doing the Work

Let's assume that a planner has a preferred specialty and organization home that is aligned with his or her core purpose. There are still more choices to be made *within* a chosen subfield. For example, a planner interested in climate change planning has options. A "builder" wants to see shovels in the ground for zero-energy buildings, while an "economist" wants to create market-based interventions such as carbon trading. A "regulator" seeks to create fair laws that allow a market economy to work with proper public-interest regulation. "Educators" and "marketers" seek to develop programs that encourage people to change "their behavior". As with the other chapters, the processes to resolve these questions use experience and reflection.

Emerging forms of planning may be more complex and/or fluid. For example, planners in current planning (zoning administration) work in a well-understood planning field. Those planners play a regulatory role, administrating a zoning code that has been written to carry out the intent of the community plan. In the minds of many members of the public, this *is* planning. But in other instances, the work does not fall into a single category. For example, there are no professionally accredited programs for those working on climate change. Climate change strategies mitigate impacts by reducing greenhouse gas emissions or adapt to inevitable changes by changing urban and rural systems, infrastructure, social services, and the like. Although a basic education in climatology and ecological systems is necessary for all climate change planners, this emerging field of planning is still being professionalized.

Good educational and career decisions are enhanced by due diligence about the options. One way of considering them is to think about the way in which change is implemented. Table 4.4 shows a two-by-two matrix that distinguishes

Table 4.4 Alternative ways to make change

	Direct Strategies	Indirect Strategies
Monetary (funds do the work)	1. Provide, purchase, program, aka "The Engineer" • Plan for dams and reservoirs to capture more rainfall • Design programs and implement projects that purify waste water and recharge aquifers	2. Tax, price, subsidize, aka "The Economist" • Price water so the cost increases with the amount used, encouraging conservation • Provide subsidies for water use efficiency, such as low-use appliances
Non-monetary (rules, convincing, agreements)	3. Require, prohibit, allow, aka "The Regulator" • Develop ordinance requirements for water-efficient appliances in new construction and renovation • Establish caps on water consumption, e.g., a maximum use per capita for households	4. Inform, implore, facilitate, aka "The Educator/Marketer" • Create residential water user public awareness campaigns • Develop advertising campaigns for water-efficient industrial equipment

between methods of implementation, using water resource management as an example. Each quadrant is associated with planning, but each one also links to other professions and associated academic disciplines. Which form of implementation is the best fit with a planner's talents and inclination? Or, does the planner want to be engaged in all four?

There's much more to selecting a professional focus than considering a two-by-two matrix, but it is worthwhile to use the table to spur reflective thinking about planning work options. Also, planners will likely change quadrants as their career evolves. The great advantage of planning's loosely defined boundaries is that it is not locked into a narrow approach—we planners move more freely among all the quadrants than those in other professions do.

The quadrant planners choose affects where they gain skills in related disciplines. Civil engineering or hydrology programs are good for quadrant 1. Quadrant 2 utilizes environmental economics, while quadrant 3 involves environmental law, political science, or public administration. Lastly, quadrant 4 draws on communications, marketing, or education. Each one provides useful contributions to addressing the problem.

Box 4.3 describes a transportation planner's transition from transit planning to the operational issue of transit workplace safety and worker's compensation. After initially doubting the applicability of her planning skills to this topic, the writer found career advancement and empowerment in an unexpected area that was critical to delivering safe and cost-effective transit services. Following an opportunity led to a new way of realizing planning goals.

Sorting out a Future as a Manager

Most planning careers move from technically oriented tasks into management. Junior planners for a consulting firm are likely to research and write reports for clients. Questions about whether to bid for projects, how to respond to client or political pressures, and personnel issues are beyond the beginning planner's scope. They take direction from above and do not decide strategic questions. At a public agency, junior planners write staff reports for zoning actions, administer zoning regulations at the public counter, or review environmental documents. Similarly, determinations about how to handle controversial issues are made by planning directors and city managers.

Box 4.3 When the Phone Rings, Answer It

By Andrea Burnside, Chief Performance Officer, Washington Metropolitan Area Transit Authority, Washington, DC

I was 28 years old when I finally figured out what to do with my life: urban planning! Two and a half years later, graduate planning degree in hand, I was up and running in my new career at the Los Angeles County Metropolitan Area Transportation Authority. I was lucky to have landed a great job just as I was graduating.

Right from the beginning of my career, I've taken chances and tried new things. I believe this attitude is key to my career success. I moved through various roles within the planning department, often being asked as the junior team member to take on projects or programs that others didn't want or couldn't complete. The best projects were generally assigned to the most senior planners. It seemed like a long road ahead.

Eight years later and growing restless, my planning career suddenly and unexpectedly moved in a new direction. A new CEO/COO team had just been selected to lead the agency. Their first mandate was to address the spiraling cost of injuries and lost time due to worker's compensation claims. Week one, I was surprised to receive a phone call from the COO, asking to meet with me. As a staff-level planner, I rarely interacted with executives. He proposed to borrow me from planning for a few months to manage the important new safety initiative within transit operations. I admit I had to think about it for a few days. What did I know about safety and worker's compensation? After some deliberation, and being asked more than once, I accepted the prominent assignment and never looked back. One opportunity led to another, and within a few short years I was a managing director responsible for corporate safety and operations central instruction. I applied my planning skills in an area that initially seemed far from planning but that was crucial to supplying safe and cost-effective transit services.

Many years later, I asked the COO why he tapped me for this special assignment. He told me that he had asked the Chief Planning Officer for the names of some of his best project managers, and my name was offered. I was pleasantly surprised to learn this! I always worked diligently to ensure my projects were successful, but I often felt invisible within the large department. Little did I know that senior management had noticed my work. I spent many years working with the COO, who became my mentor and sponsor. When he later accepted the CEO position at the Washington Metropolitan Area Transit Authority, he asked me to move east and join his new executive team.

Planners possess a unique combination of skills that are valuable in areas that may be outside of traditional planning departments. I used my planning skills to advance my career in unexpected ways because I was willing to take chances, to move out of my planning comfort zone.

Because this book is about the early career experience, these management issues are not addressed in detail. It is, however, worth thinking about management early. I have worked for planning directors who did not care for management—they longed to do the actual planning work. They may have been promoted for their planning skills but found management a poor fit with their temperaments. Other supervisors were natural managers, who dealt with team-building, personnel management, and politics with ease. Planners should test their aptitude and interest in management in school team projects and in their first years of professional work. Because moving into management is the normal career trajectory, planners benefit if they get an early sense of their attraction or aversion to management.

If management is interesting, planners can plot a career path that provides increasing management experience and seek additional training. If management is not interesting, there are paths that allow advancement with less management responsibility. These tend to be jobs that are highly technical, such as a GIS expert or app development innovator, advanced transportation modeler, researcher, or planning educator.

Box 4.4 chronicles a planner's career journey to a management role, describing progressively responsible leadership with teams and with departments. It also shares the manager's approach to supporting staff and creating a team.

Box 4.4 Do I Want to Be a Manager?
By Karen E. Watkins, Planning Manager,
San Bernardino County, California

How is the decision made to move from planner to manager? Is it found in the natural progression in a single agency, through a job change, or in an attraction to a job description that includes management? Most planners expect to move through the hierarchy, eventually reaching supervisor, manager, or director. Or on a more technical track, the planner may reach the principal planner level by managing projects, not people. For me, the progression occurred naturally as I changed jobs and my qualifications better fit management positions.

With a B.S. in Parks and Recreation and an M.S. in Forest Economics, I planned to be a Park Ranger but ended up in private consulting and then local government. I moved from planner to manager in consulting, and then again in government, with varied job duties depending on the size of the organization. I started as an Environmental Planner at a large private firm and then transferred

Box 4.4 (continued)

to a smaller firm as the Director of Planning and Environmental Services. This didn't change my workload but added supervision. The next step was owning my own consulting firm, where I was both planner and manager.

A move from Arizona to Washington changed my role from manager in the private sector to planner in local government. As I moved up from senior planner to principal planner, I expanded my subject focus from environmental planning to long-range planning. Through these changes, I managed projects and teams but did not directly supervise staff. I thought this was how I would end my career, but a move to California led to my current position as the Planning Manager for the largest county in the United States.

Adjusting to the shift from performing the planning tasks to managing planners can be a difficult transition. Initially, I missed the writing and creating aspects of planning, but I realized my values as a manager by providing support and serving as a sounding board to staff planners. The key in this transition was meeting with staff to understand their workload and how to assist them in their projects.

Staff-level planners need to be able to work unmanaged. Although some managers micro-manage, it is ideal when the staff complete their tasks with little assistance from their manager. A manager likes to be informed of the planner's progress or if there are issues, but does not have time to keep track of every detail. Therefore, staff-level planners should learn when to collaborate with other staff and when to seek assistance from management. Trust between the planner and manager is key.

An effective manager touches base with all staff frequently, even if it is a quick "good morning" to see what they may need that day. Keeping a list of potential questions for your boss will help you remember what you want to discuss with them.

Managers and planners work with staff of varying skills and temperaments. Disagreements are expected, but you can learn to work together to come to the best solution. Only by working together can a team be successful. An effective manager may say no to a recommendation or request changes in a report, but she does so in a neutral tone that does not demean the planner. For planners, learning how to treat your team in the same way is key to success. We all make mistakes, so it is best to just learn from them and move on.

Even though I sometimes wish I could take a project from start to finish, I realize that I am able to support my staff and help them be the best planners they can be. I know that this could mean that they will one day take a position elsewhere as they grow and follow their own career path. Looking at the trust given to me by my employer and my relationship with my staff, I know that I am where I should be—managing people.

More discussion about productive ways of interacting with supervisors is provided in Chapter 10.

And Now to You: It's Worth It

This chapter set out many options. It takes effort to select your path, but there's really no choice but to do so, and it doesn't have to be figured out all at once. When times are tough and life's pressures are bearing down, it is natural to take the first job available. But if you don't take charge, you may find at the end of your career that you haven't made the contribution you wanted.

Discussing your core purpose and being wary of false purposes isn't pop psychology—it's at the heart of vital questions in career planning. This is a very *practical* matter. Decisions are much easier when you know the options and can assess them against a reflectively developed core purpose. A well-developed progression of increasingly responsible planning work positions provides the greatest personal satisfaction and impact.

Discussion/Reflection Questions for Chapter 4

1. What is your core purpose (or purposes) at this point in your career? Why?
2. Think back to a job you did not like. Was there a mismatch between it and your core purpose? Or did another reason explain the dislike?
3. What form of planning implementation appeals to you the most—building things, pricing/incentivizing/disincentivizing, regulating, or educating/marketing?
4. Explain your core purpose, planning subject matter, and preferred method of implementation to another person. Ask that person to comment on whether those elements seem aligned and if you have blind spots.
5. Identify five job opportunities that fit your sweet spot of core purpose and preferred method of implementation. Conduct information interviews with people at those jobs to see if you have interpreted them correctly.

References

Campbell, J. (1968). *The hero with a thousand faces.* Princeton, NJ: Princeton University Press.
Campbell, J. and B. Moyers. (1988). *The power of myth.* New York, NY: Doubleday.

Halibur, T. and N. Berg. (2009). *Insider's guide to careers in urban and regional planning.* Los Angeles, CA: Urban Insight, Inc.

Jones, W. and N. Macris. (2000). *A career worth planning.* Chicago, IL: Planners Press; Novato, CA: New World Library.

Yung, C. (1980). *The archetypes and the collective unconscious.* Translated by R.F.C Hull. Princeton, NJ: Princeton University Press.

Chapter 5

What Work Setting?

Bureaucrat or advocate,
leverage or action.

Decisions about the type of work to do, as discussed in Chapter 4, are not the only career choices. Work settings have many dimensions, such as organization size, type (public, private, or non-profit), management style, culture, and arrangements. No particular setting is inherently superior—it is wise to try many of them. This chapter provides tools for thinking about these issues to support the search for the planner's satisfaction and effectiveness.

A Good Fit, Not a Perfect One

Of course, the *perfect* work setting doesn't exist. After all, work settings are the stage on which messy human interactions are played out. If planners are *too* picky about work setting, they will end up on the sidelines, not fulfilling their mission. There are gradations of fit, so it is wise to seek a good fit rather than a perfect one. Also, planners should be realistic—unfortunately, the perks found in tech companies are simply not available in planning.

A public-interest private investigator (the writer of Box 7.3) recently told me about a young person who approached him asking, "How can I end up like you, doing the socially progressive work that you do?" The investigator suggested an organization where that person might seek work, but the response was, "I don't agree with all the goals of that organization." Being too picky can mean not getting started. Starting somewhere provides experiences and introductions to people that help planners on their paths.

Taking this a step farther, planners should consider experiences in work settings that *aren't* a natural fit. For example, entrepreneurial planners may not like working in a large bureaucracy in the long term. They would be happier in a small consulting firm, an app start-up, or a non-profit organization. However, gaining experience in a bureaucracy provides insights into how that type of organization makes orderly decisions, ensures quality, and avoids arbitrary actions. Of course, large bureaucracies don't *necessarily* produce those outcomes, but the good ones do. Some planning work calls for orderly, consistent procedures more than innovation and change.

Working in a bureaucracy may help idealist planners temper an excessively change-first approach, or at least give a broader perspective on its dimensions. Furthermore, an experience in a large organization can teach how entrepreneurship works in that setting. As planners work in smaller organizations later in their career, they can apply the lessons learned in the bureaucracy, and they will be more effective in interacting with large organizations.

Avoid Toxic Work Environments—Seek Positive Ones

There are a number of traditional dimensions to seeking an alignment between work setting and the planner, such as a preference to work alone or in collaborative teams. We'll discuss those as the chapter unfolds. But before we get there, let's address toxic work environments. It may seem dramatic to say, but some work settings should be avoided. What kinds of problems exist that should be a red flag? I've seen the following:

- *Organizations that do not address conflicts head-on.* They are characterized by fakeness and inauthenticity in professional and social dimensions. People aren't straightforward. They use gossip, indirect sanctions, and formal grievance procedures to avoid directly addressing issues. Some of these organizations have the *appearance* of a happy, well-functioning team.
- *Organizations that speak employee empowerment language but don't mean it, or that twist it to humiliate, sanction, and punish.* It is a fine line, for example, between

supportive coaching and bullying—the same language may be used, but the way it is delivered could provide support or undermine confidence.

- *Organizations that tolerate supervisors who behave badly.* That bad behavior includes raging, verbally abusing subordinates, sexual harassment, or acting in passive-aggressive ways. Or, a supervisor may not be trustworthy, blaming a staffer when she or he made a mistake. Many "boss" problems are with people who have found their way into management but are not suited to it. They may be in survival mode themselves.
- *Organizations that do not have an ethical code of behavior.* This may include a consulting firm that adjusts analytic results to please clients, non-profit organizations whose staff lie on grant applications or progress reports, and public agencies that inconsistently implement regulations to favor politically connected developers. Idealist planners' reputations decline when they work for these organizations, even if they do not behave unethically.

These problems are not the kind that organizations advertise. Candidates should check around discretely with people inside and outside the organization to see if such problems exist. They can read news stories about the organization, its leaders, and projects implemented to gain information. The quality of an organization's website may reveal that it doesn't value transparency, accountability, and participation. If considering an offer from such an organization, planners should reflect on whether they have the inner reserves to handle these issues. Such an organization may pay a higher salary or offer more responsibility because their reputation scares away potential employees. If the stress is manageable, there may be an opportunity because of high staff turnover.

In addition, toxic isn't always toxic if it provides a life or professional lesson of value. Box 5.1 provides an example in which an apparently toxic work environment supported my professional growth. Some unpleasant organizational experiences may help planners grow in the long run.

Planners should seek organizations that have a positive team culture and active mentoring. Those organizations are characterized by having a clear focus, leaders that inspire, mid-level managers who create a culture of learning and collaboration, and a good balance of stability and change. They understand that developing young talent is part of their mission. My students have found these qualities in employee-owned consulting firms, well-managed public agencies, and non-profits guided by clear goals and strategies.

The "start-up" culture of small new organizations is informal and built around the shared desire for success (and survival). In larger organizations,

---

Box 5.1 When 'Toxic' Isn't

My earliest planning job was for the first woman-owned planning consulting firm in Canada. The firm consisted of my boss, a draftsperson, an office manager, and me. Making payroll was a continual stress for my boss and owner. She was demanding, impatient, and quick to anger at mistakes. I was in my first professional planning job, lacking experience and confidence. My boss was fighting for the legitimacy of a woman-owned planning firm against well-established competitors.

Because my boss was often out at client meetings, I was often alone in the office without anyone to ask when I didn't know what to do. If I spent one hour writing a letter to a client, she asked me why I hadn't done it in 30 minutes. When I didn't know what to do, I was aware of the clock ticking and no billable product to show for it. She wanted me to have 130% billable hours (i.e., bill clients for justifiable work 52 hours per week) and also provide unbillable business development hours. I was in a new city with few friends, living alone, and unhappy.

It was a harrowing experience, but I stuck with it, not because I was courageous but because few other jobs were available. A slightly worse experience might have broken my self-confidence. But over a year, I slowly found my footing—I understood the pressures she faced, I depersonalized the criticism somewhat, and I learned how to handle her no-nonsense approach. With experience, I became less nervous about making a mistake. I got better at my job and slowly my competence emerged. After about a year, I wrote a housing report, and she told me that was the first time I had shown an ability that exceeded her last employee.

Near the end of my time there, she sent me to represent a client at a hearing on my own, and when I messed up, she was surprisingly forgiving. Over the course of a tough year, I grew and learned how to be a professional planner. When I left the firm I was newly empowered—this apparently "toxic" boss taught me how to work hard, how to be efficient with my time, and how to hustle. She also taught me not to personalize criticism. This experience has benefited me throughout my career. Every time I meet a planner with a poor work ethic, I am grateful for my tough first planning job.

---

good qualities are more formalized. Look for evidence of staff development, which includes team-building activities, professional development and training opportunities, and meaningful performance monitoring and evaluation.

When considering a job offer, planners should do homework on the organization's work culture. There is no way to eliminate risk, but planners can usually find out whether the work environment in the new organization is toxic or positive.

Differences in Work Settings—Public, Non-profit, Private

Table 5.1 describes work in public, non-profit, and private sectors. It uses level of primary job satisfaction, personal effectiveness, and orientation to the public good to differentiate among sectors. The public sector category refers to government agencies at the local, regional, state, and federal levels, or special districts at various geographic levels. The non-profit category includes advocacy organizations, service delivery organizations such as child development centers or museums, affordable housing developers, business incubators, or environmental remediation organizations. Private organizations include consulting

Table 5.1 Satisfaction, effectiveness, and the common good across sectors

Characteristic	Public	Non-profit	Private
Primary job satisfaction	• Serve the public good; long-term • Understand context and witness implementation	• Mission-based; passion; "speak your truth" • Flexible strategies	• Mission- and profit-driven • Teamwork, project completion, quality, winning in the marketplace
Effectiveness	• Systemic (you set the rules of the game) • Long-term orientation, process-heavy, and slow pace of implementation	• Depends on stability, funding, and leverage • Short-term focus	• Tangible products, clear milestones • Quick wins, projects "on the ground" • Short-term focus
Primary orientation to advance the public good	• Assumed, but contested in reality and subject to political determination • More comprehensive approach	• Yes, but often focused on underserved constituency/ underrepresented issue • Founder/ board/funder determined	Yes/no—Yes at the staff level (perhaps), but the market orientation competes with the public good at the management level (customers, lenders, investors, etc.)

firms, real estate developers, renewable energy providers, and many other types of businesses.

Table 5.1 doesn't suggest the best work setting—that depends on the preferred method of making change and the planner's personal preferences. In the long view, the public sector can provide leverage and meaning. For immediate feedback, the non-profit and private sectors may be more satisfying. Considering this continuum of comprehensiveness-versus-focused action can help planners determine the best organizational fit.

In each subfield of planning, the most innovative work may take place in a different setting—public sector, consulting, or non-profit. In transportation planning, for example, much of the interesting work happens in the consulting world. Box 5.2 describes how a person trained in engineering found her way to transportation planning and then found consulting to be the most satisfying way of pursuing that work.

There are distinct differences among organization types. In addition to the broad criteria reviewed in Table 5.1, everyday work life differs. Table 5.2 describes these differences, addressing autonomy, work effort, and commitment. If fairness in the assignment of workload is important, the private sector offers advantages over public sector agencies, where it can be uneven. If living on the edge is appealing, the non-profit sector's financial instability can be exciting.

Consulting and non-profit work can require the longest hours, and time demands vary according to project and grant deadlines. Among the three sectors, consulting is likely to require the most travel. Although public sector work hours are more regular, there may be many evening meetings. Beginning planners should seek a right balance between working hard for their organization and working so hard that they burn out or neglect other life priorities. Box 5.3 provides an account of a consulting planner's process in figuring out how to manage workload expectations. On one hand, planners create a good impression by saying yes to every challenge, but on the other hand, in some jobs, saying yes too much can wear them out.

Home-Based, Small Organization, Large Organization Work Settings

The size of an organization is a consideration in choosing a work setting. Small planning organizations offer lots of responsibility at the junior level—often,

Box 5.2 My Long and Winding Road to Transportation Planning Consulting
By Terri O'Connor, Oakland, CA

While I was an undergraduate student, I had a passion for environmental sustainability and hoped that a career in civil/environmental engineering would support that passion. My first job out of university was as an environmental engineer at a 100-person firm in Boston whose core work was environmental and geotechnical engineering.

I assisted with the clean-up and remediation side of industrial polluting clients. I developed methodologies and conducted field environmental and geotechnical investigations. Although this was initially interesting, I became frustrated with a process that wasn't focused on pollution prevention. Moreover, I struggled with a job and clients that didn't align with my values.

I then investigated graduate programs with a sustainability focus, deciding on an engineering management Master's program that straddled engineering and business. This degree supported a career relocation to the Bay Area to work for an Internet company, where I applied my project and program management skills. With no experience in software or programming, I used soft skills and relationship management. Although I was valued by my team, it became apparent that career fulfillment required my being an integral part of the core mission rather than a supporting player.

An unexpected opportunity arose when all the project managers were laid off during the 2002 downturn. This opened a period of career soul-searching as I struggled to decide—what next? Tech wasn't the place for me and environmental engineering would be a step backwards. I considered how my education and training in civil engineering could open doors to a focus in transportation sustainability, a growing concern in the Bay Area.

I found an engineering school with a dual-degree program in planning. I did some quick research and found that I had about a month to pull everything together to apply. In retrospect, it was the best career decision I ever made. I was accepted into the program and graduated in 2006. I have been a practicing transportation planner ever since.

I found my voice and my passion in transportation policy, transit planning, and parking management. I work on projects that make an impact directly in my community. I've also learned from and worked with many smart people, clients, co-workers, and academics with similar values, who care about reducing congestion and greenhouse gas emissions. I've had a hand in building a team of young planners, and we share a collaborative and nurturing work environment. I have also found a passion for managing and mentoring young staff early in their planning careers.

Consulting is by no means perfect. There are occasionally the negative aspects of corporate bureaucracy, management reorganizations, the continual need to win more work, and occasional disappointments when a community chooses to ignore our recommendations. But overall, serving as a consultant is the best fit for me, and advancing sound transportation projects gives me professional satisfaction.

Table 5.2 Autonomy, effort, and performance across sectors

Characteristic	Public	Non-profit	Private
Autonomy in defining work assignments and products	Low—structured roles and answer to politics, with some whistleblower and civil service protections	High for the executive director if funders agree; variable at junior levels	High for owners if lenders/ investors agree; low for junior staff who must support management decisions
Autonomy in freedom of dress, schedule, work habits, and work locations	Low—public service role requires standardization	High, as long as the work gets done	Variable—low in corporate environment, high in start-up environment
Work effort and performance	• Variable (uneven effort among staff) • Defined hours but night meetings • Some people "hang on for the pension" while others work hard, which can feel unfair	• High (mission-based) • Dedication assumed—operate with day-to-day uncertainty about funding	• High (profit-based) but likely higher in small start-ups • Discipline of billable hours, profitability means lazy/ incompetent staff won't last

anything the planner can handle—but they don't have the resources for training or teach planners about the management systems. Mentoring can be weak or strong, depending on the supervisor/owner. Table 5.3 distinguishes between home-based businesses, small organizations, and large organizations. It addresses the autonomy of work effort as in Table 5.2, but adds social interaction and financial stability considerations.

Even if having a one-person consulting firm is appealing, it is difficult to start one without the connections developed by working in a larger consulting firm. A good path is to work for a medium or large organization, learn their systems, and then start a firm. An exception might be a technical area, such as a company based on a new planning app. As noted, the best environment depends on the planner's makeup and preferences—the systems that large organizations possess or the flexible setting of smaller ones.

Box 5.3 Managing the Workload
By Anonymous, an Environmental Planning Consultant, with Three Years' Experience

I started my first paid planning job the day after graduation. With no break after finishing a comprehensive exam that tested planning theory, knowledge, and methods, I dove headfirst into the real world of private sector planning.

During my first week of employment, I was assigned to an environmental document for a large transportation project. Fast forward one year later and I was still working on the same transportation project. That first year was filled with many long evenings and weekends spent at the office. Although I also had the opportunity to work on other projects, this transportation project filled most of my billable hours. The long days were exhausting, and I began to resent my job. I convinced myself that I needed a change.

I applied for a few public sector jobs, thinking that I needed to get back to the reason I went into planning: improving cities in more immediately tangible ways than environmental impact review preparation. In addition, like most young people, I wanted to have a more reasonable work/life balance. I interviewed at a handful of public agencies, but there was something holding me back from committing to this path. After much contemplation and discourse with mentors, I realized that I did not really want to leave my job.

I enjoyed the fast-paced nature of the private sector. I benefitted from being trained by a mentor with over 40 years of experience, and I appreciated the company's work environment. The opportunity to work on different types of development, transportation, and infrastructure projects stimulated me. I realized that I hated the long hours that accompanied the deadlines, but I did not hate my job. I was overworked.

My workload was partly my own fault. I was eager for project experience, so I accepted any manager's offer to work on a new project. I did not understand the timelines for environmental documents. My inexperience and desire to learn had caught up with me. My supervisors checked in to make sure I was not overwhelmed with work, but my pride never let me admit my unhappiness.

That first year of employment was draining, but it was also an excellent learning experience. Long hours may be a part of many jobs, but they should not lead one to the point of exhaustion. As I head into my third year of my planning career in the private sector, I am glad I did not give up after year one. I have learned how to prioritize projects and manage a demanding workload. In addition, being selective with projects I take on has made learning on the job more meaningful. The growing pains of a young planner's career can define the type of professional he or she becomes. Sometimes a job change is warranted and necessary, whereas other times reflection and vacation time can make all the difference. At the end of the day, your career does not belong to your supervisor, mentor, or co-worker. It is *your* career. I quickly learned that managing my workload was my responsibility. Although this lesson continues to challenge me, it has enabled me to take greater advantage of all the good parts of my job.

Table 5.3 Autonomy, effort, and performance across organizational size

Characteristic	One person, home-based	Small organization (< 50)	Large organization (>50)
Autonomy in defining work assignments, products, and work style	High—it's just you!	• Moderate, because of greater access to the boss • Depends on organizational culture	• Structured, sometime unionized • Rules and procedures necessary
Social interaction, learning, and mentoring from colleagues	Low, no mentoring, isolated	High—you may be thrown into every assignment you can handle	Variable—role is defined, but opportunities for collaboration
Security and stability	High risk, income varies, always hustling	Moderate risk	Stable, with defined advancement procedures, rules, etc.

Flat Versus Hierarchical Organizations

Management systems also affect the nature of work. Bureaucratic systems have well-defined reporting and decision systems, with little autonomy. The organizational chart looks like the root structure of a tree. Such organizations can be slow to react. Flat organizational systems are more responsive to change but require more negotiations about roles and tasks. Organizational charts for flat types have more people at similar levels working across departments, with weaker hierarchy.

The planner can look at the organizational chart of a prospective employer and ask around—in a city, for example, what is the personal style of the city manager? Do decisions work their way up the organization, filtered by the city manager, or do council members directly call on staff? Non-profit organizations tend to have flat organizations because they need flexibility and cross-training. Table 5.4 displays some of the choices in these dynamics.

Large organizations have a more hierarchical structure, whereas small ones can be flatter, but that is not assured. For example, a state department of transportation may be hierarchical, whereas a county-level transit agency less so. Also, technical/scientific organizations, such as air quality management districts, are generally hierarchical, whereas political- and implementation-oriented ones,

Table 5.4 Autonomy, work processes, frustrations, and satisfactions across organizational types

Characteristics	Flat	Hierarchical
Autonomy in defining work assignments and products	High, individual entrepreneurship is encouraged	Low, must follow the chain of command and stay within role
Work processes	Coalition-based, negotiated across department staff, less control over outcomes	Recommendations go up the chain of command and come back down; slow pace
Frustrations	Lack of coordination can lead to ad hoc decision-making	Inability to respond quickly, innovation stifled
Satisfactions	Ability to move quickly, initiative is recognized	Stable processes and fairness, deliberate decision-making and a systems view

such as redevelopment agencies, can be flat. The planner should find out about the structure in the organization being considered. Box 5.4 describes day-to-day professional activity in a non-traditional organization structure.

Office Work Versus Fieldwork

I notice uneasiness among my students when I mention that most urban planners work in office roles with tasks such as drafting memoranda. When I ask for a show of hands of how many students were worried about being "chained to a desk" for their professional careers, a surprising number of hands go up. What types of planning work are suitable for those who, by nature, like to be physically active and in the field?

There are many planning jobs that have less desk work—overseeing field work, surveying and field data collection, construction management, parking management, emergency response planning and implementation, grassroots community organizing, environmental remediation, etc. Educational and participation planning roles also provide a more active workday.

Even within the office, there are differences in activity levels. Working as a GIS analyst or researcher involves more desk and computer time than being a manager who spends most of the day facilitating meetings and decisions. Some of my consultant colleagues tell me that they enjoy travel for fieldwork and client meetings because it gets them out of what they perceive as the boredom of spending every day in the office.

Box 5.4 Matrix Management

When diagrammed, a typical bureaucratic structure resembles a tree's root structure. Requests for decisions go up the hierarchy to the top levels, where they are deliberated, and guidance comes back down for staff. Lower-level staff people are frequently not at the table for the deliberation—they frame the question as best they can and hope others above them do their job. In the 1980s, I worked for a redevelopment organization that used a flat structure called "matrix management." This structure reduces vertical hierarchies and emphasizes cross-functional and cross-department groupings. Teams are assembled around specific objectives rather than roles. These types of organizations are thought to be nimble and innovative, but they require a high level of professionalism to work well. For example, I as a mid-level planner would ask a mid-level real estate department staff member to complete a task without going to the supervisors above, and without the traditional authority to demand cooperation.

As that mid-level planner, the matrix management structure created stress because I didn't have an assurance that the analysis product I needed would be completed by a colleague at my level in a different department. I had to use personal relationships and persuasiveness to entice cooperation. On the other hand, when it worked well, a more collaborative and interactive environment existed. We could respond faster than if upper management had to meet to develop a cross-department team, make work assignments, and monitor and manage the effort.

It was also true that in this particular setting, a mid-level planner could pitch an idea to the executive director, going behind the back of their direct supervisor, the planning director. This would not be permissible in a traditional bureaucratic organization. In some organizations, this would be an unacceptable breach of protocol, but it was accepted in this organization and allowed innovative ideas to get to the top quickly, unfiltered by layers of management conservatism. The question for idealist planners is whether they prefer a work environment with a clearly defined chain of command, where rules are followed but access to decision-makers is limited, or one that is more chaotic but permits policy "free styling".

Creativity

Many young planners view themselves as creative, innovative change-makers. Some are apprehensive about the regulatory world of conditional use permits, sign ordinances, and parking requirements. They want to be creative. Once in practice, the mundane tasks typically assigned to junior planners may lead them to feel that their jobs don't tap into their creativity. So what can a creative planner do?

The first point is to recognize the availability of new opportunities in contemporary planning practice. Planning work has expanded to include creative, implementation-oriented activities. Rather than wait for proposals to come to the zoning counter, planners are making things happen by being proactive. Instead of being limited to administering zoning and subdivision regulations, planners are creating improvements in the field. Books like *Start-Up City* (Klein, 2015) show how the quick world of start-ups can be brought to urban planning through public entrepreneurship.

In Los Angeles, young planners work inside and outside government on active transportation, greening the Los Angeles river, and local placemaking projects. Sometimes the initiative comes from community stakeholders, with the public sector getting out of the way, and in other instances, creativity is happening *within* bureaucratic agencies. City departments are designing programs that incentivize and support communities in developing bike corrals, road diets, parklets, and other temporary public spaces uses. Furthermore, young entrepreneurs who develop apps, such as those that direct parkers to available spaces, are engaged in creative work.

In short, there is opportunity in creative, non-regulatory planning work, but the creative planner needs to go get it. Entrepreneurial planning can lead to a renaissance in the profession, pushing us out of whatever regulatory stodginess we might have possessed.

The second point is about planners who work in a regulatory setting. This work is essential to ensuring that development outcomes support the community vision. It fulfills the profession's aspirations of rationality, comprehensiveness, and fair process. Can implementing planning regulations be creative? I think so. It is easy to underestimate the problem-solving creativity in regulatory activities. For example, imagination and creativity are required to write zoning regulations that fulfill public goals while allowing for design innovation, changing conditions, and technological innovation.

There is creativity in implementing codes as well, as occurs when a planner finds a resolution between competing interests in a development proposal. Planners at the zoning counter imagine and negotiate project modifications, seeking win-win solutions, inventing new ways to mitigate impacts, and crafting new strategies that realize public benefits. Moreover, creativity is in evidence in people-work that planners do. A planner facilitating an internal design review team uses creativity in bringing different departmental perspectives into the discussion and finding resolutions that move projects forward.

Creativity is everywhere in planning. It may not look the same as it does in art, architecture, or app design. Planners may need to work their way a bit up the career ladder to find it, but we are a profession of creative problem-solvers.

When Planning Isn't Well-Established

The discussion about work settings assumes that planning is a well-established activity that presents planners with work setting options. That is not always the case—in some cases agencies, planning requirements, and standard planning products do not yet exist. In those instances, planners work in provisional circumstances to create new forms of planning and new work settings. The following provides two examples.

The first example concerns climate action planning. This new type of planning has emerged in the last two decades, particularly in states like California in which state law prescribes that it must occur. AB 32, the California Global Warming Solutions Act of 2006, was the primary force in bringing about new forms of plans—local greenhouse gas mitigation and climate adaptation plans—as well as new staff roles. Because planning does not have rigid disciplinary definitions, it can respond quickly to new issues that demand innovation.

In California, climate planning has evolved from creating policy statements, to greenhouse gas inventories, to greenhouse gas mitigation plans that include reduction targets. Then, some cities went further to develop climate adaptation plans, and later, developed integrated mitigation and adaptation plans. Lately, planners have recognized that these plans should not stand alone from other plans, so mitigation and adaptation are being integrated into General Plans, the overall policy guide for each city. This evolution has taken place very rapidly, with new sustainability ideas coming from city planning departments, consultants, and non-profits such as ICLEI—Local Governments for Sustainability, a global network of cities, towns, and regions working on climate change planning.

Idealist planners may find the chance to create new forms of planning and new planning institutions among the most exciting opportunities. Finding such opportunities means being attuned to the latest challenges and pressing issues in society and the profession, and considering ways of bringing planning methods to them. It also requires a willingness to work in fluid organization settings, where roles will change as the new forms of planning become established.

The second case occurs when there is not a strong local or regional government planning tradition in national planning legislation and practice. The status of local planning varies globally, with developing countries generally having less-developed local planning institutions. In these cases, the primary effort may be making the case for local planning, building planning institutions, and supporting the development of professional expertise. Box 5.5 provides an account of one planner's work to develop local planning institutions in Ecuador.

Box 5.5 Building Planning From Scratch: A View From Ecuador

By Carlos Jiménez, General Manager, Rocalvi Brokerage, Groupo Calderon, Guayaquil, Ecuador

I was raised in an upper-middle-class family in Ecuador. I spent most of my childhood in Esmeraldas province, one of the poorest provinces in Ecuador, located close to the border with Colombia. Growing up, I saw lots of things that seemed unfair, and being a rebel kid, I wanted to get involved in a field that would allow me to change the system.

My bachelor's degree was in industrial engineering, with a focus on business process modelling. I wanted to find something useful for systemic thinking, and considering that cities are complex systems, I felt planning was the answer. I went to the United States to get a Master's degree in urban planning due to the lack of such programs in Ecuador. I then moved back to Ecuador after spending eight years abroad in Mexico and the United States.

In 2016, Habitat III a United Nations Conference on Housing and Sustainable Urban Development, took place in Ecuador. The Global Planning Education Association Network (GPEAN) sponsored a talk that showed that the UK has 38 accredited planners per 100,000 population, compared to 1.44 in Nigeria and 0.23 in India. The study did not have data for Ecuador, where local government planning is not well-established. This lack of professional planners has shaped my efforts.

To illustrate this issue, one time I visited a very poor municipality where the main square had a huge fountain; however, the fountain was empty because they did not have potable water. When I sat down with the mayor to explain master plans, how land uses affect public utilities, and how he could benefit from geographical information systems (GIS), he told me that with the money a good plan requires he could build soccer fields, put asphalt on roads, and that he did not care about what might happen after his term. I worked all around Ecuador, experiencing things that did not make sense from the planning standpoint. Later, I worked for federal agencies pushing for national legislation, getting answers like "people did not vote for paper, we need tangible stuff." Finally, out of frustration I switched to the private sector, getting a job with a logistics operator, realizing that bad planning has a direct effect on the firm's daily operations and all other businesses.

I could have kept complaining about mayors, the president, and the system, but after taking several deep breaths, I concluded that the root cause of bad urban planning and design is the lack of educational programs in planning. Architects, landscape architects, civil engineers, or urban designers are not urban planners. To change the system, I got involved with universities, working for a low salary, teaching at nights, and spreading planning knowledge. In some cases, I worked for free in order to start continuing education programs. I'm

Box 5.5 (continued)

not giving up and keep pushing for planning education to cultivate a cadre of professional planners.

It is hard to change the system by oneself—one urban planner is not going to make enough noise. Hence, critical mass is important. I keep knocking on doors and drinking coffee, not with mayors but with university chairpersons, deans, and professors in order to move planning forward. In the near future, Ecuador will likely have its first B.S. in urban planning, a vital first step considering there are 23 *provincias* (states), 221 *municipios* (counties), and 4,079 *parroquias* (cities), all of them needing help. Assuming one planner per agency, we need at least 4,323 planners. These planners will be able to change the built environment in the long term to improve communities.

My advice for planners living in developing nations is to keep pushing for educational programs to build the critical mass of planners. No matter how good a master plan is, things will not get done until good plan managers and implementers get involved. For my colleagues from the U.S. who would like to work in Latin America, come with an open mind and do not assume that Latinos living in Ecuador or any Latin American country would behave or react the way they might do in the U.S. People will always tell you it cannot be done, but if you cultivate patience and a positive mental attitude, it can be done.

And Now to You: Find a Fit

Organizational settings vary greatly, even in similar subfields of planning. That's why deciding on the subject matter and implementation form of your work, as discussed in Chapter 4, is not enough. During internships and initial positions, try different work settings to learn about them and assess how you perform in them. Your assessment may consider multiple factors—how you feel about going to work, feedback on your performance, and your satisfaction with your work products. Be insightful about how organization culture functions in your work setting, formally and informally. Look at your options, compare them to your best ways of working, and find the work setting that supports your growth and effectiveness. Long-term, position yourself in an organizational setting in which you will be inspired and effective.

Discussion/Reflection Questions for Chapter 5

1. Think back to a work setting you enjoyed. What were its characteristics? How were decisions made? How did information flow? How were problems addressed?

2. Consider the continuum of management settings between large conventional organizations and nimble small ones. What associations come up for you? Imagine yourself in each extreme. What would be your greatest challenge and where would you be most effective?

3. The grass often seems greener on the other side of the fence. Brainstorm ideas about how a large organization could be made nimble and innovative, or if you prefer, a small one could be made less chaotic.

4. Develop a strategy for gaining experience in different types of organizational settings in the first decade of your career. Ask around, attend conferences, and find out the exemplars in each type of organization in your planning field. Conduct information interviews with top prospects.

Reference

Klein, G. (2015). *Start up city: Inspiring private and public entrepreneurship, getting projects done, and having fun.* Washington, DC: Island Press.

Chapter 6

Career Plans Are Useless

The further I go,
the faster the current.

Young planners are advised to have a career plan. Universities ask about goals in application essays. Employers ask for five-year plans. They want to know if the candidate is thinking beyond the present. This is sensible, of course, but how can career planning be most useful? This chapter proposes a different way of thinking about career planning, given changes in technology, economic organization, and social context for planning. It suggests contingent planning methods as an alternative to the "blueprint" idea, emphasizing processes that support robust career decisions under many conditions. Career plans may be useless, but career planning is not.

Planning, Context, and Chance

Thinking about career planning naturally leads planners to reflect on the theories and methods they use in planning for communities and clients. As planners know, long-term planning is often undermined by changing conditions and unanticipated events. This chapter suggests that career planning should be done in a way that respects context and chance. Hopkins's conception of development planning provides a metaphor for understanding the setting for career planning:

> Planning in the complex systems of urban development is like paddling a canoe in moving river water. Your learned canoeing skills are the actions available to you to include in plans, and the river is the system in which you plan. If the water were still, you could point your canoe in the direction you wanted to go and paddle. In moving water, however, you will not end up where you are pointed because the movement of your career results from the direction in which you paddle and the direction in which the river is flowing.
>
> (Hopkins, 2003, p. 16)

Planners don't control the flow but they can react, change direction in response to conditions, and chart a path in a dynamic environment. This suggests that "real-time" career planning has validity.

Extending Hopkins's metaphor, the planners—the paddlers in this case—are also changing as people and professionals as they move down the river. For example, a planner may discover an imperfect fit between planning school knowledge and what happens at work. With experience, planners gain a sense of what they like and don't like, the way in which they want to make change (e.g., on the ground or systemically). They also learn through experience about their need for money, stability, autonomy, and other job attributes.

The role of chance must also be considered. Looking back on his career in architecture and planning, theorist Ernest Alexander attributes an important role to chance: "the sporadic impacts of chance that determined my biography have made me acutely aware of contingency, and the limits of purposeful action" (Alexander, 2017, p. 93). A rigid career plan may be insensitive to opportunities that arise by chance. Many of the accounts of career paths in the book describe an element chance.

Changes in Planning Employment

Long-term government employment used to be the norm for planners. A planner could chart a path from Assistant, to Associate, to Senior, to Director and accomplish that by moving up in one organization or similar organizations. Loyalty was expected, so frequent moves were frowned upon. A similar, somewhat less predictable path was available in consulting and the non-profit sector. Many consulting firms of the prior era had stable employee ownership. The planner was expected to work at a single job; freelance ventures or outside employment were discouraged. Financial stability was promised through a pension or an ownership stake in a consulting firm.

Conditions are different today. Career plans as a "blueprint" for the future doesn't match reality. Although prospects for planning employment are good, there is uncertainty about future economic conditions, restructuring among planning firms, contracting out of local government planning functions, and technological disruption of planning work. Long tenure and traditional promotion paths are less available, and short-term, task-based teams and entrepreneurial work settings are more common. Technology and globalization are disrupting the traditional structure of all professions, so it is difficult to predict the environment in which planners will be working in five years.

Now, governments outsource planning work for studies *and* for temporary city staff. Consulting firms are consolidating, reducing the number of employee-owned firms and subjecting firms to financial targets established by owners with a weaker connection to the local business environment and employees. Some consultants complain that the billing model no longer supports reasonable overhead. As non-profits continually compete for funding, with some donors unwilling to support overhead and baseline costs.

Compared to the previous period, more planners are freelancers with a portfolio of work. Freelancing means the freedom to choose work hours and arrangements, but less stability, less early career mentoring, and fewer benefits. Teams are assembled for projects and then disbanded. Some planners entering the workforce must have more than one job, especially if they face high college debt.

This is a different context for a planning career than when I started out as a planner, requiring more frequent job decisions, less reliance on a predictable future, and a proactive, entrepreneurial strategy for advancement. Even though career progressions are less predictable today, for some older planners, they were never that predictable. Just as today, fluctuating economic conditions dictated opportunities, career launches were delayed, and unexpected opportunities emerged. Box 6.1 outlines how uncertainty and stability are woven in my career progression.

Box 6.1 Graduating, Job Markets, and Advancement

I graduated from undergraduate planning school into a lousy job market. In 1978, Canada's unemployment rate was over 8% and was headed to 12% six years later. Most of the available planning jobs were in western Canada, in Alberta, stemming from oil extraction–based growth. Three internships and good grades didn't prevent me from being underemployed the first year after graduation. I completed a small consulting project for a small town with two classmates, then was unemployed, and then landed a summer internship a year *after* I graduated. That was embarrassing. I landed my first full-time job 18 months after I graduated. Although I was averse to networking and making cold calls to firms, I had made one cold call to a small consulting firm and had an informational interview a year earlier. My resume had stayed on my future boss's desk for a year until a position opened up, and she remembered me. Launching my career was difficult, confidence-challenging, and proceeded without a plan. I would have taken any planning job—the idea of a career plan seemed laughable. I was in survival mode, held back by poor networking skills.

Despite this rough start, I learned as I went. Getting started in the field provided confidence that I could have a career and a game plan. Later, I finished my Master's degree in 1983 when the U.S. unemployment rate was over 10%. The path was smoother this time, but my first job was part-time for a consulting firm, for an hourly wage with no benefits. Soon after, I found a job with a redevelopment agency on a former professor's recommendation. With an improving economy, a predictable career progression became possible. I was inspired and satisfied; there was the possibility of career advancement at that organization. Things seemed set.

After a few years on the job, though, I soured on the work (as described in Box 6.2). That's how I usually explained my leaving. But there was also a pull—a vague sense that there was a better way to focus my career. This thought was in the background, not something that I could fully articulate, and I didn't know what the other thing was. I investigated getting an MFA and becoming an artist.

About this time, I saw a job posting for a tenure track professor position at my current employer. I didn't have a Ph.D. and hadn't considered being a professor. Nonetheless, I applied and was hired based on my experience and a commitment to get a Ph.D. Moving from practicing planner to professor brought a cut in salary and uncertainty that I could succeed in this new realm. But by that time, I was ambitious and embraced the challenge. In my case, there was no game plan, but a purposeful and enjoyable work life as a professor came about from paying attention to what I was doing and following opportunities.

Does Planning Theory Have Relevance to Career Planning?

Planners are used to experiencing the need *for* and the impossibility *of* long-range planning. Planning issues require a long-term perspective, such as assessing ecosystem sustainability, selecting capital investments, or understanding how demographic changes affect housing needs. Indeed, long-term plans are mandated by national and state governments for land use, transportation, housing, and environmental plans. Major capital projects, such as roads or public facilities, cannot be built in small increments and therefore require long-range planning as well.

The traditional planning process also prizes comprehensiveness. Transportation plans affect land use patterns, housing affordability, and environmental sustainability. Land use patterns drive transportation demand. In fact, planning is characterized by interconnections between systems. Comprehensiveness means examining those interconnections.

Classic rational comprehensive planning embraces the long-term, comprehensive perspective. It seeks rationality in promoting clarity about ends (goals and objectives) and logical correspondence between ends and means (policies, programs, projects, or in this case, career decisions) (Brooks, 2002; Levy, 2003). It is also committed to considering alternative courses of action. Rather than adopt the first good idea presented, planners develop alternative courses of action and evaluate them against goals and objectives.

Rational comprehensive planning is the default "common sense" planning method in practice. Plans based on this model are essential, but some of them may collect dust while incremental decisions are made. At their worst, these plans are process-heavy, disconnected from decision-making, and exclusionary in their need for simple, non-conflicting goals. In fact, contemporary planning theory largely ignores rational comprehensive planning despite its prevalence in practice.

So what about career planning? Should the idealist generate career goals and objectives, develop alternative career plans, and evaluate them? Is that responsive to the dynamic nature of the profession? Given the job market realities discussed earlier, the five-year career plan has an archaic, Soviet-era, blueprint-plan feel.

An Alternative Career Planning Approach

New planning approaches respond to planning uncertainty. For example, scenario planning considers choices under multiple futures. Rather than define a "right" plan, it assesses the robustness of strategies under a variety of probable scenarios. By considering a variety of contingencies and responses, scenario planning provides guidance under uncertainty.

Under an alternative conceptualization, career planning becomes a learning process. It provides intelligence for ongoing decisions rather than a blueprint for the future. It is contingent and emphasizes making good decisions in an unstable environment.

I suggest three attitudes to support this alternative planning approach: (1) self-knowledge as a basis for making decisions as described in Chapter 3, (2) attentiveness to the work done in the here-and-now, and (3) alertness to opportunities.

Self Knowledge

The decision-making process discussed in Chapter 3 helps idealist planners assess and pursue career opportunities. The process is built on self-knowledge gained in the reflection techniques reviewed in Appendix B. What is the planner's passion? What are his or her skills? How do they align with what the world needs? Of course, this assessment is strengthened by having knowledge about types of work and work settings, as addressed in Chapters 4 and 5.

This self-knowledge can draw upon others' insights obtained through formal work evaluations, feedback from clients or elected officials, or advice from associates. Sometimes, an external perspective is just what is needed. The process of gaining feedback isn't necessarily comfortable, because acknowledging a poor fit means change, and change can be scary.

Some people thrive in the stable environment of a government position in a large organization. That environment fits their temperament. Others want the excitement of collaborating with a small, close-knit team. In this context, self-knowledge means being clear about preferences like those. It includes the planner being clear on values, preferred work style, and talents. It requires a commitment to authenticity, to being true to one's core self.

Pay Attention

Paying attention to the work planners do in the "here and now" may seem obvious. Doesn't everybody do that? Although this may seem sensible, this attentiveness is not universal. It is easy to put a professional career on autopilot. To perform at a high level, live an interesting life, and attend to friends and family is a lot. For busy planners, paying attention to their career path may just seem like one too many things.

Fortunately, there are simple ways to pay attention. Although some forms of multitasking can lead to unproductive distractions, reflective planners think about what they are doing while they are doing it. They observe themselves as they work. Self-observation is cultivated as a habit, if just for a few hours per week. The planner may be able to develop an observational ability that will operate in the background, most all of the time.

The planner's physical body offers information, of course, such as anxiety or rapid aging in poor job settings, and conversely, a feeling of vitality and health in good ones. Heart rate, blood pressure, and a general state of wellness are useful indicators. Being a professional planner comes with unavoidable stress, but off-the-charts stress is a sign that something is amiss. Interesting assignments, collegial work arrangements, and workplace fun can make planning practice a pleasure.

Paying attention also means alertness to opportunities, through networking, professional participation, and staying in dialogue with supervisors and colleagues. This often means showing up, developing new networks of colleagues and collaborators, and prioritizing face-to-face communication.

Alertness to Opportunities

I stay in a job as long as I am learning, but I stay aware of opportunities. Seeking continual learning simplifies career move decisions. The 30 years at my current job could be seen as evidence of someone who never makes a change, but my job provides continual learning. The opposite of this model, of course, is complacency, where a planner is satisfied with day-to-day activities but is not learning or stretching. If that's true, it may be time to make a change.

Box 6.2 provides an account of a time in my career when a desire for continual learning was not realized in a job, prompting a change.

Jobs can be kept fresh by seeking opportunities for learning. Planners can seek new responsibilities or tasks outside their job description. It is possible to change what seems like a boring job into an interesting one with initiative and a supportive supervisor. Learning also occurs outside the job, with participation in professional organizations and networking at conferences. Once all opportunities for growth are exhausted, though, a new job may be appropriate. Strategies for finding that job include conducting informational interviews with those in interesting jobs and always having a resume and business card

---

Box 6.2 When to Leave

My switch from professional planner to professor resulted from paying attention to how I felt about my work and being attentive to opportunities. I held a transportation planner position in a redevelopment agency. The agency had prestige and political clout. The salary and benefits were good; we had sleek furniture, art on the walls, and free, watered-down coffee. In these circumstances, there was a strong rationale to hang on to a good thing. When I was younger, I hoped to find a job where "I would have it made." This job offered stability, good prospects for the future, and a comfortable life.

Initially, the work was very interesting. I had a great boss and opportunities for advancement. The work, creating new travel demand management and parking requirements for office development, was innovative. At the time, the pace of office building construction in downtown Los Angeles was fast and seemed to be poised for continuous growth.

Over time the agency came under high scrutiny of the city council, whose members felt that it had too much money, too much autonomy, and a non-collaborative style. Although I found the agency executive director inspiring and engaging, others found him imperious. Agency staff had an attitude that we could implement in ways that other city departments could not, and that they should agree to our development deals without question. As a consequence of this perceived arrogance, the city council curtailed the agency's autonomy. The executive director was ousted and oversight increased. The agency posture moved to a more defensive one. My work became more focused on organizational defense than on producing good planning outcomes. One day, I gazed in a daydreaming way at a staple remover sitting on my desk, and it reminded me of a set of jaws. Those jaws represented the conflict in the agency's day-to-day work. That's when I began my search for a new job.

Much later, the agency, as with all redevelopment agencies in California, was disbanded as part of state budget reform. My possible "for life" dream job no longer exists.

---

ready. The planner intending to move should alert mentors, monitor job posting sites, and apply.

These three elements—self-knowledge, paying attention, and alertness to opportunities—are an effective guide to deciding about job changes. This is a more proactive approach than letting things slide or believing that fate will take care of things. I don't rely on fate, but perhaps there are synchronicities, situations in which goals, environment, and people line up to create opportunities. To allow for synchronicities, planners should be open to new ways of thinking, be curious, and remain attentive to their situation.

An Example of Scenario/Contingency/ Anticipation Analysis

Although conventional wisdom is that planners have a "blueprint" or "master plan" for their career, this chapter emphasizes the dynamic context for such a plan. Advances in community planning process, as discussed, address the weaknesses of blueprint-type planning and are applicable to career planning. This section illustrates how a scenario and contingency planning concept can be used to guide career decisions. Scenario planning considers multiple possible futures to avoid zeroing in on a future that does not come to be. Contingency planning focuses attention on responses to disruptions, allowing for the reality of uncertainty but developing response mechanisms in advance.

Anticipatory governance is a planning model built around the concept of resilience, using scenario and contingency planning ideas. Planners anticipate a wide range of futures, develop multiple strategies, monitor conditions over time, act, and evaluate progress. A typical use is outlined by Quay (2010) to address open space acquisition. If these methods are helpful for traditional planning, can they be applied to career planning? The following paragraphs provide an example of how they can.

Let's say a planner is considering an offer to become the director of a non-profit organization that works on environmental remediation in a low-income community. The job is in her hometown. She is currently working at a lower level in a similar organization in a different city, learning as much as she can about effective strategies and how environmental advocacy organizations work. Assume that the planner has "non-profit director" and "give back to my hometown" in her career plan. Taking the job would fulfill those goals. Let's say that she has done due diligence on the organization by checking in with board members, the organization's customers, and those who interact with the organization. The planner thinks it is a good fit.

Scenario and contingency planning comes into play when she considers that the organization may change from the good fit it is today. To make sure the decision to take the job is a robust one, the planner assesses plausible future conditions, considering factors internal and external to the organization. Table 6.1 shows how contemplating just two variables—the level of visibility about an issue and the status of the organization—affect the nature of the job and the prospect of satisfaction. Having imagined these scenarios, she can estimate their probability and assess how each one fits her goals. This provides a more robust assessment of prospects for success.

Table 6.1 Anticipatory career planning—roles under different conditions

Scenarios	A public health emergency produces high public visibility	No public health emergency, low public visibility
Strong grant support, stable board of directors	1. Emphasize technical expertise and the political work to position the organization in negotiating remediation plans. Provide quick responses to take advantage of opportunities for organizational growth.	2. Commission and manage studies to build a science basis for change, conduct education, and use legal tools to make change. Develop readiness tools and activities (e.g., convene stakeholders for table-top exercises on response plans).
Weak grant support, unstable board of directors	3. Network with other non-profit organizations, universities, and public agencies to secure a role for the organization. Build board capacity and seek crisis-related and sustainable grant funding. Focus on efficient operations and keeping the doors open.	4. Focus on public information and organizing for a grassroots awareness campaign. Seek to create a movement that will build board capacity and support grant applications.

Such an analysis may show that role #2—the more technical approach—is what the current executive director is doing, supported by a board that favors that approach. In that case, the job description has been written along these lines. If the planner excels at this type of work, then the job seems a perfect fit. It is also true that in the first month there could be a public health emergency, such as a lead contamination issue, that produces a different environment. This new issue could generate conflict among board members about the organization's mission. Assume that a longtime board member leaves along with an substantial annual donation. Now the planner could easily find herself in role #3—networking and capacity building. That could be an exciting growth opportunity, or a disappointment, depending on the planner's goals and skills. Thinking about the probability of each of the four scenarios will help the planner decide whether to take the job (i.e., the current circumstances are a good fit), understand how the role may change over time, and think about the type of job she will be looking for after this one.

Of course, personal factors may come into play in considering scenarios about this job, such as:

- Readiness to move into the executive direction position, given experience, training, and capacity for stress
- The level of mentor support and the *type* of mentoring support (technical, leadership, management, etc.)

- Personal situation, such as raising a family, caring for an elderly parent, or wanting to move on a frequent basis
- Feelings about returning to the planner's hometown—empowering or settling?

Applying scenario and contingency planning supports wise decisions that are guided by broader values. This is akin to turn-by-turn directions provided by GPS—often the driver doesn't see the whole map but just the corners that lie ahead. At the outset, there was a route plan, but with attractions, opportunities, or obstacles, the route changes. As the planner gets closer to the final destination, the route may become clearer, or she may choose to reprogram the destination.

Career Path Stories

This section includes three text boxes describing the career paths of planners in the early stages of their careers. Their stories illustrate how varied career development steps are, and how in each case the planner's current job was not anticipated when he or she started. All three have found a "dream job," at least for now. Common themes in the stories include the role of mentors and champions, openness to new experiences and types of planning, a willingness to accept uncertainty along the way, and willpower.

The first story is from a planner working on healthy communities planning issues at the county level. This planner developed an infographic to reflect on his career path, something I recommend that all planners do. Figure 6.1 shows the experiences, jobs, role models, champions, professional service, and organizations that influenced his path. Supporting the thesis of this chapter, the path was not the result of a master plan but a process of responding to conditions and intentional discovery. Box 6.3 provides further details on his experience. It is difficult to conceive how any planner might have mapped such a path out at the beginning of a career.

The second story (Box 6.4) is from a transportation planner who decided to take a Scandinavian study tour as part of her graduate degree and fell for Scandinavia and its active transportation systems. Participating in the tour turned out to be a pivotal experience, as it produced an idea of becoming a professional in Sweden. This was not part of the planner's initial career plan, as she already had a "dream" job. The rest of the story is an account of moving forward, step-by-step, toward a new experience.

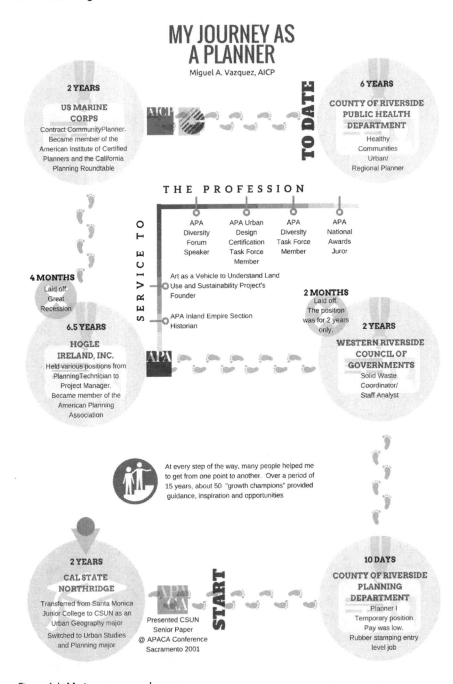

Figure 6.1 My journey as a planner

Box 6.3 Hoping for the Best: My 15-Year Planning Journey

By Miguel A. Vazquez, AICP Healthy Communities Planner, Riverside University Health System-Public Health, California

Growing up, I wanted to be an artist. That longing was squashed by my mother's wisdom when I was 14 years old. "If you want to starve, go for it," she said. Although she never discouraged me from using my creativity and artistic abilities, she made me consider other options. She also worked hard to provide me with opportunities so that I could graduate from college. Life took many turns and finally, at age 31, I honored my late mother's dream when I received my undergraduate diploma.

Although my degree was in Urban Studies and Planning and I loved what I learned, I knew little about the realities of the profession. Nevertheless, I trusted that I would find employment. After searching for a few months, I landed my first planning employment: a temporary entry-level job at the County of Riverside Planning Department. It was a dreadful 10 days of reading internal planning procedures and rubberstamping lot-line adjustments.

Around that time, I interviewed for a Solid Waste Coordinator position at the Western Riverside Council of Governments. That job was more in tune with my interest in environmental stewardship, and the pay was twice as much, so it was a no-brainer to accept it. Although I wanted to stay there, the grant-funded job was only for two years.

I found myself again looking, and was lucky enough to land work with a consulting firm that provided contract-planning services to none other than the County of Riverside Planning Department. I went back to square one, but this time with higher pay, clout, and opportunities to move up. I was in charge of entitlement projects for an area that in 2008 became one of the newest cities in California. Around the same time, the recession began to take its toll on planning employment, and regardless of my success, I was one of the casualties.

Again, I was searching for a new opportunity, but this time it was tougher. After four months of uncertainty, I landed a contract planning position at Twenty-nine Palms U.S. Marine Corps base, where I was in charge of a livable community master plan for the base.

Nearly two years after that, I received a call from a colleague from . . . where? The County of Riverside Planning Department! She let me know about a vacancy at the Public Health Department and encouraged me to apply. The position was to lead a community planning effort in Coachella. Now, six years after: I am living my dream job, straddling the realms of planning, community development, public health, social equity, active transportation, affordable housing, community engagement, and more. I never thought that this job existed. I guess it had to materialize first for me to believe it, to understand it.

Box 6.3 (continued)

How was I able to sustain my career facing uncertain times and many "launches"? I credit a network of colleagues, mentors, and friends in the field who gave me opportunities to grow, to express myself, and to contribute. They are the ones to whom my mother would say "Gracias" because they have made a difference in my life and in my career. They inspired me with their mere presence, positive attitude, and wisdom. Some of them were my champions who helped me grow to my fullest potential. Most of them came into my life by chance, at workplaces. Also, I developed my most valuable connections through my involvement with the American Planning Association.

As for the desire to be an artist, I did not desist. I combined it with my planning practice. In 2010, I convinced 15 planners and 15 artists to collaborate with me on artwork that depicted planning concepts. The project was called Art VULUPS (Art as a Vehicle to Understand Land Use Planning and Sustainability), which the American Planning Association California Chapter recognized with an award 2011. In the spirit of paying it forward, the artworks were auctioned off for the benefit of the California Planning Foundation, which provides scholarships to planning students.

The third story (Box 6.5) is from a planner who discovered a niche in planning that might easily be overlooked—campus planning. It shows the value of building on existing work experiences, although not directly in planning, allowing a lateral move without starting all over. This account is important for planners who return to planning school after another career path and seek to repackage their past experience so it counts toward planning.

And Now to You: The Elevator Talk

Making good career decisions is vital to your success and effectiveness. It is worth the time to find organizations where you shine, are supported by supervisors and mentors, and feel inspired to go to work. You will excel in these situations. To return to the canoeing metaphor, avoid the dangerous rapids of poor job fits, toxic work environments, and the wrong paddle for steering the canoe. Find your way to the place in the river where the current is carrying you along with your own paddling.

Boxes 6.3–6.5 describe planners who have found their way to fulfilling jobs. Their stories warn against using the canoeing metaphor to rely *too* much

Box 6.4 A Plan Interrupted

*By Arianna Allahyar AICP, Transport Analyst, WSP,
Stockholm, Sweden*

I remember the day I got the call from my dream consulting firm in Seattle. Everything was going just as I had planned: the undergraduate planning degree, networking, mentoring, volunteer internship hours, and late school nights had paid off. I signed the contract with a company pen and began the job before starting a Master's program.

Later, when the Master's degree was near completion, I faced a decision. Transfer a course into my program to finish early or apply for a travel study program studying public spaces and public life in Scandinavia. I tend to be a "what's next?" person, moving forward by executing never-ending plans. As such, my immediate desire was to be done with the degree. For whatever reason, the question "why not?" came to mind. I already had my dream job. I'd earn the degree either way. Why the rush? I applied to the program and was accepted.

I travelled with a group of 20 graduate students for one month to cities in Denmark and Sweden before returning to apply lessons learned to Seattle. There I was in Copenhagen, riding a Dutch-style bicycle on a warm, late-summer day touring with an urban designer who showed how Scandinavian cities are designed for people. How could I not fall in love?

When I returned, I obsessed over the idea of getting back to Scandinavia. The thought was both frightening and exhilarating—studying abroad, let alone moving abroad, was never in my plans. I knew the work I wanted to do and the company I wanted to work for. I had career plans and strategies to make those plans come to life. Yet after this trip, I found myself utterly compelled to move abroad.

Day in and day out, I looked for opportunities in Copenhagen and Stockholm, imagining what daily life would be like. For awhile it was merely an idea, a fantasy that consumed me but would likely never happened.

Months later at a Transportation Research Board (TRB) meeting in Washington, D.C., I met someone who worked in Sweden, so I (only half-jokingly) said I loved Sweden so much I would board a plane for Stockholm tomorrow. That's where it started. We went home to our respective cities, and he forwarded my CV to his manager. After numerous video calls, a visit to Stockholm that I initiated and paid for, and months of slow conversation, I got the job offer—the golden ticket I needed for the work permit. It was real, after all.

With excitement came other emotions, including anxiety, sadness, and nervousness. Saying goodbye to friends and family was no small feat. Prior to leaving the U.S., people questioned why move to Sweden, especially because it was so unexpected. Now living here, it's the same question. One response is "why not?"

Box 6.4 (continued)

Sweden has turned my planning mindset inside out. Making the move halfway across the globe involved complicated logistics and learning a new language and culture. Naturally, actually living in a new country brings situations and challenges that I simply could not plan for.

Rather than make plans, I now favor making opportunities. I wouldn't have been on the travel study if I hadn't applied. I wouldn't have attended TRB without coauthoring research with my former professor. I wouldn't have established my first Swedish client if I hadn't talked to an international speaker at a national planning conference. And so the story goes. One cannot experience something great and unexpected without showing up and cultivating opportunities.

I felt unsettled throughout this process, unable to tell if things were progressing or regressing. Pursuing a job in my native language and country is one thing; knowing little about Swedish language and culture made communications all the more uncertain. I had self-doubt about how to present myself, and I encounter feelings of insecurity in everyday challenges at work and elsewhere.

Sometimes, planners' career plans are interrupted when they realize a new perspective. I've learned that no matter how much I plan, I can't know for sure where I will end up. Moving to Sweden has undoubtedly been my most rewarding *derailing* of my career plans to date. Who knows what's next?

on the current. These planners had willpower and took risks. Many planners have figured out that planning for healthy communities, active transportation, and university campuses is fun and fulfilling. They will be following their dreams too, so you'll have to compete.

Because the five-year career plan is such a standard expectation, be prepared to offer one when asked. It has an important place in considering opportunities and job choices. Use the dynamic process described here for making choices as they come, and reconsider the five-year plan as frequently as needed.

Knowing if you are on track is simple: ask whether any job opportunity moves you closer or father away from your motivating values, as discussed in Chapter 3—love, justice, truth, or beauty. If you are on the right track, you will sense an alignment, and that alignment will make you effective and inspired. A simple compass read can take you a long way. Returning to the chapter title, the traditional career plan is useless, but career planning is essential.

Box 6.5 Embracing the Sum of My Experiences
By Jaime Engbrecht, Planning Specialist, University of California, Riverside, California

Until a year ago, I thought my "official" career as a planner would never happen. I had been out of planning school for two years and had not applied for a single planning job. For the previous seven years, starting in my mid-twenties, I worked in facilities planning at a community foundation with a great mission, culture, and benefits. The work-life balance enabled me to work full-time and attend a Master's of planning program in the evenings—I did this for three years.

I learned about facilities management from the ground up. My undergraduate degree was in communications, but here I learned about building systems, contract procurement, and project management. Through the years I was promoted and sought to incorporate my newfound planning knowledge into projects, supported by my supervisor. Working within the confines of my role I tried to be innovative, developing a waste diversion program, a staff community garden, a reclaimed water system, and bicycle parking.

Many of my graduate school classmates were working at interesting planning jobs: this was not my reality. Valuing my knowledge and experience, I still assumed that I needed direct planning experience to be competitive. I became restless after completing graduate school, but my complacency impeded action.

It wasn't until I connected with a mentor that I realized my experience was an asset, and that I needed to explore career paths that built upon that experience. I had been too focused on the traditional planning career path—do x, y, z to get a planning position—and didn't recognize that the sum of my experiences could lead me to a planning career that fit me well.

Working with my mentor, we searched for jobs and ranked them in order of preference and knowledge and skills alignment. Campus planning seemed to be calling my name. I applied to jobs that I would have considered to be a longshot. To my surprise, I was invited to an interview that led to my current job as a campus planner. My experience in facilities management, communications, and event planning, and my background in planning were seen as valuable assets. My new supervisor valued my potential for growth and felt any planning experience I lacked could be learned on the job.

My campus planning work includes capital planning, physical planning (siting of new buildings, public realm improvements), and environmental planning. As someone who likes to have a wide breadth of knowledge versus one specialty, this fits me well. My lack of experience has been a catalyst for learning. Sometimes I have felt unprepared when particular issues hit my desk, and other times I've felt one step ahead. I've accepted discomfort as a normal part of growing professionally and personally.

Through this process, I learned to embrace and repackage experiences that did not seem relevant, to seek mentorship, and to acknowledge that luck and timing are working for me, too.

Discussion/Reflection Questions for Chapter 6

1. Select a planner you admire. Ask him or her if you can have a 30-minute informational interview to discuss career paths. What advice does he or she offer on career planning? How much was planned and how much was opportunistic?

2. Read the biography or autobiography of a person you admire, planner or not. Pay attention to how this person found his or her way to making a contribution. What lessons might apply to your career path?

3. Do you think that the contingent planning model described in this chapter gives up too much on vision? Could it lead to a meandering career path rather than a deliberate one? If so, how could the meandering path be avoided?

4. If you have started your career, develop a career infographic such as the one shown in Figure 6.1 for yourself. What's missing and what steps can you take to fill in the gaps?

References

Alexander, E. (2017). Chance and design: From architecture to institutional design. *Journal of the American Planning Association* 83(1): pp. 93–102.

Brooks, M. (2002). *Planning Theory for Practitioners*. Chicago, IL: Planners Press, American Planning Association.

Hopkins, L. (2003). *Urban development: The logic of making plans*. Washington, DC: Island Press.

Levy, J. (2003). *Contemporary urban planning*. Upper Saddle River, NJ: Prentice Hall.

Quay, R. (2010). Anticipatory governance: A tool for climate change adaptation. *Journal of the American Planning Association* 76(4): pp. 496–511.

Part II

SUCCEEDING

Chapter 7

Principled Adaptability

For growth, the self,
must leave its shell.

There is a way to practice planning that honors idealism and realism. Although idealism is a driving force in the planning profession, it's not an either/or question—often, but not always, an idealist planner can compromise without selling out. And seeing the world as it is, a realist's view, contributes to effective strategy. The preceding chapters provide ideas on how to launch a planning career, starting with a degree in planning or a related field that provides knowledge and techniques, project and studio experiences, and internships. Education isn't enough, however. Similar to professions such as architecture or medicine, there is an art to professional practice. This art of planning is learned by doing.

Questions about planning practice abound. What technical information should be brought to bear? How should competing interests be addressed? What values apply? Whose values apply, and in what combination—those of the planner as an individual, a member of a profession, a member of a community, and/or a member of an organization? Do commonly used methods have a bias? Effective planners reason and learn through experience to resolve these questions. They don't hit the "autopilot" button in practice. Rather, they embrace technical, strategic, and ethical questions every day.

Planning practice questions cannot be decided in advance because the context is an important part of the resolution. Experience helps planners develop a workable "theory-in-use." Coined by scholars Argyris and Schön (1974), this term describes how professionals act as they encounter complex problems. New planners, consciously or not, are engaged in a process of developing their own theory-in-use.

A theory-in-use is synthetic and intuitive, and is not easily explained. Unlike tightly defined technical fields, planning deals with "messes"—instances where pure technical knowledge is not sufficient. Planners often manage a mess rather than solve a clearly defined problem. Russel Ackoff (1999) coined this term for organizational planning. Applying this to planning, Rittel and Webber (1973) explain how planning problems are "wicked" in the sense that they cannot be definitively described and do not have decisive, isolatable solutions.[1] The context for the "mess" includes politics, administrative or financial issues, history, prior decisions, stakeholder alliances, uncertainty, instability and feedback loops, incomplete or contested technical knowledge, relationships with other policies and plans, and community perceptions and experiences.

In contrast to theory-in-use, espoused theory is a formal axiom taught in school or upheld by a professional organization. Espoused theory can concern either knowledge or process. A planner may espouse microeconomic theory, for example, leading to market-based analysis and planning solutions. Others may espouse Marxist structural theory, understanding how the processes of capital become urbanized and leading to plans that seek social control of community assets. Theories also include design concepts such as new urbanist behavioral theories. Furthermore, advocacy planners advance a theory of justice, such as that asserted by John Rawls (1971), who postulated that policies should favor those with limited choice.

There are also espoused theories of planning process. For example, the classic rational planning model of matching means to desired ends is embedded in planning's technocratic professional identity. In contrast, disjointed incrementalism, which asserts a non-optimized search for short-term amelioration of problems, posits a different theory of process and action. And finally, the planning workplace may reflect the presence of other espoused theories, such as those of community and teamwork.

Planners graduate from school having learned some or all of these theories. But planning practice draws on too many theories, of too many types, that are too contradictory for a universally agreed-upon and uniform theory to exist. Even if there were a single theory, practice would not accommodate its unambiguous application. The setting for planning varies across places and people over time, making it difficult, if not impossible, to recommend the cut-and-dried application of theory. In practice, planners find ways to frame issues, make recommendations, and take action that resolves theoretical dimensions and disagreements. Said simply, theory-in-use is "the walk" rather than "the talk."

Reflective planners develop and modify a theory-in-use through their practice. It may not be visible or articulated, but it exists in the background. The more aware planners are of their theory-in-use, the better they can assess its efficacy over time and make adjustments. The important issue is that there are good theories-in-use and bad ones. The good ones produce intelligence that guides practice, relying on continual learning, reflection, and assessment. The bad ones have a narrow, self-referential character, such as basing all interactions with developers on one experience with a crooked one.

This chapter introduces a framework for gaining awareness of the planner's developing theory-in-use. It shows a range of practice approaches and comments on the efficacy of the choices. Planners benefit if they seek to understand the assumptions, theoretical bases, and practices in their planning career. Of course, they may also learn from other planners by observing and borrowing from them.

The Principled Adaptability Planning Style

Principled adaptability is a planning style that responds to professional planners' reality: dealing with messes and wicked problems. It is a framework that I have developed in my planning practice and have observed among planners I admire.

In some ways, principled adaptability is an oxymoron—it juxtaposes elements that appear to be contradictory. Don't principles argue against adaptability? Doesn't adaptability undermine principles? An oxymoron juxtaposes terms to contain a concealed point—that planners find effectiveness in the tension between principles and adaptability. Planners engage these apparent opposites in their everyday practice.

A principled adaptability style helps reconcile the idealism/realism tension discussed in Chapter 1. It allows for strongly held convictions about planning values and vision—the idealism part—and an ability to be effective in environments of uncertainty, controversy, and structural limitations—the realism part. It contrasts with an approach where planners are *so* principled that only one "right" solution can suffice. "Right" refers to either the technical rationality of the approach or the values that guide selection of the approach, or both. A principled adaptability style is perceptive and seeking of feedback and learning. It keeps planners engaged within their organization and with external stakeholders.

The adaptability part is not intended to suggest that there are not better and worse planning answers—there are. Planners should not cave in to self-interested or uninformed forces. Rather, the call is to think strategically about how to plan. Adaptability does not mean throwing up one's hands in the face of overwhelming challenges. That's too far on the other end of the spectrum. Planning is an ethical practice, day-to-day.

Figure 7.1 organizes the terms involved in the principled adaptability planning style. The top of the diagram shows planning practice not as a rote activity, but as a professional practice in which each engagement begins anew. This doesn't mean that knowledge, skill, and experience are not important, but that the planner considers *how* to plan in reference to the particular context and situation.

The realms of idealism and realism are central to this model, as introduced in Chapter 1. To review, idealism is the notion that planning forms and pursues noble principles such as love, justice, truth, or beauty. In contrast, realism is the concept of accepting a situation as it is and being prepared to deal with it accordingly. Few planners act exclusively in either realm, hence idealism and realism appear in the dashed circle. Some planners may lean to one realm more than another, and there are differing degrees of idealism and realism in every action. The challenge is to acknowledge and reconcile each of these realms in specific planning instances and contexts. Should values or an evidence approach drive this planning activity? Or, how will these dimensions interact? These decisions affect each planning episode, whether it be writing a plan, completing a staff report, or responding to a city council member in a hearing.

There are four other terms in the "philosophical approach" row in Figure 7.1 representing approaches that I argue are less effective. The dreamer has wonderful ideas but is unrealistic and unprepared to overcome the challenges of implementation. On the other hand, the hedonist acts only for personal gain, disregarding larger planning aims. Shown farthest from the ellipse are the most extreme approaches: fundamentalist—a self-contained system of thought that does not allow for other voices or reference points, and nihilist—a rejection of all principles and meaning.

Consider a planner working in design. Let's say the planner's idealism is expressed in values concerning beauty, community, and human self-realization.

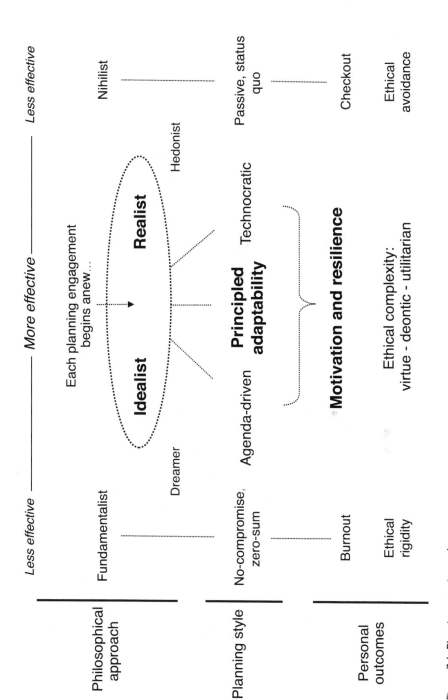

Figure 7.1 Planning practice styles

She is an advocate for restorative public spaces. This planner is aware that design theories such as having "eyes on the street" inform design concepts, but she takes a skeptical view about universal design prescriptions. She knows that local context and culture must be considered, and requires that behavioral research validate design theories. She is an idealist in promoting restorative spaces but also a realist in not "drinking the Kool-Aid" of the latest urban design fad.

If the community for which she is planning values public spaces, then the planning challenge is to use behavioral research to support the most effective designs. But what if the community does not express interest in public spaces? Can this planner impose her values about restorative public spaces on the community? This is the point at which planners should reflect on their own values, allegiances to profession, community, and institutional affiliation, and consider whether their right answer is universal. Chapter 8 explores this issue further.

The next row of Figure 7.1 concerns planning style, suggesting principled adaptability as one in which planners have a firm compass direction in terms of values and goals, but are adaptive to the context for planning—political, economic, social, and environmental. Using this approach does not produce wins on every issue but is focused on progress, considering the political space available, evidence about planning solutions, and strategies for creating change. The principled adaptability style does not recommend a *balance* of idealism and realism. Balance is an overused planning word, often used because it promises all interests with something they want. It may be that evidence-based realism should rule the day on a particular issue, whereas a more idealistic values approach is appropriate for another. Because these tensions are resolved in practice, rather than a priori, this planning style is an unstable position; the planner does not have a "game plan" ready for each planning issue. The planner is neither solely value-driven nor reliant on apparently value-free evidence. It is a hybrid position in which planners may operate in political and technocratic roles. Encountering these tensions requires reflection, which challenges planners more than the seemingly clear-cut approaches at the far left or far right of the diagram.

In addition to principled adaptability, planners may adopt an agenda-driven or technocratic planning style. Agenda-driven planning styles are propelled by advocacy for issues, whether that be greenhouse gas reduction, social justice, affordable housing, or creating places that restore human well-being. That style is rarely comprehensive and tends toward advocacy; the planner is more likely to play a political role. The technocratic planning style, on the other hand, values comprehensiveness and emphasizes evidence as a driving force in decisions.

These three styles—principled adaptability, agenda-driven, and technocratic—are all effective in the appropriate settings, but principled adaptability is the one I favor. The inspiring supervisors I have worked for and the effective planners I have observed practice this form of planning.

As mentioned, the extremes at either end of the planning style continuum are less effective. Let's say a planner seeks to increase the supply of affordable housing. If the planner's social justice idealism fuels moral outrage at the inequity of housing availability and misdistribution of political power, then that planner may adopt a no-compromise, zero-sum planning style. See planning as dividing up a fixed-sized pie leads to a focus on fighting for the biggest piece. Such a style could limit the planner's influence in his or her organization or prevent him or her from landing a position with an organization that could make change.

On the other hand, a planner may understand the power of entrenched community groups in resisting affordable housing to be greater than it really is. Although this condition clearly exists in some communities, there is a choice in to how to respond. Seeing reality as unchangeable may lead to giving up with the fight, with the thought, "I know that community groups will oppose whatever affordable housing plan I develop." Such a planner is dominated by existing power relations. This view may lead to a passive, status quo planning style and joining the ranks of those "putting in the years until retirement."

The third row of Figure 7.1—"personal outcomes"—emphasizes that motivation and resilience is brought about by achieving change, whether it be transformational or incremental. A community organizer empowering a community to fight an environmental toxics problem is engaged in transformational change. The organizing process may create new community leaders who carry the fight for more resident clout in regulatory processes and remediation. On the other hand, a planner working in a large bureaucracy may reform permitting and environmental review processes to reduce environmental hazards and ensure remediation. A regulatory change inside an influential organization may have a large, systemic impact. The best approach depends on the context and the planner's strengths and weaknesses.

Outside the middle ground, the no-compromise planning style often yields burnout because the opportunity for transformations that increase the size of the pie is not realized. On the other extreme, a passive, status quo planning style leads to checkout, allowing problems to continue and potentials to be unrealized.

Principled adaptability works. Being effective motivates. Success produces confidence and inspires. It generates resilience that helps planners recover from disappointment if an issue doesn't work out as hoped. The result is motivated planners engaged in a most amazing type of work—being paid to make the world a better place.

So why don't all planners practice principled adaptability? The last row in Figure 7.1 provides a hint: principled adaptability requires ongoing ethical reasoning and living with uncertainty. Sometimes, compromise is being a "sell-out," and sometimes it is exactly what is needed to get things moving. Reason is needed to sort these choices out. As Chapter 8 discusses, competing ethical concepts of justice such as virtue, deontic (following process), and utilitarianism (greatest good) may be in tension. Becoming a person who thinks well about ethical questions is invaluable. It benefits both professional and personal life.

Consider the alternatives. The passive, status quo planner goes through the motions at work and avoids ethical reflection. The no-compromise, zero-sum planner, on the other hand, is ethically rigid, applying one ethical maxim regardless of context or issue. This is also an easier ethical path, because the world is measured against that unchanging, unambiguous standard.

Much of the idea of principled adaptability hinges on the question of how much to compromise. When should one push hard for a virtuous ideal and when should one compromise or wait, recognizing the reality of the power structure and the process of change? There is no universal answer: only the answer for a particular planner in a particular instance.

To illustrate these ideas in concrete terms, three boxes provide instances that reflect on the idea of principled adaptability. Box 7.1 deals with assessing how hard to push for something—in this case, fighting for resources for the good of an organization. Because the issue seemed so clearly an injustice to the writer, his first instinct was an uncompromising path. By holding off on a risky strategy, a more strategic approach became apparent by considering the risks and benefits under different scenarios. Compromise turned out to be the best path.

Box 7.2 is a case where *too much* compromise produced a failed program. It illustrates the degree to which success of a program depended on implementation details, and how self-interested stakeholders used compromise to undermine a plan. In short, this is a case of too much adaptability.

Box 7.3 addresses a professional circumstance outside of planning—that of a public-interest private investigator. Planners are not alone in facing

Box 7.1 Fighting for a Cause—How Hard?

As chair of an academic department, one of my jobs was to ensure that there were enough tenure-track faculty to meet the accrediting body's student/faculty ratios requirements and standards of teaching quality. When a faculty member retired before an accreditation self-study was due, I requested a search for a new faculty member. I believed that we needed to have a search underway before the accreditation review team visited the campus. Rather than have it automatically granted, the department had to request permission for a replacement position. The decision rested with the Provost, a person whom I respected.

The Provost declined the request, stating he would consider it in six months during the regular search request process. I was livid—by that time, the accreditation report would be submitted. I wanted a guarantee. The department had performed well, and the replacement would not increase costs.

My initial reaction was to fight. I stated that the department would lose accreditation if the position was not granted immediately. This was partly a bluff—not certain, but possible because student/faculty ratios were an issue. The decision seemed unfair and disrespectful to my efforts. I could engage alumni and employers to put pressure on him and appeal to the university president. My ultimate recourse was to resign my position in protest.

My sense of personal outrage made it difficult for me to think clearly. I learned through experience that when I feel this way I should slow down, calm myself, and think strategically. I conducted a decision-tree analysis, similar to that described in Chapter 3. The "guns blazing" approach had risk, however satisfying it would feel. If I succeeded, I might alienate the Provost so that the department would suffer in the future. If I was unsuccessful, I would be out of the leadership role, with no more political capital to help the department. As is common in these issues, my thinking encompassed my desire for personal respect and for what was good for the department. Another option on the decision tree was to accept the decision and wait six months—it wasn't optimal but left my options open. By not pursuing all the options in that moment, I would preserve them for the future, should need be.

The Provost met with me to explain his decision and rationale. I made my case but respectfully accepted his decision. By being reasonable, I gained credibility. I negotiated a one-year visiting professor position and agreed to wait for the decision on the permanent position. That turned out to be a good choice—the permanent position was authorized six months later, the accreditation team was satisfied, and I gained legitimacy. I did not follow my first instinct—the idealist demand that justice and fairness prevail and my reasonable request be granted. Instead, I allowed enough realism to develop a better response.

Box 7.2 Too Much Adaptability

I worked for a redevelopment agency overseeing extensive downtown development. This development generated traffic impacts; the agency sought to reduce them by requiring that some parking be built at intercept points around downtown, lessening on-site parking and shuttling office employees to their jobs. This would reduce traffic on downtown streets. The program was proposed long before I arrived; when I got the assignment, it was late and overdue. We hired consultants, engaged stakeholders, and began to build the program. In order for it to work, intercept structures had to serve all key access points from the freeway, and structures needed to be large enough so that frequent shuttle service could be economically provided. The logical way to do this was to have office developers pay an in-lieu fee to the city to fund the intercept parking and the shuttles. In this way, efficiently sized and appropriately located parking structures could be built and be served by a convenient shuttle network.

The scheme promised to save money, as building parking structures was cheaper than constructing parking under the office buildings. It was the ideal system from a transportation planning point of view. If the intercept parking was not properly located and the shuttles not convenient, however, office workers might not use it. Commuters do not like to change travel modes, especially when they are close to their destination.

The ideal solution encountered an effective opposition strategy from developers and property owners. Rather than oppose the program, which would have required a lot of political support, they agreed to the concept and negotiated a "minor" point of implementation. Great, I thought, we're on our way. However, the implementation detail was a Trojan horse designed to kill the program. They said, "we like the program but would like to build and control our own peripheral parking facilities." This seemed like a minor point to elected officials, and it was not unreasonable for them to seek control of the parking for which they were paying. But this small change undermined the logic of the program—no single development could build a complete set of intercept facilities or run an efficient shuttle because each individual building was too small. Participation would decrease and commuters using them might drive *more* by having to go around downtown to get to an assigned structure.

There was great political pressure to get this program adopted. Redevelopment staff did not have the support to resist the developers' proposals. So, to get *something* adopted, the program went forward as proposed by the developers. Only one parking structure was built, which is underutilized to this day. The shuttle system was never created. Lawsuits were filed. The issue slipped off the front burner because the office market collapsed; no one was building offices anymore. The flawed peripheral program stayed on the books for years. The program had to either be done properly or abandoned for another approach. Too much adaptability led to failure.

Box 7.3 A Case of Competing Principles

By Keith Rohman, President, Public Interest Investigations,
Inc., Los Angeles, California

I am a private investigator, a field you may not think of as having a strong ethical code. You would be wrong. Perhaps because we often work on the margins of society, it is all the more important that we have a sense of right and wrong.

It was that sense of right and wrong that drew me to investigations. I'd been a community organizer working in low-income areas and a union organizer working with low-wage workers. My route to investigations was circuitous, but when I opened my own firm, I called it Public Interest Investigations (PII), and my goal was to use my investigation skills on behalf of the social justice causes I supported.

Over the years, PII has worked for defendants in death penalty cases, investigated allegations of sexual harassment in the workplace and on campuses, and investigated allegations of torture at the Abu Ghraib prison. Mostly, my idealism and ideology matched the work that I did. But one case challenged that smug assumption. I was hired by a civil rights group to investigate claims by a respected activist that he had been attacked by members of an unidentified neo-Nazi group. The activist was found in his car, tied up by the roadside in a rural area of Mississippi. (Identifying details have been changed.) Local police investigated the allegation but took little action.

Some of the group's leadership wanted to issue a strong statement of support for the activist, whereas others seemed more skeptical about his report. I was hired to help the group sort out the facts. I first researched the activist. I learned he had stellar credentials and had been working on civil rights issues when I was still a kid. He was the kind of person I would have liked to meet and learn from, not investigate.

But investigate I did. I interviewed people in the community, determined his whereabouts before the incident, and had several lengthy meetings with investigating detectives. The police surprised me by being open and cooperative, and I found they had conducted a thorough and professional investigation.

I can still remember sitting in my dusty hotel room, with the police reports and crime scene photos laid out in front of me, as the truth slowly dawned on me: the activist was lying. He had made this story up. I felt a chill go up my spine. I didn't know why he'd done it, but the evidence was clear. He had engaged in a "self-kidnapping," arranging the scene to make it appear as if he had been attacked. Numerous pieces of physical evidence were completely inconsistent with the activist's story. Other evidence raised more questions than it answered. When I did a follow-up interview with the activist, he could not account for the inconsistencies and accused me of being biased.

I was a social change advocate-turned-investigator, and the idea that I was about to create a report that would label this life-long activist as a fabricator was hard to swallow. I knew that if I told the truth, my report would expose this well-respected

Box 7.3 (continued)

civil rights group to public criticism. But as I thought about it, I realized something about me had changed. My idealism and my thirst for social justice had evolved into something different: I was an investigator now, and it was important to me to follow the facts, even if they led to an uncomfortable conclusion.

In the end, my report told the truth as I understood it. Many of my worst fears were realized. Right-wing talk radio hosts had a field day talking about how the civil rights group's "own investigation" revealed the activist's claim was a fraud. The group's board was split, and the faction that supported the activist won out. Those who had hired me ended up being fired or resigning, along with a number of board members.

The group eventually overcame this hurdle and remains a well-respected group. My report is probably long forgotten. But I still think about that case and how it awakened me to the investigator I had become.

ethical dilemmas about their practice. In this case, the investigator experienced two kinds of idealism: his profession's commitment to truth-telling (deontic, rule-based ethics) and his commitment to the cause of civil rights (outcome, utilitarian ethics). The investigator knew the reality of how truth-telling would affect the cause of civil rights. Planners frequently face this tension—when pursuing one ideal would harm another.

Labelling Versus a Dynamic System

Figure 7.1 is not intended to label any planner as falling into one category or another. In some instances, I bring a realism to well-intended (and sometimes self-interested) planning proposals that are not grounded in the evidence. In my transportation planning work, I use evidence about human behavior, context, and economics to realistically understand whether a proposal will shape travel behavior toward more sustainable travel choices.

This work opposes transportation "boondoggles"—expensive projects that don't advance mobility and access as they should. Engineering and construction firms seeking lucrative contracts and land speculators and developers seeking enhanced land values often line up behind a flawed project. Then, elected officials seek to spread investment to all parts of a jurisdiction, regardless of efficiency. Compounding the problem, these schemes are sometimes accompanied by regressive taxing schemes. The way in which politics, infrastructure development, and travel behavior interact leads me to a skeptical perspective.

Realism about these issues keeps me from flights of fantasy about how well a transportation project may work.

A second example is climate change, where I argue for the need for the realism that science provides. The severity of the climate change problem is such that I assert that scientific evidence should override a person's or elected official's view that climate change is not a human-caused problem that demands immediate attention. For climate change planning, I claim the necessity to heed the science as forcefully as I can.

In other situations, I am an idealist. In the area of human interactions and management, I have a vision of the transformative and positive impact of discourse. When it is undermined by lying, obfuscation, insincerity, or false claims to legitimacy, I don't accept that as a normal aspect of human interactions. It pains me personally; I seek to move discourse toward that ideal communication environment that Habermas (1984) proposes. Having experienced the transformative effect of dialogue, I hold an ideal vision of what it can be. This serves my commitments to bring repair in the world, promote interdependence, and advance mutual care. Of course, a realist recognizes how personal self-interest and group dynamics can derail conversation and dialogue, but I take an idealistic approach, seeking opportunities for transformational dialogues that generate opportunities.

More broadly, when the planning efforts in which I am involved don't support my interpretation of universal values of love, justice, truth, or beauty discussed previously, and when that happens over a period of time, I become discouraged. There have been times in my career when I felt burnout and/ or the impulse to check out. Fortunately, they have been brief. The reflection process discussed in Appendix B can help achieve perspective. When I have faced those instances, I usually respond in one of three ways: changing the way I interpret the situation, changing my role within a job, or changing jobs.

Lastly, idealism and realism may apply differently to stages in the planning process. Idealism may drive the purpose of the plan. Then realism may inform strategies for implementing the plan—being realistic about politics, interests, and strategies. And of course, planning and implementation are not separate steps but should inform one another.

And Now to You: Passion and Reason

Using different terminology than the idealism/realism tension described here, Abraham Lincoln refers to a related tension. In an address entitled "The

Perpetuation of Our Political Institutions," he said: "Passion has helped us; but it can do so no more. It will be in the future our enemy. Reason, cold, calculating, unimpassioned reason, must furnish all the materials for our future support and defense."[2] Idealism might be associated with passion. Realism might be associated with reason. In his speech, Lincoln called for reason to predominate in the context he faced. In your planning career, and for the times you face, how will passion and reason inform your work? How will you engage idealism and realism in your day-to-day planning efforts? How will that engagement translate into your approach to a particular planning problem? As the quote attests, this demand and these questions are not new.

The way in which idealism and realism operates in your planning career will evolve over time. The planner starting out may be driven primarily by idealism and be frustrated by the slow pace of change. But planners may not be aware of how their role contributes to the bigger picture, know the dimensions that inform change, or have the power to make change—the realism part. Box 7.4 provides an account of an environmental planner who experienced the ebb and flow of idealism, feeling it challenged at first but having a plan to find work that more directly addresses idealism. This ebb and flow is a normal aspect of a planning career. My point is to advise you to recognize this tension, reflect on it as you plan, and steer your career to the place on the idealist–realist continuum that makes you most effective.

Over the course of my career, I have worked in contexts in which planning values have been embraced and contexts in which they have been under attack. As I write this manuscript, populist movements in the U.S. and other countries are challenging planning values such as sustainability and social justice. Exclusion and "me-first/us-first" values are being expressed, counter to traditional planning values of inclusion, community, and bringing repair to society and the natural environment. Regarding realism, the so-called post-truth era contests planners' reliance on science and rational thought to justify recommendations. From either idealist or realist perspectives, this is a tough time. As a beginning planner, you may wonder if you will be able to make a contribution and question whether society values your contribution. Yet history shows that these challenges have been present before, in different terms, and overcome. The challenges require planners to be as effective as possible.

I suggest using reflection to move practice choices and strategies from a background, unexamined level to an explicit one. In addition to helping develop a planning style, the principled adaptability diagram can guide

Box 7.4 The Rhythm of Idealism and Realism
By Anonymous, an Environmental Planner,
with Four Years' Experience

My idealism is on pause. It hit its peak during my senior year in college. Once I discovered urban planning, I felt as if it were too good to be true; this was the answer to "wicked" problems such as climate change, social inequality, and environmental conservation. What really fueled my love for planning was sustainable development. I was determined to find a job that would help reduce human contribution to CO_2 emissions. Upon graduating in 2012, I searched for a sustainable development position and didn't find much. After a six-month stint in retail, I landed an environmental planning internship at a large consulting firm in Southern California. Having no connections to the company, and feeling like the least qualified candidate in a group interview, I felt as if I had won the lottery when I was offered the job.

A few months in, I realized that environmental planning is not exactly about what's *best* for the environment but rather writing a strong justification for projects to meet the requirements of the California Environmental Quality Act, the National Environmental Policy Act, and the resource agencies. Most agencies knew exactly which project alternative they wished to build, regardless of the environmental analysis. This realization was disheartening but not a deal breaker—at least for me. Although I was astounded at the amount of regulatory processes, I was set on getting a few years of experience before moving onto something else.

Fast forward four years, I am still working at the same firm, now as a mid-level environmental planner, and am wrapping up my Master's in Urban and Regional Planning. Even though this field of planning doesn't promote my ideals as directly as I would like, I do love my job (most of the time) and the people I work with. At this point in my life, I need a realist perspective in order to balance the life of an employee, student, wife, (new) mom, and homeowner while keeping my sanity. Even though I'd be happier in a job closer to my purpose, I've accepted that bureaucracy is inefficient, slow to change, and frankly, doesn't care what mid-level planners think.

For me, staying positive through what I would consider a transition period is a must. I remind myself how beneficial it is to have a four-year work history with important agencies, as well as having leadership roles on regionally significant projects. I enjoy being part of a team that delivers high-quality products.

I reject the notion that one must be naïve or unrealistic to retain an idealist spirit. Though it's taken some time, I recognize that early in my career, I don't get to call all the shots. I am still gaining experience and have sacrificed seeking a job that directly addresses climate change in order to finish my Master's degree. Now, four years in, I am optimistic that my next career move will be in the right direction to my truer, more idealistic self.

selection of planning work settings. Consider the predominate planning style of an organization (transformational or incremental) to find alignment with your preferred planning style. Also, use Figure 7.1 to better diagnose and interpret planning discussions. Listen for notes of idealism and realism, and for arguments in favor of taking strong positions and those for compromise. With this framework, you can see how the work of planning is accomplished by engaging this tension. Planners work out idealism/realism tensions in real time, as do planning teams. Principled adaptability supports planning effectiveness.

Discussion/Reflection Questions for Chapter 7

1. Reflect on planning situations where you were sure you were right and were unwilling to compromise, and those when you saw the validity of different points of view and acted more as a facilitator of compromise. What distinguishes the two situations for you? If your strategy for acting varies in those situations, how did you act differently?
2. Search the American Planning Association website for planning awards. What styles of planning are lauded? Does transformational change get more attention than incremental change? If so, why might that be? Are there awards for planning efforts that reflect a principled adaptability style?
3. How does the planning profession deal with disappointment? Ask a seasoned planner about her or his experience.
4. Interview a planner about her or his position on idealism and realism. How do they bring these elements into their work?

Notes

1. The 10 characteristics of a wicked problem, defined by Rittel and Webber (1973), are: (1) no definitive formulation; (2) no stopping rule (for finding a solution); (3) solutions are good/bad, not true/false; (4) solutions cannot be fully tested; (5) "one-shot" operations; (6) no ability to enumerate all solutions; (7) each problem is unique; (8) each problem is a symptom of another problem; (9) explanation of the problem determines its resolution; and (10) the planner has no right to be wrong.
2. Lincoln, A. (1838) "The perpetuation of our political institutions." Accessed at http://teachingamericanhistory.org/library/document/the-perpetuation-of-our-political-institutions/

References

Ackoff, R. (1999). *Re-creating the corporation: A design of organization for the 21st century.* New York, NY: Oxford University Press.

Argyris, C. and D. Schön. (1974). *Theory in practice: Increasing professional effectiveness.* San Francisco, CA: Jossey-Bass.

Habermas, J. (1984). *The theory of communicative action.* Translated by T. McCarthy. Boston, MA: Beacon Press.

Rawls, J. (1971). *A theory of justice.* Cambridge, MA: Belknap.

Rittel, H.W.J. and M. Webber. (1973). Dilemmas in a general theory of planning (PDF). *Policy Sciences* 4: pp. 155–169. doi:10.1007/bf01405730

Chapter 8

Being Right

*My pact with the good
is prior to my choice.*

Few choose a planning career to tinker with mundane problems. Planning has exciting aspirations for design, the environment, the economy, and social justice. It is inspiring to have this commitment to the public good. With lofty aspirations, however, comes the possibility that idealist planners believe they know the "right" answer for a planning challenge but encounter political, economic, or administrative resistance. They may find themselves frustrated with the distance between the "right answer" and what happens in practice. As discussed in Chapter 7, the notion of principled adaptability argues for clear thinking in making a claim to rightness. But sometimes, planners must draw a line in the sand. How do idealist planners decide these issues?

The question of a planner "being right" is complex. Success metrics in other fields are often clearer. For private companies, metrics include return on investment, market share, growth rate, and so on, and employees are expected to contribute to the organization's vision and goals. An employee may have the "right" answer about a corporate strategy or program, but if the supervisor doesn't agree, he or she must toe the line. Public agencies and non-profit organizations have more complicated and sometimes contradictory goals, such as tension between economic growth and the quality of the environment. There is also room for personal advocacy in many planning organizations, so idealist planners may seek to change the organization along the lines of their "right answer."

Planners have different ways of understanding problems based on their training and their ideological commitments. They may draw on design theory, economics, political science, policy analysis, public administration, geography, critical theory, or sociology to understand problems and propose solutions. One planner may use neo-liberal theory to identify externalities and public goods while another uses a Marxist approach to understand how capital is urbanized. If these two approaches are applied to the same problem, they will generate different ideas about solutions. There is no straightforward way to determine which approach is correct, and so one planner's "right" answer might be another's "misguided approach."

"I'm right" situations require reflection and discernment. Sometimes we are right and sometimes we are wrong in the full context of the issue, and the more discernment we gain, the better. This chapter explains the types of disagreement, such as those concerning goals, strategies, or tactics. Then, two examples—"right" in relation to what a supervisor wants and "right" in relationship to the needs of elected officials—are explored.

Next, the chapter introduces the larger context for being right. Focusing on the immediate issue might neglect subtle dimensions of change that occur later, or that occur as second- and third-order impacts. If planners recognize the complexities of change, they are better equipped to decide on strategy. There is a way to practice planning that lessens the feeling that "I alone carry responsibility for the world," without reducing motivation and effectiveness. The chapter concludes with strategies for acting, including staying loyal to the organization, voicing the planner's opinion, or exiting the organization.

"I'm Right" Situations

"I'm right" situations are inherent in the idealistic and change-oriented field of planning. An obvious first question is, "right about what?" Right about the definition of the problem? Or, right about the *values* (basic aims) that should apply, *technical matters* (different views of cause, effect, risk, and unanticipated consequences), or *means* of accomplishing those ends (strategy, tactics, disclosure)? Right about *tactics* or unique context factors associated with planning decisions? The better planners can isolate which of those elements apply, the better they can consider their claim and level of certainty. Achieving clarity and distinguishing among these elements is a vital skill.

Issues of "being right" are tricky when it comes to technical matters, but they often can be resolved with reference to research. Does evidence support a particular planning solution? How certain are the causal factors in the issue? What implementation strategies avoid policy failure?

"Being right" about values is more complex. In this regard, planners may be moral realists or moral relativists. A moral realist believes that there are better and worse answers to moral questions, and that certain values are universal. This leads planners to assert correctness about the values that a planning decision should serve. A moral relativist, on the other hand, believes that laws and the values from which they are derived are a consensus of opinion in a particular place and time and do not reflect universal notions. In this view, planners should not claim correctness based on a universal value but support the majority view.

Many planners are moral realists. This is embedded in the AICP Code of Ethics' aspirational values related to rights, social justice, the environment, participation, and value of considering the long-term future. These are a form of virtue ethics, concerned with the moral character of the planner. What is challenging for moral realist planners is that the values they think should apply in a planning issue may conflict with those of supervisors and decision-makers.

Although many planners are comfortable with the moral realist position, there is a risk of going too far with an "I'm right" attitude. Moral facts cannot be observed as can material facts, which generates a demand for justification that is not easy to provide. In contrast, deontic ethics suggest that planners should follow accepted rules of behavior in relation to the profession, elected decision-makers, and the AICP Code. Perhaps planners should concern themselves with process rather than outcome. This tension is why I counsel due diligence on conclusions about being right. Planning's professional values may differ from those established by the decisions of advisory boards, political bodies, or boards of directors. Furthermore, the planner's personal values may be different than those of the organization. In their practice, idealist planners weigh how much they are willing to bend their values to the organization's values, because they are not the decision-makers and are not directly accountable to the electorate.

Lastly, tactics may be a point of tension. For example, a supervisor may tell a planner that certain quantitative model results will help the organization compete for funding from an external agency. The planner may agree with the goals of the organization and know that other competing applicants will use favorable data. If the organization doesn't play the game, it may lose out. Such an approach stems from utilitarian (consequentialist) ethics, where the goodness of the outcome is prioritized over the process. But this is set against the planner's commitment to presenting unbiased numbers as they are produced by analysis.

Table 8.1 arrays a variety of issues and contexts where that perspective may be present. As the table shows, there are many ways that a planner may disagree with the direction given by a supervisor, elected official, or client. Most of them involve all three conceptions of ethics mentioned

Table 8.1 "I'm right" examples

Issue	Example	Nature of the disagreement
Social justice	Planner is directed to write regulations that make it difficult to build affordable housing because of community opposition linked to fear of crime and property value decline.	Values
Environmental sustainability	City manager considers a wetland a useless swamp and directs planner to prepare community plans and development regulations that allow for its degradation, whereas the planner wants to preserve it.	Values and technical matters
Rail transit development	Planner is directed to support a regional transit agency's sales tax measure that focused on rail transit rather than bus rapid transit, in opposition to research on cost effectiveness of those modes and needs of transit users.	Problem frame and technical matters
Cost effectiveness	Project proponents "buy" support for initiatives by providing community benefits for a wide range of stakeholder groups, even if the extra elements are only tangentially related to the main proposal.	Tactics
Wastefulness	Planner is advised to purchase unneeded equipment at the end of the fiscal year with a "use it or lose it" perspective.	Efficiency versus department interests
Bureaucratic impediments to change	An otherwise worthy proposal to reform zoning codes is thwarted because entrenched city department interests want to keep their roles from changing.	Competition among interests

(Continued)

Table 8.1 (Continued)

Issue	Example	Nature of the disagreement
Avoidance of decisions	Planners agree that park space needs to be improved in inner-city locations, but managers do not act to avoid disagreement about resource allocations between competing neighborhoods.	Strategy
Manager is incompetent	The manager makes policy decisions that are inconsistent and without rationale.	Competency
Insider developer connections	Planner is encouraged to give good ratings to a flawed development proposal in which the mayor's relative is an investor.	Ethics
Management is engaged in fraud and abuse	Planner in public agency is asked to inflate budget requests and hide certain costs from city council and the public.	Ethics
Challenge to loyalty and trustworthiness	Planner is asked to leak information to the media in order to sway public opinion about a proposed development project that will create jobs and sales taxes for the city.	Ethics
Inclusion and participation	Planner's request for translation services for a community meeting is denied by supervisor even though the majority of residents are non-English speakers and planner privately makes case to director.	Ethics

above—virtue, deontic, and utilitarian—and planners must sort them out in specific instances.

Upstream and Downstream From the Entry-Level Planner

Most planners lack a complete view of project conceptualization, planning and design, and implementation. For example, municipal planners are not privy to the deliberations of development teams as they consider the type of project to propose. A municipal plan could influence the developer's project idea without it having a direct regulatory function. Similarly, consulting planners on a development team do not fully know the political and community concerns about the project. The municipal planner they interact with may insist on an apparently ineffective mitigation measure because it has symbolic value that will pave the way for community and political approval. Finally, those involved in project mitigation monitoring may not know the tradeoffs in project design and cost that were made before those mitigation measures were adopted. They may wonder why better project planning did not alleviate the need for mitigation measures.

The higher the management level of planners, the broader the view they are likely to have of the upstream and downstream decision-making in the planning process. Entry-level planners have a limited view, as they may not be at the table for negotiations between the parties, management strategy meetings, and elected official briefings. Entry-level planners generally complete defined tasks after they have been decided by managers. Without the full picture, entry-level planners may underestimate the positive impact of their work because they don't know how it affects the overall process. They may feel that a task is a waste of time or ineffective, but it may have impacts in ways that they do not understand.

The following example considers environmental planners' work. Environmental review laws require that alternatives to the proposed project be considered. Because much political and technical work has been invested in bringing a project to environmental review, alternative analysis work in an environmental impact report (EIR) rarely leads to the adoption of anything but the proposed project. Of course, it certainly may lead to modifications to the preferred alternative or the development of mitigation measures.

To entry-level planners, alternative analysis may seem like "going through the motions." Alternative projects are rarely selected. It may seem to them that the process is an expensive and analysis-heavy form of rubber-stamping projects. Without a broader view, planners may conclude that they "know better" and that their work isn't having an impact. This can be discouraging.

In my view, the EIR is the wrong place for substantive alternatives analysis—this should occur upstream in the planning process. Entry-level planners may not know how the EIR requirement shaped project definition and design. It may have done so at project conceptualization—where developers, planners, scientists, and designers sought to avoid environmental impacts, knowing that the downstream review would occur. The entry-level planners' role may have contributed to reducing environmental impacts in ways they don't directly know about. This understanding can lead to tolerance for planning and regulatory processes that don't appear to affect outcomes.

The Misunderstanding: Being "Right" in Relation to Supervisors

It is common for planners to disagree with their supervisor. If a supervisor rejects a recommendation, they may be making decisions based on an unarticulated theory-in-use, as discussed in Chapter 7. At the same time, the supervisor's compromises, failures of courage, or unwillingness to take a stand against public harm may be apparent. One thing is sure: staff planners' view is narrower than that of those higher in the organization. Supervisors have more information on the context for the decision.

Sometimes a supervisor is weighing a larger set of goals than staff planners are. Or a context factor unknown to staff planners may explain the supervisor's position. If planners straight out of school see theory as the highest form of knowledge—and application/practice as a degradation to theory—then they may struggle with understanding a supervisor's decisions. That supervisor may be seeking to impose coherence on a complex planning "mess" or may be guided by a different planning approach (e.g., incremental versus comprehensive).

Most planning situations have shifting, ambiguous ends and unstable institutional contexts. Planning cannot be firmly bounded or standardized, or based solely on scientific evidence. It shares these characteristics with other professions, such as education. There is artistry in effective practice that is difficult to simulate in planning education. Therefore, a supervisor could be practicing a form of planning artistry that staff planners do not recognize. The supervisor may have no way to describe or account for this artistry other than that which is revealed in what they do. If it could be detailed and described, then it would be taught in planning schools.

Frustrations with supervisors are not limited to planning decisions. Box 8.1 provides an account of a common frustration for staff planners—supervisors or clients who don't provide clear assignments.

A complex professional practice like planning, therefore, does not provide certainty—more than one answer can be correct. As discussed in Chapter 7, some planners choose apathy when there is conflict over the right answer. Other planners adopt a tight ideology to banish uncertainty. Lisa Schweitzer uses the

---

Box 8.1 Why Can't Clients Give Clear Assignments?

As a consultant, I sought clarity on the problem definition so my work could be on point and efficiently completed. I wanted to deliver a good work product within budget and responsive to technical demands and the decision-making process.

Despite this wish, many of my clients did not give clear assignments. With experience, I realized that this was the normal process with complex problems. Clients were not withholding clear assignments, but rather they were searching for an acceptable problem definition. Planning problems are usually wicked problems, lacking clear definitions or solutions. My clients were also considering multiple interacting systems: relationships in and outside of the organization, administrative politics between departments, the political dynamics of the decision-making body, knowledge and data limitations, the likelihood of future legal challenges, and tactics such as incremental versus systemic change.

It is easy to think clients don't know what they are doing, but planning consultants should consider the complex problem the client is facing. I learned over time not to judge this process; I could be of the greatest value if I could help my client discover an acceptable problem definition for moving forward. I did this by synthesizing ideas and issues and presenting them back to the client to see if they said "that's it" enough to begin studying it, knowing the second round of analysis may redefine the problem yet again.

---

term "Smartest Boy Urbanist" to describe the person who *knows* the answer, has built a personal brand around it, and is prepared to bludgeon the world with it:

> The Smartest Boy Urbanist in the Room knows that cities run like little clockworks, and that if People Would Just Do As He Says, cities and every service, space, or interaction in them would be So Much Better.
>
> (Schweitzer, 2016)

Better relationships between planners and supervisor are possible with more understanding of each other's role. In fact, planners are bound up with their supervisors in that each determine the other's success, and that web of connection passes up the line to other managers. If planners fail, their supervisor fails by not having a productive department. If the supervisor fails, planners fail by not having influence in the organization. Framing being managed as a mutually beneficial activity makes it a bit easier to "be managed."

Or . . . a supervisor could be wrong, an opportunist, or corrupt. Supervisors aren't always right. The challenge for idealist planners is to discern the difference between being adaptable and deciding that things are flat-out wrong.

Espoused Theory and Theory-in-Use

Planners' early careers involve a transition from relying on the espoused theories learned in school to developing their own theory-in-use. As mentioned, espoused theories vary widely—from a new urbanist design agenda, to one that favors market pricing in transportation systems, to a neo-Marxist perspective that embraces public ownership of assets. Each theory has clear and well-developed ways of understanding and offers defined policy and design prescriptions. But one cannot simply *apply* a theory to the complex setting of public planning. Other stakeholders and constituents have their own theories that they want to advance.

A desire to cleanly implement a single theory can lead to an excessive "I know I'm right" perspective. A colleague from a progressive urban planning program told me that their graduates could not stay employed in the more conservative, suburban cities in the region. For those graduates, with a progressive change agenda, the suburban city setting, politics, and planning traditions were too far from their vision. It is understandable to avoid a work setting that is at odds with a planner's values, but it is also worth taking the long view on change.

Planning involves problem definition—naming the things we wish to attend to, and framing—assessing the context in which we will attend to them. All of the stakeholders involved in planning bring their own "naming and framing" to the process. Rather than there being a single right answer, more often, we communicate and seek resolution about those different conceptions.

As their career progresses, planners develop a knowing that is not derived from easily explainable rules or procedures. Because planning involves complex, multifaceted problems, an optimization procedure that might apply to a simple decision will not work. Designers, for example, may be able to recognize a bad fit of a form to its context, but they may not be able to explain the rules by which bad fit was recognized and redesigned (Schön, 1973, from Alexander, p. 52). Similarly, planning managers working in large organizations may recognize a way forward in an administrative "mess" without being able to clearly articulate the reasons. In other words, planners may be incapable of writing the "textbooks" that are written in their minds (Barnard, 1968, p. 306).

"Knowing you are right" blocks an openness to learning from unexpected, non-linear, and surprising events. Donald Schön (1983) describes this as follows:

> The practitioner allows himself to experience surprise, puzzlement, or confusion in a situation he finds uncertain or unique. He reflects on the phenomenon before him, and on the prior understandings which have been implicit in his behavior. He carries out an experiment which serves to generate both new understanding of the phenomena and a change in the situation.
>
> (p. 68)

Planners who are sure they are right are rarely willing to be surprised, puzzled, or confused. Being certain, angry, and self-righteous does not lead to learning. Of course, some of this feeling may stem from legitimate outrage over a manager's corrupt practices, disagreeable values, or incompetence. Outrage is not an excuse for idealist planners not doing their best.

The Prophet: Being "Right" in Relation to Decision-Makers and Community

A second "I'm right" situation occurs if idealist planners work for a community whose values, as expressed through the political system, are different from theirs. For example, an environmental planner who understands the threats of global climate change may conclude that radical, systemic economic reforms are the only valid path. That planner's sense of urgency is certainly justified by the science. Having good ideas for climate change mitigation and adaptation motivates action and generates hope, but progress can be stymied if the planner seeks more change than is politically feasible in that moment. Seasoned idealists are also frustrated with slow change, but they have seen it occur over the longer arcs of their careers. They may be more tolerant of the time required. Barring revolution, compromise is a part of reform.

A reform-minded environmental planner may encounter climate change deniers on the city council and at community meetings. I get angry when climate change deniers lie about science at a city council meeting or when scientists are told their peer-reviewed papers must be reviewed for compliance with political positions. The key is to avoid being blinded by righteous anger. Strategic, tactical thinking is required for these situations. When opponents to climate change action provoke a planner into being angry or arrogant-sounding, they then characterize the planner as an arrogant bureaucrat with a radical agenda.

Sometimes change seems to take forever, while many problems demand solutions now. Deeply understanding a problem and its interconnections with natural and human systems naturally brings a sense of urgency. As well, that understanding reveals structures that impede change. For example, understanding globalization could lead an environmental planner to conclude that no local action can counter climate change.

Fueled by visions of the ideal developed in a planner's education, the hard-scrabble reality of practice may shock the planner, especially if there is a large gap between the vision and local conditions. One response to the messiness of planning practice is to judge others to be inferior, intellectually or morally. The critical thinking perspective learned in school may make idealist planners *too* critical. Impatience motivates reform, but it too can be overdone and lead to errors.

The first type of error is technical. Using economic development as an example, planners working on community revitalization programs may use retail sales data to track progress and guide efforts. If they don't have the time to collect data from the target community and a control-group community, this shortcut could lead them to falsely conclude that a façade program was successful because retail sales increased in the target community, but if sales went up in places without the program, the conclusion is faulty. Those planners might recommend continuation of a program that isn't working.

A second type is process errors. For example, planners may take a shortcut by copying the business improvement district (BID) charter from a highly regarded BID in another state. If they fail to do the legal due diligence to ensure that the provisions are enforceable in their state, the BID could be dissolved because of a legal challenge that would have been avoided with better homework.

Ethical failures are a third type, such as when planners decide that the ends justify the means. For example, a goal of revitalizing a district might justify a shortcut in the public notification process and time frames for the BID vote. It could include falsifying the results of a retail study to support a desired course of action, or manipulating a bidding process for service companies to ensure that the preferred firm wins the contract. Feeling the virtue of a planning agenda, combined with impatience, could seem to justify cutting corners. The planner may then "dress" questionable practices in a robe of self-righteousness.

Loyalty, Voice, and Exit

What can idealist planners do when they've given careful thought to values, diligently sought evidence about facts and circumstances, avoided arrogance and impatience, and have a strong position in opposition to decision-makers? The policy analysis literature identifies the options as loyalty, voice, and exit (Hirschman, 1970).

Loyalty means placing the organization's goals ahead of personal goals. Obviously, loyalty is carried too far if the organization is engaged in unethical or illegal activity. In less stark choices, loyalty may preserve career advancement, yielding future influence, and it may be the right answer if planners are not *sure* they are right. Loyalty might be chosen if overlooking an immediate disagreement brings longer-term gain. But always choosing loyalty over personal conviction, regardless of circumstance, produces worn-down, uninspired planners who don't develop a reputation as independent professionals.

Voice means arguing for change along the lines of the planners' assessment of desirable action. Voice occurs with fellow staff members, immediate supervisors, senior supervisors, and decision-makers. Voice can also occur in a collective sense, as in unions representing planners in an organization. Whether and how planners exercise voice, and at what organization level, depends on the organizational culture (is productive dissent welcomed?), the management style of supervisors, the planners' social capital in the organization, and protections against retaliatory actions, such as whistleblower laws.

Choices about voicing disagreement are tricky. Depending on how planners exercise voice, they can either be viewed as thoughtful, ethical, independent thinkers who help the organization stay honest or as complainers who aren't happy unless they get their way. It takes wisdom to discern the first path from the second.

Planners should try different ways of expressing voice, such as developing arguments regarding legal, health and safety, fiscal prudence, or unanticipated consequences. Even if a city council was, for example, opposed to affordable housing, the planners could warn that not complying with a state affordable housing requirement could lead to the city being sued by an advocacy organization. In this way, the planners don't seek to change the council members' values or convictions but rather to appeal to their fiscal prudence.

The success of the voice strategy has a lot to do with how it is delivered. It is worth learning how to disagree without rancor. Unpack the disagreement. Is it about values that should guide a decision? Is it about the weighing of the different values that guide a decision? Are values in agreement but a disagreement exists in the technical analysis supporting a particular means? The more precisely the disagreement is diagnosed, the better planners can avoid personalizing it. The planner's voice can be more precise, pinpointing the nature of the disagreement rather than criticizing or attacking the whole process. It is possible to disagree in a friendly way that preserves relationships.

Exit means exit, as planners leave and seek a setting in better alignment with their views. For many planners, with mortgages, student loan debt, and family obligations, exit sounds like the end of the world. Yet it is always an option. Although there may be a financial price to pay in income or a promotion, the reward is personal integrity. If exit is being considered, planners should make it their last step, not their first.

The other consideration in exit is making sure that what seems like a failure to influence outcomes is indeed a failure. Judith Innes and David Booher (2010) explain first-, second-, and third-order impacts in collaborative work. A first-order impact is the adoption of the policy but is not limited to that. Let's say that a recommendation was not adopted. Was that a failure? On the surface, perhaps, but the planners may have built a new relationship with the city attorney (political capital) or become more trusted members of the team (social capital). These impacts might produce benefits down the line. Second-order impacts include immediate changes beyond the interaction on the particular issue, such as partnerships or coordination with other agencies or changes in perceptions in the broader community. Third-order impacts are changes that might happen later based on the groundwork laid in a current effort. It could be that an initial effort to increase understanding about an issue fosters conversations and underpins the change that occurs later. Today's action may have unanticipated effects and provoke system changes that support the intended reform.

Box 8.2 describes a circumstance where this perspective was lacking.

And Now to You: The Happy Warrior

Working for change requires an interpretative framework for the change process and the impact of your work. If you reach an "I'm right" assertion after due diligence, then you have choices of strategy. In this process, effectiveness is increased if you can avoid arrogance and impatience. Consider the value of the old expression: "perfect is the enemy of the good" in each instance.

Appreciate the dignity of the mundane struggle for good. This occurs in less-visible actions that support planning systems: interactions at the zoning counter, generating dialogue with the city council, and nitty-gritty regulatory reform

---

Box 8.2 Sell-Out?

Years ago, I developed a research associates (RA) program in a public agency. It was designed for students who had completed their Master's degrees, to bring a research perspective into day-to-day policy-making, encourage new thinking, and mentor young professionals. Students came straight out of school, some of them with little knowledge of the politics of decision-making.

The policy issue being addressed was how this agency spent funds on different travel modes—driving, bicycling, walking, and the like. The historical pattern favored those who drive, part of the long, post-war approach of accommodating private vehicle transportation. One of the research associates, armed with the latest academic critiques of transportation investments, saw the position as an opportunity to correct the historical bias toward private automobile travel. The research assignments were intended to provide information that would inform the legislative body's decisions in these matters.

I advised the research associates that the change process is incremental. It relies on issue "frames" (the way people perceive causal relationships), cooperation between agency departments, the positions held by the elected board members, and the chief administrator's strategy for presenting issues and moderating disagreement among board members. Policy shifts occured slowly and only to the degree that the elected officials felt they had local support for the change. These conditions suggested a light touch, one that supported incremental changes that produced quick but partial wins. Then, support could be built for more comprehensive change.

The idealistic RA wanted to expose the inequity of the current policy to different transportation modes by calculating a cost per each mode served believing that sheer force of evidence would produce change. The RA's theory of change was that logic and insightful technical analysis produce desired results. I offered that exposing the inequity could hamper change by hardening resistance by the elected officials who favored the status quo. Rather than starting a war between those supporting different modes, my counsel was to seek incremental improvements in pedestrian, bicycle, and transit modes without taking on the solo driving mode head-on. The RA thought I was a sell-out.

---

that make decisions transparent and rational. Sometimes, these seemingly minor arenas have more leverage than lofty but unimplemented policies and plans.

A rational person sees the world as it is and has a reasonable theory of transformation. Don't beat yourself up over a vision that is unreasonable. See things as they are. Some possibilities are structurally constrained, such as interventions that challenge private property rights, but there are more and less effective ways of moving forward. If you lean toward idealism, build a capacity for wise discernment. One way of navigating this is to "be an ethicist first, activist second."

Considering yourself as on the right side of history offers the moral high ground. It is better to admit flaws—be part of the human race—than seek to be above it. If you avoid feeling morally superior, even in the face of disappointment, you can manage anger and resentment. In most situations, be willing to compromise.

My read of world history suggests that evil exists in human affairs. Even though planning does not normally act at the global level, even minor local government corruption has a negative effect on public trust in government. After a highly publicized corruption case in a Southern California city, constituents across the region came to their own city councils with anger, which undermined public deliberation and reason. It produced a backlash against professional discretion in planning, such as when voters demand ballot box control over planning decisions.

If you need to fight evil, do it. As Alexander (2017) says, "circumstances determine whether a planner should apply communicative practices and aim for consensus, or use Machiavellian strategies to oppose power" (p. 97). Make a clear-eyed assessment of which strategy is appropriate, assess the potential for success, and select good tactics. Find allies: the press, community organizations, the city attorney, state law and state agencies, or the constitution. Even though you may hold yourself to a higher standard, your opponents may not. You may be called to decide whether to fight dirty. In cases where there is wrong-doing, work for justice but don't be the sole dispenser of it. Bad people may get away with stuff, especially in the short run, but history tells us that their long-term prospects are poor.

These ideas are a call for authenticity on the part of idealist planners. Authenticity is having a clear understanding of your values and then standing in the predicament of this flawed world. It is considering what is moral, experiencing the pain of things not being right, and having courage to work for the good nonetheless.

Discussion/Reflection Questions for Chapter 8

1. Take a recent planning controversy in your local community. Use the framework of assessing values, technical rationality, and tactics to create a more insightful understanding of the conflict.
2. Planners should ponder the dividing line between an approach in which they respect their opponents' values and knowledge, and when they are

prepared to unilaterally resist their opponents' initiatives. Reflect on a situation in which you have such a dividing line—does it vary by issue? How do you mark the line?

3. Interview a respected planner about how he or she determines when to compromise for partial gain rather than hold out for what he or she considers to be the best solution. How does this planner decide? Reflect on how you make these decisions in practice.

4. Review the write-ups for recent plans and projects that have won American Planning Association awards. These narratives represent the collective "knowing" of the profession. Critique those narratives from a free-market, anti-government planning point of view. Can you articulate the opposition's facts and arguments? What can you learn about effective strategy based on that critique?

References

Alexander, E. (2017). Chance and design: From architecture to institutional design. *Journal of the American Planning Association* 83(1): pp. 93–102.

Barnard, C. and K. Andrews (1968). *The functions of the executive.* Cambridge, Mass.: Harvard University Press.

Hirschman, A. (1970). *Exit, voice, and loyalty: Responses to decline in firms, organizations, and states.* Cambridge, MA: Harvard University Press. ISBN 0-674-27660-4 (paper).

Innes, J. and D. Booher. (2010). *Planning with complexity: An introduction to collaborative rationality for public policy.* New York, NY: Routledge.

Schön, D. (1983). *The reflective practitioner: How professionals think in action.* New York, NY: Basic Books.

Schweitzer, L. (2016). The smartest boy urbanist in the room. *Blog post.* Retrieved from https://lisaschweitzer.com/2016/06/03/the-smartest-boy-urbanist-in-the-room/ 2/18/17.

Chapter 9

Avoiding Wrong

Virtue beckons quietly,
asking to speak.

Because planning practice links knowledge to action in the public domain, as discussed in Chapter 1, it generates complex ethical questions. Dealing with these questions can be stressful, but if properly addressed they develop character. After all, professional life might be boring if it was just straightforward application of technique to problems. If my planning practice means something, I accept that there will be tough choices. Developing an ability for ethical reasoning in the planner's professional life also supports good choices in the personal realm. Perhaps there is no greater satisfaction than to look back at the end of a career and feel peace with the choices made.

This chapter makes a simple point: planners should allow an inner moral compass to exist in their practice. This can help them avoid wrong and respond appropriately *if* they've done wrong. This is the path of virtue.

Planners' Ethics

A planner can avoid ethical mistakes by listening for the voice of an inner conscience, thinking clearly, and taking planning professional ethics seriously.

Although avoiding missteps should be the planner's first priority, the chapter also addresses what to do *after* making one. Although we all seek to avoid mistakes, they are an occupational hazard in change-oriented professions like planning. In fact, planners who deny the possibility of misstep are often the ones who get into trouble.

Case studies help planners consider ethical obligations and generate useful dialogues with other planners. They are regularly presented at conferences and offered in planning ethics books (Barrett, 2001; Weitz, 2013). These cases provide scenarios and interpretations of rules. This chapter takes a different direction. Surely, most of us will decide to do the right thing when nothing is on the line. Yet, ethical standards that we readily endorse may be ignored in times of stress. Ethics becomes most necessary when planners are at their worst, not their best—when they've been betrayed, when they've made a humiliating error, when they've sought personal benefit, or when their house is about to be foreclosed.

Ethics play a modest but important role early in a planner's career because managers define work tasks, parameters, and make the critical judgments. Even so, entry-level planning work presents ethical choices, and it is advisable to establishing a pattern of ethical thinking and action early on. As planners move up the ladder, more ethical choices await—in interacting with politicians and the community, pursuing work as a consultant, and seeking funding as a non-profit organization.

The chapter suggests a three-part process for avoiding missteps and dealing with missteps that may occur: (1) sensing a pang of conscience, either before or after an action; (2) thinking rationally about that pang of conscience; and (3) avoiding the mistake or making amends if it has already occurred.

About Ethics

Allowing a pang of conscience is easier to say than to do. It takes self-esteem to anticipate or admit a mistake. Feeling a pang of conscience is a signal that something is amiss, but it's only a signal. Thinking rationally requires consideration of that pang in terms of ethical principles, context and situations, and culpability. With that, the idealist can avoid or discern wrong. This is the work of virtue, used here to mean a willingness to feel a pang of conscience and a commitment to use that feeling to stimulate rational thought about how to correct the action.

The chapter uses *ethics* to mean a system of principles to guide behavior. An example of ethics is Emanuel Kant's concept of a duty to respect other rational beings (Honderich, 1995, p. 438). All ethical systems are built on concepts of morality, ultimate rightness or wrongness. As discussed in Chapter 8, accepting this idea means ascribing to moral realism—the existence of right and wrong beyond individual opinion. Most planners are moral realists, but this is not universal. Of course, moral realists will disagree on what constitutes rightness or wrongness, in abstract terms and specific situations.

Philosophers have argued about ethical systems and morality over millennia. Some ethical systems are based on virtue—a quality such as fortitude or self-restraint that serves a larger purpose. Other systems refer to rules of behavior or *process*, such as an admonition to tell the truth. These systems are called deontological. Following state law in environmental review procedures is an example of this. Other systems refer to the *outcome* of behavior and are termed consequentialist or utilitarian. In that case, environmental ethics is about avoiding damage to the environment. Of course, there are different views about outcomes in consequentialist ethics—is the best plan the one that provides the most aggregate utility for all or the one that serves those with the least agency and choice?

All professionals face ethical and moral questions, but planning's idealistic and political nature produces situations that challenge simple definition or resolution. The first distinction needed is between appropriate professional behavior and broader moral questions about the rightness of plans, programs, or their outcomes (Wachs, 2013). As with most professions, planning has an ethical code for professional behavior that guides planners in making good choices and avoiding mistakes with clients, supervisors, and elected officials (AICP, 2016). This is difficult enough, but now consider the impact of plans—is there such a thing as a plan that was developed with proper process that produces harm? Of course there is. And to add further complication, a plan may produce both harm and good at the same time—in different realms, to different groups of people.

Planning "wrong" can occur for many reasons, ranging from a technical error, to inappropriate professional behavior, to participating in a plan that produces harm. Planners may be confused about standards of professional conduct, or think they are doing right when in fact they are doing wrong. These are mistakes of knowledge or logical thought. Wrong can also occur if planners have weak moral character—they know what is right but transgress anyway. This may stem from greed, excessive deference to authority, or lack of courage. Obviously, planners do wrong if they corruptly pursue personal gain or personal agenda over process, rules, and professional standards as might the hedonist described in Chapter 7. This may occur when planners' internal ethical compass is disabled or their view of the public interest(s) is idiosyncratic.

Considering whether a plan creates harm or good is a complex undertaking. Planning "ends" may be in conflict, such as tension between short-term job creation and long-term greenhouse gas reduction. Of course, planners want to find the sweet spot where tradeoffs are lessened, but that isn't always possible. There are also tensions between ends and the *means* used to achieve them. For example, reporting on a climate model that produced anomalous results compared to the majority of models gives those opposed to climate change responses fodder to claim scientific disagreement, and therefore resist action. Should ethical planners withhold those results?

Do good goals (ends) ever justify otherwise inappropriate means? If so, what warrants such an action? How does that line up with the obligation of a professional to be honest? This question raises the virtue/deontological/consequentialist split in ethical systems. Here is a practical example: Is it permissible to selectively present data or modeling results favorable to a land use reform agenda, in order to resist powerful forces motivated by narrow self-interest?

Nihilists reject the idea of a moral law and the notion of an internal moral compass. They may make decisions from self-interest, destructive impulses, or follow rules of society out of prudence so as to avoid punishment. My view is that there *is* moral (natural) law (Honderich, 1995, p. 586). Some things are right and others wrong, universally. Although this may be discredited in contemporary philosophical circles, most planners act as if moral or natural law exists. Of course, people (and philosophers) will differ on what that natural law is. Values commonly ascribed to natural law that relate to urban planning include social life, rational conduct, justice and fairness, knowledge of truth, physical and mental health, the natural world, and experience of beauty. Idealist planners can gain clarity on their compass directions if they reflect on which of these aspects motivate their work.

The Planner's Internal Compass

Values guide thoughts, feelings, speech, and behavior. The latter two are the primary subjects of professional interest. My view is that planners should seek to cultivate and follow an internal moral compass, as it is a guide when complex ethical questions arise. I see this as the aspect of a person that produces good decisions. I cannot prove that a moral compass exists, but I know there's one in me. I seek to make myself open to it when I stand at a critical decision. My moral compass helps me make good decisions and avoid mistakes. But when I fail, it also helps me own up to mistakes after I have made them.

The idea that certain values are an authority may be held by both an atheist secular humanist and a religious person. The humanist may refer to human dignity as an ultimate value, whereas the religious person may refer to values based on religious texts. In contrast, a relativist conception suggests that values are not universal but exist only in relation to culture, subculture, personal experience, and context.

Engaging these issues has provoked many philosophical debates and is certainly beyond the scope of this chapter. The simplest way planners can resolve the question of values for professional practice is to develop a rough distinction between values that are universal and those that are relative. For me, issues of urban design are primarily matters of taste and culture, and therefore relative. I don't expect my point of view on urban design to win the day universally. On the other hand, values related to human rights, social justice, and environmental sustainability are universal to me. I seek to realize those values in my work and convince others of their validity. Of course, reasonable people will differ on how we move from a value to action in the public domain, so this doesn't mean I avoid compromise or conflict.

The Planning Profession's Compass

If planners receive American Institute of Certified Planners (AICP) certification, they agree to live by the values espoused in the AICP Code of Ethics (AICP, 2016). Even if they don't have AICP certification, the Code is a useful external reference point on ethical behavior. Having a code of ethics is part of what makes planning a profession—a set of expectations that the public can count on for the planner's behavior. Furthermore, the planner's code is a product of the deliberations of planners as to their conduct, and so differs from those for architects, landscape architects, city managers, and engineers. It is our profession's unique statement.

The Code's narrative examines both process-oriented and outcome-based ethics and provides guidance for making tough decisions. It includes the following:

- Aspirational principles—ideals to which AICP planners strive. Failure to achieve these principles is not a violation of the Code.
- Rules of conduct—rules to which AICP members are held accountable.
- Procedural provisions—what to do if there is a violation.

Key aspirational principles regarding the public include respecting the rights of others, considering long-range consequences, and providing accurate information. The Code indicates that planners have a commitment to public participation, social justice, and fair process. Lastly, it stipulates aspirational values regarding design excellence and environment.

With regard to clients and employers, the Code exhorts planners to exercise independent professional judgment. The code advises planners to accept employer decisions *unless* they are illegal or inconsistent with public interest; it requires that planners avoid conflict of interest or appearance of conflict of interest. Regarding the profession and colleagues, planners have an obligation to respect the profession, think, reflect, and train.

The Code also includes 26 rules that define good professional behavior. These concern issues such as providing clarity, refusing assignments that are illegal or violate rules, not using information or power for personal advantage, disclosure, avoiding perceived or real conflict of interest, transparency, avoiding misrepresentation and plagiarism, and other provisions. Violation of these rules can lead to a charge against an AICP-certified planner, which is a rare but serious occurrence. The Code does most of its work in shaping planners' day-to-day activities and decisions.

Planning's professional rules are not straightforward nor can they be. First, as Weitz (2013) suggests, rules of conduct provide little context, so a narrow interpretation of them could lead to an ethical violation when the full context is considered. He suggests that planners consider the intent of the rule when applying it to a particular situation.

Another interpretation issue is that a planner's work serves the public interest, which is a contested idea. The Code, therefore, requires judgment between differing "goods" involved in planning. For example, loyalty to an employer (a process-oriented ethical mandate) can be set against loyalty to the public interest (an outcome-based ethical mandate). Rather than artificially resolving this, the Code leaves responsibility to the individual planner to reason through these dilemmas, hence the previous suggestion that the planner cultivate a personal ethical compass. Here's how this issue is addressed in the Code:

> As the basic values of society can come into competition with each other, so can the aspirational principles we espouse under this Code. An ethical judgment often requires a conscientious balancing, based on the facts and context of a particular situation and on the precepts of the entire Code.
>
> (AICP, 2016)

Finding an Inner Guide

Planners need an inner guide to help them make ethical judgments. Situations require it. For example, because zoning changes affect land value, interests seeking to influence zoning for private gain. They will seek to draw planners into their scheme. These are cases of clear-cut wrong. More complicated situations are those in which there are competing values to which the planner ascribes. These situations require ethical reasoning that helps the planner assess the situation. A strong inner guide supports good decisions and the planner's integrity.

Despite efforts to do the right thing, planners make missteps from time to time. It is better to not be in denial about that possibility. If the planner's inner guide fails or is ignored, the planner may feel shame. Shame has a bad connotation for many, evoking a parent shaming a child for a minor transgression. Some people are held back by shame that they don't deserve to feel. I'm also not talking about it in the sense of one person shaming another to control them. Rather, I mean an internal experience of distress caused by an awareness of the potential for wrong behavior or wrong behavior itself. Instead of avoiding it, ethical planners allow an internal sense of shame to operate.

Biographies of planners and other public officials who go off-track suggest that some blocked their feelings of shame. Once blocked, self-justification and distraction rushes in—a planner makes one mistake and then compounds it with further ones. I certainly know how hard it is to admit when I am wrong. I sense my desire to self-justify—my need for self-esteem wants to make the feeling go away. Because society values self-worth, it is hard to admit mistakes, flaws, or brokenness.

When we err, it is difficult to accept the damage we do. It's natural to run from shame, avoid it, go to sleep, repress it, or go on the attack. It is an uncomfortable feeling, but it can be metabolized in a healthy way to serve as a catalyst for positive change. Shame is a challenge to self-worth, but in fact, a healthy respect for shame is key in following an ethical path.

Ways of Being Wrong

A planner's inner guide may be experienced as a vague feeling that something is not right as he or she faces a decision or considers something already done. As long as that feeling stays vague, there is nothing to be done about it. Precision is vital for clear ethical reasoning. The planner should connect the vague feeling to a specific issue. To illustrate that, the examples that follow show how varied the types of issues may be.

Technical Errors

A simple case of being wrong is making a technical mistake. This could be transposing numbers in a spreadsheet or incorrectly citing the facts on a staff report. This is an affront to the planning value of providing technically valid information for decision-making, so planners shouldn't underestimate the seriousness of technical mistakes. Making a traffic impact analysis error in an environmental review document may lead to its rejection under court challenge, costing money or halting a project. A financial projection error could lead to the termination of an otherwise valuable program. Attention to detail is the starting point for professional work.

We all make technical mistakes, despite our best efforts. This is not the territory of complex ethical questions. What to do when that happens? The temptation to hide the mistake is strong—perhaps no one will notice and the planner will avoid embarrassment. If it is noticed, and if the planner hasn't brought it to his or her supervisor's attention, he or she has done a disservice to that supervisor, the organization, and the planning profession. It is not for a staff planner to decide what to do about a mistake—it is up to the responsible manager. By hiding a mistake, the planner denies the manager the opportunity to determine what to do about it and harms the client's or public's interest.

Professional Behavior

Mistakes in professional behavior are common, running the gamut from seemingly inconsequential to job-threatening. It may seem a minor point, but being chronically late is poor professional behavior. In effect, the planner adds a concern and a task to his or her supervisor's already busy schedule, who must now pay attention to punctuality rather than the substantive elements of work. Missing a meeting because a planner entered an incorrect date on the calendar may result in the company losing a consulting client. More serious, and usually grounds for dismissal, is exaggerating qualifications. This could occur if a planner put a Master's degree in planning on a resume when the terminal thesis was not filed, misstated the order of authorship on a multi-author research publication, or fraudulently wrote a letter of recommendation posing as the recommender. In the interpersonal realm, let's say a planner has a frustrating co-worker who doesn't follow through on work assignments. This casts a negative light on the entire team. The best course of action is to directly address the issue with the person, and if that doesn't work, bring the matter to the attention of a direct supervisor. Less appropriate is gossiping about the person while socializing with other co-workers. That person, in turn, could tell the co-worker, resulting in a negative work environment.

More seriously, there are professional behavior situations where a planner personally benefits, financially or otherwise, from insider planning knowledge or powers to approve a request. This is a direct ethical contravention. It can ruin the planner's career and it undermines public trust in planning institutions, which affects all planners. Even if money isn't involved, it is unethical to use insider planner knowledge to have power or undue influence over others.

When it comes to policy choices, planners can make the mistake of exaggerating the benefits of a proposal or catastrophizing about what will happen if a policy is not adopted, thinking that the greater "end" of getting a policy adopted justifies the "means" of suggesting outcomes beyond what the evidence suggests. Mistakes can also be those of omission. For example, a planner might not speak up at the staff meeting when a planning analysis is misinterpreted. Because the planner did not speak up, decision-makers may approve a course of action that creates harm. More subtly, the decision-makers may be confused over the evidence and analysis, but the planner doesn't correct them because they are about to select the planner's preferred policy.

Lastly, professional behavior includes conflict of interest. The AICP Code of Ethics says, "We shall avoid a conflict of interest or even the appearance of a conflict of interest in accepting assignments from clients or employers" (AICP, 2016, 2c). Direct conflict involves accepting a golf club membership in return for approving a development proposal that otherwise would have been denied. Appearance of conflict of interest is being seen on the golf course playing a round with that developer, even though there is no quid pro quo. The planner's actions create a reasonable suspicion that there may be one.

Those who violate conflict of interest rules may be intentionally corrupt, but for those who intend to honor them, the slippery slope of self-justification can interfere. "I deserve this holiday gift from XYZ developer because . . . I'm underpaid . . . worked so many uncompensated overtime hours . . . am unappreciated by my manager . . . could have made a lot more money in consulting . . . take a lot of crap at the zoning counter every day . . . have gone out of my way to help the community but my efforts have not been recognized." The list of possible justifications is long. In these instances, a *version* of justice (reward for effort) is used to justify unethical behavior. The human power of imagination can propel us into actions that aren't grounded in the real world.

Box 9.1 provides an example that illustrates potential conflict of interest and perceived conflict of interest concerning my role on an advisory committee.

Box 9.1 Conflict of Interest

My job involves teaching, research, and community service for a state university. I also do independent consulting on transit-oriented development (TOD) for public and private sector clients. One of my clients proposed a TOD at a bus terminal in Southern California. I worked for the developer on an hourly basis and did not have an equity position in the project.

In 2006, California voters approved Proposition 1C, an affordable housing fund that included $300 million for mixed-income housing in TODs. State officials were developing criteria to allocate these funds to TODs across the state on a competitive basis. They hired a northern California based consultant to develop criteria based on factors such as density, type of transit service (rail versus bus), impacts on transit ridership, private/public partnerships, walkability, etc. As with any allocation system, the factors, measurement, and weighting system can explicitly or inadvertently include bias.

State officials created an advisory body of academics and public agency officials to advise state officials in developing the criteria. I was appointed to the advisory body and participated in a four-hour meeting by telephone. I was not paid for the work; my comments were provided as community service advice to the state agency. Unlike other planning roles, such city council and some consulting situations, financial disclosure statements were not required. During the introductions at the meeting, participants did not disclose their consulting relationships.

My view was that the first draft of the criteria was biased. Although the law prescribed a split in funding allocations between northern and southern California, the criteria reflected a northern California perspective, favoring rail systems over locations with advanced bus-on-freeway programs. The state officials and their consultant team were based in northern California. I successfully argued for some changes in the criteria system to recognize bus-on-freeway situations, but even with the revisions, my view was that they still did not fairly reflect TOD opportunities in southern California.

In separate meetings with my developer client, I indicated my view that the draft criteria were biased. I also provided strategic advice to the developer on preparing a funding application. The developer contacted state politicians representing southern California to complain about this bias, and they in turn pressured state agencies to revise the criteria. I participated in this meeting.

State officials later called me to complain about my involvement in a private development project that was intending to apply for funds. Even though I had sound technical reasons for my position, the lack of disclosure was a problem. There was the appearance of conflict of interest. My actions lacked transparency. I believed that my position had technical justification, but the event undermined my reputation with state agencies. I should have disclosed my consulting relationships. I learned from the experience and vowed to go out of my way to disclose early on in those relationships in the future and to step down when the appearance of conflict of interest is present. Disclosure is critically important, even if it seems awkward in the moment.

Content of Plans

Understanding ethical missteps in the content of plans requires clear thinking, as debates over plans relate to axioms, values, and facts. Axioms are taken to be self-evident and cannot necessarily be proven—for example, an axiom might be compassion. A planner may view compassion as a starting point for considering right and wrong. A plan that treats homeless people harshly would then be said to be mistaken. If an axiom is clear, then a person with a different axiom, like personal responsibility, can understand how the other person's thinking starts from a different place.

A more specific expression of axioms is values. Plans can be examined in terms of the values they serve. There will be differences of opinion about these values, but as with professional behavior, the AICP Code of Professional Conduct outlines aspirational principles that can be considered along with the planner's own values. Lastly, a plan might be faulted on a factual or analytical basis. Does it ignore long-term environmental consequences? Are the projections of travel demand flawed? Assessing a plan's "rightness" or "wrongness," therefore, can be achieved by considering axioms, values, and facts and the distinctions between them. Sometimes when we say we are arguing about facts, for example, we are really arguing about values.

In plan development, let's say the city engineer asks a planning consultant to remove all alternatives from a commissioned report that (a) aren't feasible right this moment or (b) aren't in agreement with what the engineer is willing to do. The reason is to prevent anything from appearing in a document that a member of the community can use to pressure the engineer to implement a disliked option. It is understandable that the engineer does not want to build up expectations for an infeasible idea, but if the consultant edits the report to the engineer's preference, then the product may not be the consultant's best professional opinion. Rather, the document is the engineer's report masquerading as an independent consultant report. The education role of planning is lost as alternatives are truncated and eliminated. Figuring out how to respond to this type of situation is a common challenge for planning consultants.

Implementation of Plans

Well-designed plans may go "wrong" in implementation. The benefits of a policy choice could be counteracted by a single aspect of implementation. For example, a streetcar system whose forecast ridership and resulting financial feasibility are based on its travel time may fail because the assumed traffic signal prioritization is not implemented. This slows service, reduces ridership and fare revenue, and places the project in a financial bind. Or, a plan or policy intervention may produce an unanticipated consequence. For example, setting high value-capture taxes around streetcar stops may produce an undesirable consequence of shifting development to sprawling locations away from transit access. Box 7.2 provides an example of a poison pill that was included in a policy that made it impossible to efficiently implement.

After a Mistake

As discussed above, there are many ways of being "wrong" as a planner. They range from personal examples, such as gossip, to complex situations in which the planner is part of a team that collectively misjudges outcomes, such as the streetcar implementation example above. Planners seek to avoid mistakes, but try as hard as we might, they are inevitable. What should planners do when they have made a mistake, personally, or in plans and their implementation? I suggest allowing the feeling or anxiety to occur rather than rationalize it away. An error doesn't mean that a planner is a bad person, just that he or she made a mistake. In fact, a sign of virtue is to own mistakes and make amends.

My first suggestion is to diagnose the pang of conscience. For some, a knot in their stomach is a physical indication that something is off. For others, a heavy feeling or sense of gloom occurs when attention is drawn to the wrong that occurred. Still others may feel jittery, annoyed, and ready to pick a fight. Regardless of which feeling is an indicator, it should stimulate rational thinking.

Ethical planners use a methodical process to understand what happened—naming it—and then assessing how to respond. First, what was the nature of the "wrong" or error? As noted above, it could be technical or related to professional behavior, the content of plans, or the effect of plans. Then, the details of the error should be enumerated—developing a factual understanding of what happened without emotional interpretation. Was the error one of commission (something the planner did) or omission (something the planner didn't do but should have)? Was the wrong committed by the planner individually or as part of a group? Is the issue about process, outcome, or both? Then the planner can assess who was harmed and how. It may be that multiple parties were harmed. Lastly, the planner can consider possible remedies and ways to prevent such occurrences in the future.

I battle my tendency to self-justify by seeking objectivity and withholding feelings so that I can get the facts. This might be called the "police report" version. Although there are certainly bad police reports, either incomplete or biased, the best version of the police report is just the facts, who said what, to whom, when, and who did what. This avoids the possible distortions of feelings.

Table 9.1 illustrates two examples of situations that have "gone wrong" relating to a planner's personal behavior. Using this table format can help planners be precise about what happened. This counteracts a tendency to be too general, when a planner deals with error by saying, "I'm a bad person." The more specific, the better. In this reflection, the planner seeks a reasonable conclusion about his or her role and culpability in the error. Then the planner can consider what to do about it—how to disclose it, make amends, and to take steps to prevent it from reoccurring.

If "wrongs" or errors occur in team or group efforts, identifying culpability is more complex. There are difficult tradeoffs between personal conceptions of the good, organizational goals, norms, and loyalty to the team and/ or organization. Table 9.2 provides examples of these dilemmas, in situations concerning the content of plans and the effects of plans through implementation. Similar to Table 9.1, a step-by-step process can shed light on the best course of action.

Table 9.1 Diagnosing a pang of conscience for an individual wrong

Type of wrong	What happened?	Details	Who is harmed? How?	Remedy
Technical error (modeling example)	Used the wrong data set in specifying a travel mode model, which led to selection of a suboptimal transit mode.	An error of commission (accidental). An outcome concern.	Transit users and taxpayers, through an inefficient project.	Disclose, reissue study. Institute quality control procedures for data or data use procedures.
Professional behavior (advisory board example)	Participated on an advisory board without disclosing that a client was affected by the grant program being deliberated (see Box 9.1).	An error of omission. A process concern.	Other advisory board members and the public, through lack of transparency.	Disclose. Recuse oneself from those deliberations. Make a habit of identifying conflict of interest, or appearance of conflict of interest, and disclose.

Table 9.2 Diagnosing a pang of conscience for a team wrong

Type of wrong	What happened?	Details	Who is harmed? How?	Remedy
Content of plans (consulting example)	Developed transit-oriented development plans that had the effect of distracting attention from the poor ridership performance of rail transit projects.	An error of commission. A process concern.	Transit users and taxpayers, through an inefficient project.	Educate client on ridership issues. Deliberate with team and management. Consider opportunities to improve outcomes.
Effects of plans (public planning example)	Negotiated agreements with developers that compel vehicle trip reductions, used these reductions in traffic impact calculations, with the knowledge that enforcement mechanisms do not exist and compliance is unlikely.	An error of omission. An outcome concern.	Public stakeholders affected by higher trip generation levels the predicted.	Disclose implementation concerns to managers. Seek ways of strengthening agreements and agency enforcement commitments.

If a planner concludes that he or she has erred, the best response is to seek a remedy with a contrite spirit. A contrite spirit may be hard for idealists who feel strongly justified by the rightness of their cause. They might feel that they deserve an exemption from normal ethical standards because of the importance of the issue at hand. Idealist planners can be working for the good and also be unethical.

Experienced managers tell me that what happens *after* the mistake can be the most important thing. Hiding mistakes or blaming others is tempting, but it makes things worse. The planner should acknowledge the problem and allow other parties (managers, clients, elected officials) to be upset. Apologies, should they be in order, should be heartfelt—it is frustrating for managers to hear "I apologize" and then the word "but . . ." soon follows. Planners shouldn't rationalize or blame others after they apologize. They should accept the consequences—but not go overboard by deciding the consequences for themselves—and make amends to a reasonable level. When idealists own up to mistakes, they are perceived as planners of good character.

The idea of broken-heartedness may seem quaint, but it is an appropriate response to doing wrong. It is appropriate to sit with sadness associated with a mistake. Planners shouldn't grovel or ask the outside world for something to ease the pain. We should learn how to suffer properly, mourn losses, and move on. Then we can renew a commitment to allowing the self-correcting mechanism of shame to function. Let's be honest: planners have multiple motivations—lofty commitments to the public interest, but also getting their needs met by looking good, career advancement, or exercising power. Here's a new take on an old expression: "I will not sully my purpose by getting my needs met." That places purpose first, where I think it should be.

And Now to You: Your Deeds Define You

Planning is replete with ethical choices. Sometimes all interests line up with good planning. Sometimes your challenge is to determine *whether* to resist what you perceive as a wrong, and then determine *how* to resist it. You may experience consequences to resisting client or decision-maker directions that go against planning's values. As I write this, federal government employees have been told not to communicate with the public as they have in the past, and scientists have been told their research will be reviewed for compliance with the views of the government. These employees face a dilemma between following directions and serving their conceptions of the public good.

The consequences of resisting bad plans or owning an error could include job termination, missed promotions, or being sidelined in the organization. You may think the world will end if you get fired from a job or are pushed out, but life goes on. The sun comes up in the morning. If your internal compass fails in the heat of the moment, you may make a poor choice that goes against professional ethics or your own personal commitments. Ethical behavior in that case is to own the choice and make amends. You are more likely to do that if you have made a habit of virtue.

Ultimately, your deeds and professional reputation define you. They are worth investing in. You deserve a stellar ethical reputation. Making good ethical decisions creates confidence and empowerment. A commitment to improve your moral character elevates you, sustains you through tough times, and is treasured throughout your career. Having the respect of your professional colleagues is one of the great satisfactions in life.

Discussion/Reflection Questions for Chapter 9

1. Reflect for a moment and write down the top five elements of your moral value system (e.g., truthfulness, compassion, justice, etc.). How do you want to be known? What do you want people to say about you at the end of your career?
2. In your understanding of the world, are morals (right or wrong) culturally determined or universal? What is the implication of your position for planning ethics?
3. The AICP Code of Ethics does not define the public interest. Should it? What is your conception of it?
4. Reflect on a moment in your personal or professional life when you felt a pang of conscience. How did you move from that initial feeling to determining what to do about it?

References

American Institute of Certified Planners. (2016, December 22). *Code of ethics and professional conduct.* Adopted March 19, 2005; effective June 1, 2005; revised April 1, 2016. Retrieved from www.planning.org/ethics/ethicscode.htm

Barrett, C.D. (2001). *Everyday ethics for practicing planners.* Chicago, IL: American Planning Association.

Honderich, T. (ed.) (1995). *The Oxford companion to philosophy.* New York, NY: Oxford University Press.

Wachs, M. (2013). The past, present and future of professional ethics in planning. In N. Carmon and S. Fainstein (Eds.). *Policy, planning and people: Promoting justice in urban development* (pp. 101–119). Philadelphia, PA: University of Pennsylvania Press.

Weitz, J. (2013). *The ethical planning practitioner.* Chicago, IL: American Planning Association.

Chapter 10

Navigating Managers, Organizations, and Teams

Listening,
doesn't mean agreeing.

Planners continually navigate interactions with managers, organizations, and teams. This chapter suggests strategies for those interactions. For example, staff-level planners benefit if they understand how managers see things differently. Since planning occurs in organizations, navigating their cultures also requires insight. And because planning is done in teams, good interpersonal skills helps the work get done. The chapter addresses these themes and concludes with suggestions about how to temporarily endure less-than-perfect working conditions.

For planners, knowledge and technical skills don't mean much if they are not accompanied by an ability to collaborate. Having an innovative idea is only a start, because virtually all planning occurs in interaction with people and organizations. Collaboration starts with communicative competency that supports engagement with supervisors, elected officials, team members, allied professionals, and teams. This involves self-expression, listening, interpretation of direct and indirect communication, and proficiency in facilitating, negotiating, and inquiring. Teamwork also requires reliability, reciprocity, and forthrightness.

In discussing career planning, Chapter 6 argues for an approach that provides intelligence for ongoing decisions rather than a blueprint for the future, paralleling a shift toward contingency planning. This chapter also draws from planning theory in considering communicative competency.

Planning theorists take inspiration from the sociologist Jürgen Habermas's (1984) communicative action theory. It provides new ways to understand communication practices, from which theorists developed a communicative model of planning practice (Healey, 1992). In this view, discourse supports a form of rationality that is broader than instrumental rationality, namely a rationality that includes substantive concerns such as vision and goals. At its core is an ideal of undistorted communication, in which those engaged in discourse seek speech that has qualities of accuracy, legibility, sincerity, and legitimacy. Communication—speaking, listening, and interpreting meaning—is the primary tool that planners use to do their work. Communication competency applies equally to work with managers, organizations, and individuals.

Poor communication practice and accompanying misunderstandings, in contrast, undermine the planner. Four examples are provided here, one for each of the possible distortions. An accuracy distortion is as simple as missing a work task deadline without explanation, generating uncertainty for managers. Inaccurate information about schedule can be worse than the actual delay because those depending on the tardy planner must devote mental energy to keep track of that person.

An example of a legibility distortion is technical jargon. Let's say that *Local Moran's I* and *Getis Ord I* are the best tools for analyzing immigrant spatial patterns for a community development plan. If the planner's manager and other team members haven't studied spatial statistics, they won't understand the terms, and furthermore, they may be annoyed that the planner is pointing out their ignorance. A simple solution is to say in plain English what the tests do—measure the statistical significance of spatial patterns and detect hot spots.

Sincerity is also a foundational element of dealing with teams and fellow professionals. What, no sarcasm? (Queue an eye roll here . . .) I agree, life wouldn't be fun without sarcasm—it can liven up interactions and create team solidarity if it is shared and fun. In person, the planner needs a good connection with all those in the room before delivering a sarcastic comment. But if there is any confusion about the nature of the sarcasm, it can backfire. If a manager uses sarcasm to sanction staff planners instead of providing constructive, actionable feedback, it undermines trust. Sarcasm is even trickier in computer-meditated communication such as emails or group texts—emoticons can only do so much. Compared to sarcasm, sincerity requires a level of vulnerability, which can have a positive effect on communication. Sincere planners' ideas are taken with the seriousness they deserve.

The fourth dimension is legitimacy. In a community meeting about economic revitalization strategies, for example, legitimacy is realized if planners make a claim to "know" a community issue that is borne out by their direct experience. Of course, data can tell much about the issues, but a planner's lived experience in a community creates an understanding of the diversity of narratives that comprises identity and vision.

With that introduction into the four dimensions of communication, let's start by addressing interactions with managers.

Dealing With Managers

Most planners work in organizations with institutional hierarchy—and managers. Depending on the organization, the workplace management and power structure may be jarringly different from egalitarian, self-organizing group projects in planning school. Of course, school team projects can be challenging because teams lack a formal structure and may have free-riders. In planning practice, a manager is able to solve a lot of those problems. But then, of course, the downside arises—there is a manager!

I suggest tolerance for managers. Tolerance may sound like an odd word because managers *appear* to have all the power. They give assignments, carry out personnel evaluations, and control access to decision-makers. The idealist planner is subject to the manager's formal and informal power—why would *they* need tolerance? To be more specific, by tolerance I mean understanding and appreciating the pressures they face. The more the planner understands the manager's world, the better equipped the planner is to be managed. Of course, I don't mean tolerance of abusive managers—certainly there are bad ones. I recommend tolerance for the more typical well-intentioned, flawed manager.

What is it like being a manager? First, managers no longer do the planning work themselves. I started my career when land use maps were colored with pencils, and I recall the principal planner leaning over the drafting table when I was creating a land use map. He picked up a pencil, sighed, and commented how much he missed land use survey tasks and making maps. And coloring. Being a manager means giving up such pleasures and direct control over the product.

Second, managers make difficult decisions. For example, they decide when to ask a staff member to redo a flawed work product and when to allow that product to move forward to give the planner an experience of the consequences. Managers act as intermediaries between decision-makers and staff.

Third, managers have a view above and below their position in the organization that staff-level planners do not have. Usually, multiple people report to them, so they divide their time between their own work and their "direct reports." Managers do not have time to do everything properly—they make triage-like decisions about how to use their time. Of course, managers also have bosses too, so they don't get away without supervision.

Different Types of Managers

Managers, then, have different roles. If they are of an older generation than the planners they supervise, they may have different cultural reference points. They may be technologically savvy, but that technology was not part of their formative experience as it was for the current generation of planners. Moreover, they may not represent the gender/race/ethnicity/sexual identity composition of their staff. Some may delight at young planners' technical skills and enthusiasm, whereas others judge them because of differences in their styles of working or communicating.

Varied experiences and motivations are present among managers. Some stumble into management roles by progressing through the organization. They may not be suited or prepared for management, and they may not even like it. As a thought experiment, imagine what it would be like to be in a management position that doesn't fit your temperament. Since the normal planning career progression leads there, a planner's manager might really rather be doing planning work. Managers like this are unlikely to use an inspirational, team-building approach. More frequently, they base their influence on positional authority—their title and place on the organizational chart, territorial rights of a department, protocol, tradition, and expected respect for position.

Effective managers inspire their staff and manage with a light touch. Open to new ideas and interested in mentoring, they are willing to take risks and empower their staff. As a result, working for them is motivating. Effective managers create a meaningful professional relationship; they respect the planners as people. They take pleasure in their staff members' growth and are sought out by others in the organization and the profession. These managers would inspire loyalty *without* positional authority. By offering criticism in a constructive way, they allow staff members to absorb the criticism, develop responses, and improve. They do not belittle staff.

Even though I've listed desirable manager qualities, an individual planner's experience may differ. Notably, the best manager for one person might not be well-suited for another. For example, some planners like the structure, sense of fairness, and consistent rules associated with a traditional manager. Performance evaluations are done on time, provide constructive feedback, and are used to help the planner improve. Job roles are well-understood and relatively stable. Assignments are clear.

A person who values creativity might prefer a more freewheeling manager. That manager may enjoy brainstorming, a loose team structure, and entertaining a healthy competition of ideas, but he or she may not get performance evaluations done on time. There are choices and tradeoffs when it comes to managers. Of course, planners starting out take the manager that comes with the job, but understanding that managers have different strengths may help when the planner has one who isn't the best fit.

Boxes 10.1 and 10.2 enrich this discussion by providing the perspective of two planning managers—an assistant city manager and a community development director. Box 10.1 provides that manager's approach to supervising staff and his tips on succeeding as an entry-level planner. The more planners understand a manager's approach, whether explicit or implicit, the better they will relate. Box 10.2 describes how a manager learned his craft by being willing to be wrong, which naturally led to valuing the contributions of staff.

It's worthwhile for idealist planners to develop ideas about characteristics of a good manager. Planners can reflect on previous supervisors, read biographies of

---

Box 10.1 Tips for Career Success
By Al Zelinka, FAICP, CMSM, Assistant City Manager, City of Riverside, California

Planners work with a diverse array of people to make their communities the best they can be. Likewise, most planners work with a spectrum of colleagues representing different disciplines, talents, generations, interests, and personal attributes and backgrounds. Over the past 25 years, in private and public sector capacities, I have led and managed a diverse staff including most of the generational groups. I stay away from generalizing about these groups; rather, I accept people at face value and seek to learn their attributes first-hand.

Box 10.1 (continued)

My approach to leading planning staff is captured in the following:

1. Share broadly my mission and statement of values
2. Convey an expectation of performance
3. Facilitate the widespread planting and sharing of "seeds" of information and ideas
4. Show appreciation and compassion for those around me
5. Participate in developing collective wisdom with my team (i.e., leave ego at the door, be vulnerable by asking questions, suggest different approaches, invent and innovate, etc.)
6. Take care of myself and my family (i.e., when one's personal life is healthy, work prospers)

Planning provides unlimited opportunities for professionals to expand knowledge, grow responsibilities, and make positive impacts. For planners entering the profession, quickly learning how to be successful in your organization can pay long-term dividends. Although you must know the technical, procedural, and legal dimensions of planning, invest time in having effective and valued relationships with your boss(es) and peers—it is through teamwork that innovative planning occurs and great outcomes are realized. Following are a few qualities and habits of young planners I have observed:

1. *Be dependable, reliable, and "on top of things."* Track work responsibilities and set/agree to realistic deadlines; track and prioritize tasks and, generally, under-promise and over-deliver.
2. *Do the unexpected and be viewed as an innovator.* Listen to the challenges expressed by your boss or other leaders; in addition to your expected responsibilities, either volunteer to take on an additional assignment or, on your own, proactively invest thought and energy in suggesting ideas, tools, resources, or solutions. In so doing, you'll add value to the organization and your reputation will grow.
3. *Celebrate the work of others.* Promote your organization by writing or co-authoring articles or delivering presentations on planning efforts, completed plans, or built projects that celebrate the work of your organization and inform and educate others. By taking interest in the work of others and "telling their story," you become an appreciated ambassador to your team, organization, and profession.

A career in planning is immensely gratifying and rewarding. Dedicating yourself to collaboration with others, as well as to continuous self-improvement, heightens your ability to make a difference and reach your career potential.

Box 10.2 Letting Go to Grow

By Patrick Prescott, AICP, Community Development Director, City of Burbank, California

I'm writing this as a Community Development Director with 17 years of experience in planning. It wasn't until recently that I realized how much my experience with previous bosses and managers influenced my management style and the manner in which I approach planning. Each new boss required some accommodating and each new personality challenged me.

One of the most challenging professional relationships I had was painful at the time, but looking back I understand how it taught me a lot about myself. It initially seemed like intergenerational conflict, but it boiled down to two people with very different life experiences, approaches to managing people, and ways of doing planning work. This was the first time in my career that I faced such a challenge. I had to make a decision. Was I going to fight, resign, or be humble and try to work together? My first inclination was to move on, but I initially chose to work together. As time passed and the relationship evolved, it became clear that there were irreconcilable differences and that I would need a survival strategy to remain productive.

I'd like to say that I found a universally applicable answer to this challenge, but it was really just a matter of hunkering down and getting the work done as best as I could. I am happy that in the midst of it I was able to realize my own approach to planning and a management style. I could now clearly describe it. Until then I could really only speak theoretically about my ideal management style. I learned from that relationship how important it is to be open to being wrong and not assuming I knew (or even *had* to know) all the answers.

This experience has helped me manage other planners. Not knowing everything is liberating. It's the first step in working with others because you acknowledge that you need and value them. Recognizing the limits of my expertise doesn't always feel good. It takes humility, which I sometimes (okay, often) lack. As I've grown as a planner, accepting when I'm wrong or when I don't know something frees me to focus on developing my own strengths. I have enjoyed letting go of things and giving younger planners a chance to grow professionally and prove themselves. This has allowed me to evolve into my role as a Community Development Director. In my case, letting go allowed me to shift from planner to "director."

leaders, and ask peers for their experiences. They can observe how managers do their work, noticing when a particular approach works well and what methods backfire. This knowledge can assist in selecting among job offers and avoiding bad management situations. Poor management practices are not normal or inevitable. Knowledge about managers means that the next job move will be better informed. Moreover, knowing the qualities of a good manager also helps planners cultivate good management qualities when they become managers.

Communication Styles and Attitude

Communication styles vary across individual people and generational groups. Here we add to Chapter 1 and Appendix A by addressing communication between planners and managers. Young planners today grew up during an unprecedented transformation of communication methods and technology, and differences in communication styles can be a source of tensions with managers. Even though "dinosaur" managers who don't use computers are now retired, there may be generational differences in the type of desired communication, such as in-person, phone, email, text, blogging, tweeting, and other social media, and the level of formality sought in interactions. It is good practice to ask a manager about preferred ways of communicating and then to adjust to the organization's norms. This may be quite different from how the planner normally interacts with peers.

The communication practices described below can be used as prompts to think about topics the planner may wish to discuss with managers. The first issue is the preferred *form* of communication for each function. When should the telephone, face-to-face discussion, email, online discussion forums, texts, or other written forms be used? Here are some instances to consider:

- *Issues that require dialogue.* Solving a complex, value-laden planning problem requires a back-and-forth conversation and active facilitation that doesn't occur in written communication. Community meetings are similar. Emails are not immediate enough to work through a complex issue or problem.
- *Issues where misunderstanding could occur with computer-mediated communication.* A manager may prefer face-to-face meetings regarding controversial planning issues so that discussions are supported by the full range of formal and informal communications, including non-verbal cues. A joke about an issue on an email, for example, could be misinterpreted, and it is permanent. Some managers don't know what LOL means. And emojis provide opportunities for misunderstandings to occur.
- *Matters of record.* When a matter is in a preliminary form, it may be advisable to avoid creating a permanent record through an email, text, or other

method that is subject to a public records request. Later on, a record of emails revealing uncertainty about how to interpret a piece of data that is resolved through further study could be used by the public, members of the media, and lawyers to challenge a technical document.

The second issue relates to the level of formality and hierarchy in the organization. This may vary widely by sector and organizational size. Possible issues include:

- *Professional norms.* This includes norms of dress, timeliness, and standards for office organization and tidiness. It might include use of first names versus more formal ways of addressing a manager.
- *Level of deference to hierarchy and positional authority.* New planners have ideas, new tools, and lots of energy. The planner should find the right level of initiative for the organization to avoid being characterized as impatient or rude. If a manager says, "that's been tried before and didn't work out" that person may be risk averse, but it is possible that the manager *is* correct.
- *Acting as if a manager is a peer.* It grates on managers if a planner says "let's agree to disagree" as if they and their supervisor have the same level of experience. Planners shouldn't act like they expect their manager to collaborate with *them.*
- *Level of commitment to the profession and the organization.* I've worked for organizations where the culture was "devote your life to this organization" and for others with a more open view. Determining which culture predominates can support a decision, for example, of whether to talk to a manager about a dream of being an actor or asking for time off for auditions.

Frustrations and Conflicts With Managers

Idealist planners may have frustrations with managers, and vice versa. Given differences in roles, life experience, and age, it would be surprising if this didn't occur. Furthermore, not all managers are in the same place—executive managers may have their professional identity sorted out, financial stability, and be seeking a legacy. Entry-level planners and those executive managers may share a change agenda, fewer family commitments, and flexibility to try new things. Mid-level managers—the likely bosses of new planners—are likely to be more risk averse. They are in the process of developing their management style and are cognizant of the politics of change within the organization and with its decision-makers. Bold but risky moves might negatively affect their advancement or job security at a time when they may be paying a mortgage, raising a family, or caring for an aging parent. A reticence to take on an idealist's "good fight" may be frustrating, but may be understandable if the mid-level manager's context is considered.

As with many issues, frustrations and conflicts are not a problem in and of themselves; rather, the issue is how they are addressed and resolved. The following provides perspectives on three examples. The first is a mid-level manager's complaint and the next two are young planners' complaints.

The first example is what the manager wants: the planner's ability to quickly determine what is important concerning a given planning issue. This means distinguishing a small number of core questions from those that are less important. In law, for example, junior lawyers write briefs on legal cases for senior attorneys. No matter how interesting a case may be, the lead counsel needs a page or two, not a 50-page analysis. Similarly, a planner charged with writing a staff report on a conditional use permit may become lost in tracking down minor and non-critical issues. In every planning case, some issues are minor and others are critical. The critical issue may be new, without precedent, or controversial, or *the* factor upon which the decision will hinge. Managers want their planners to find the core issue, frame it in a way that they and others can understand, and then present it so that it can be resolved. They don't want to spend time hearing or reading about the whole process. They are not interested in the planner's thought process, from beginning to end, but seek the bottom line. Time-constrained, managers want to focus on the critical issues.

Due to their experience, managers understand implications and interconnections faster than new planners can. They know more about how clients, city managers, and city council members will perceive and react because they have more direct contact with them. If a manager interrupts a staff planner presentation in a meeting, it could be bad manners, but it might also be that he or she got what was needed to resolve the issue. They may not have enough time for the planners to explain their process. The analysis may have "done its work" even though the presentation wasn't completed. Although good manners are important, if the planner's work led to the resolution of the issue, then that's a contribution. Reflecting on what information brought the manager to the stage where she or he could see the solution can help the planner improve future presentations. The main thing the manager will remember from such an encounter is that the issue was successfully resolved.

How to know what is of crucial importance and what is not? Obviously, experience is the primary teacher—the more experience, the better the planning intuition. Planners can accelerate this process by asking lots of critical and relevant questions. What process do more senior planners use to get to the core issue? Do they make a list of issues and prioritize it? Do they diagram the problem? Does the critical problem come to them intuitively? Asking good questions of managers encourages them to explain their processes and may inspire them to be a mentor.

The second example is a complaint made *about* managers—that they are excessively critical or blunt, or don't provide sought-after support or encouragement. Box 5.1 describes a manager who was like that. A planner's first reaction might be that the criticism is a personal attack—that the manager is part of a "toxic" work environment. That may be true. I've been fortunate to not have experienced it, but I've witnessed it. In the private sector, I've seen a manager humiliate and belittle a planner in a development team meeting with external consultants present. In the public sector, the toxicity can also exist, but it is less direct and possibly more insidious. Mean public sector managers may tell a planner that no one in the office likes them and suggest or require a personality "remaking" workshop. In addition, good ideas, like being a team player, can be twisted into a form in which bullying occurs. Indirect forms of meanness, such as shunning, exclusion, and gossip, also occur.

Having acknowledged that genuinely bad management practices exist, it is possible to be too sensitive. Constructive criticism is an important aspect of professional growth and shouldn't be confused with abusive behavior. A planner's self-defense mechanisms may whisper "toxic manager" when the critique being offered is on target. Furthermore, the level of support and encouragement that is appropriate naturally lessens as the planner moves from the first planning position, to a developing professional, to a seasoned and mature professional.

In criticism, a manager may have a planner's best interests at heart. The manager might be testing the planner's reaction to stress and criticism. The "test" may be out of respect, as the manager sizes up and vets a planner for a promotion. Also, a manager might be assessing the planner's character rather than challenging planning knowledge. Donald Schön wrote about the kinds of tests a manager might give a planner (Schön, 1982, p. 301):

- *Challenge the planner to see how they respond.* Rather than criticism meaning that the analysis is wrong, the manager seeks to learn about the planner's openness to challenge, willingness to take a point of view, ability to parry back and forth in a constructive way, and level of interest in inquiry and discussion.

- *Admit ignorance and ask for help.* The manager tests the planner's willingness to help the team succeed. This does not mean the manager will ask for help on everything, or is incompetent or abdicating responsibilities.
- *Ask about sources of risk.* The manager assesses risk in a decision. Thinking about unanticipated consequences is a normal strategy for assessing state of knowledge. This is not the same as disputing an analysis.
- *Seek a second opinion.* The manager asks a fellow staff member for an analysis of the same thing the planner analyzed. It is possible that the manager is pitting the planner against his or her peers, but it is also a strategy of getting a second opinion before a decision. People get second opinions from doctors, so why not from planning staff?

A third staff complaint of managers is that assignments are not specific enough, or stable enough, to be efficiently completed. A specific assignment allows planners to succeed and prove themselves in a timely manner, whereas vague assignments are challenging. It is frustrating to redo an analysis, so why doesn't the manager think it through and get it right the first time?

Assignments can be vague because the manager doesn't have time to give detailed, worked-out ones. Running between meetings, they hope the planner can pick up the fragments provided and solve the problem. It could also be that the manager is unsure of the problem and the way forward, and beginning the analysis is the best way to move forward. And finally, a manager may be aware that the context for the decision may change as the analysis is being completed. My experience as a consultant is doing many re-dos of work that I thought was done. Sometimes that can take as much time as the original analysis.

Vagueness may also be strategic. A manager might use it as an instrument of control—to keep options open until he or she knows the best course of action. Or, a manager could be vague to make staff dependent, necessitating checking on every step. Vagueness may also be used to *avoid* decisions, such as when a manager won't give a clear assignment so as to avoid the expectation that the resulting recommendation will be followed. Lastly, the manager may be in the process of assessing the political "room" that is available for certain solutions. Even in this brief example, it is clear that there are many possible reasons for vagueness. Planners shouldn't jump to a conclusion about the reasons for vagueness, but tolerate and work with it until they can get a sense of the reasons.

Are You Your Manager's Servant?

I have been fortunate to have good managers. Starting out, I saw my job as making my manager look good. That meant taking care of details to allow her to pursue the big-picture vision. This role came naturally because I was serving a person I respected and who treated me well. She didn't have to say "your job is to make me look good." I wanted to make her look good. As she was successful, so was I. Box 10.3 provides some details on that role.

Box 10.3 Figuring out What the Boss Needs

In one of my early planning jobs, I realized that my boss was an idea person. At the time, I didn't really know if I was an idea person or not, but that wasn't my primary role. I was organized, conscientious, and able to imagine how things play out through implementation. I realized that she generated many ideas, but other divisions in the organization were frustrated with my unit for poor follow-through. Quarterly budget reports were not done on time, and some good ideas didn't get implemented. Our unit was seen as getting away with breaking rules—not an entirely bad thing but this undermined our credibility.

I realized that my job was not to be an idea person but to accompany my boss to meetings, listen carefully, and "catch" the ideas before they hit the ground and rolled under the photocopy machine. I organized the ideas, wrote briefs about them, created systems to track implementation, took care of budget reporting, and pushed back when too many ideas were in play. In this way, my boss and I had synergy—this was not discussed explicitly but was worked out in practice.

Some managers might explicitly tell you they want help in areas that are not their strengths, whereas others may not clearly see their weaknesses, but in either case being attentive to this dynamic can garner a manager's loyalty and support over the longer arc of a career. Being an organized, logical person does not sound like a lofty attribute, but in this case, it was exactly what was needed. Finding this function gave me a vital role in the organization. It wasn't just my boss who was appreciative—her superiors knew that my presence made her more successful and therefore supported the organization. There was plenty of time for me to become an idea person later in my career.

Planners should seek to understand their manager's style and shape their behavior and work strategy accordingly. For example, some managers appreciate being challenged in a meeting and are eager see what their planners know. Others don't have the time to even ask the planners a question. Still others may think that planners don't know their place because they haven't put in the time to establish professional credibility.

At some point, planners may find themselves with a difficult manager. It is often possible to find a way to a better relationship, but Box 10.2 reminds us that that is not always the case, and that there may be something to learn from the difficulty. That could be as simple as what *not* to do when a planner becomes a manager. In the middle of a difficult situation, though, problems with managers can be overwhelming. It may seem that the problems will go on forever, but they do not. Even if treated unjustly, a planner can seek some detachment. It's the difference between holding a view that managers should live up to an ideal role and accepting a world where flawed people are trying to get through the day. In short, planners should respect the greater experience of managers, tolerate a reasonable amount of unreasonableness, and seek to find a working accommodation.

In the case where a planner has made an effort without success, engaging an external management expert to provide short-term one-on-one coaching services might make sense. A coach can objectively assess the situation and provide support for the planner to learn new strategies to achieve positive outcomes with the manager. The coach can also confirm that organizational change is unrealistic, and the best option is for the planner to exit the organization. Such a professional development opportunity could be valuable not just for the current issue but for long-term career success, as the planner may acquire new or refined interpersonal and communication skills.

Organizational Culture

Planners need to succeed in an organization's culture, whether it is a bureaucracy or a nimble non-profit. Discerning and responding to organizational culture generates a compatible and productive role.

Organizational culture is defined as "shared assumptions of individuals' participation in the organization. Often taken for granted by the actors themselves, these assumptions can be identified through stories, special language, norms, institutional ideology, and attitudes that emerge from individual and collective behavior" (Tierney, 1988, p. 4). Importantly, this definition does not rely on the organization's mission statement. Although a close alignment is expected, organizational norms may be different from the organization's mission statement or code of behavior.

The mission statement of an organization devoted to social change, for example, likely emphasizes participation, empowerment, and speaking out. Coming out of school, idealist planners are eager to voice their ideas about reform. But if the executive director's management style does not reflect the official mission statement, a planner could be fooled into thinking that it is appropriate to openly challenge the executive director's ideas. It is wise to be attentive to both the official and informal cultures. A planner can assess whether the written mission statement is actually practiced by listening to the organization's stories, identifying norms, and other attributes mentioned above. The planner should make sure that the organization walks the talk in their strategic plan before acting like that plan defines the culture.

Organizational Culture Types

Planning organizations' cultures vary greatly. A small non-profit is less formal than a large federal agency. There are also differences in culture across departments in large organizations. In local government, for example, planning and public works departments do different work (policy versus operations) and have different dominant disciplines (planning versus engineering). As a transportation planner, I encountered this clash of cultures when trying to reform traffic impact analysis practices for infill development. The planners made research-based arguments to change practices based on local context, whereas the engineers held on to uniform procedures, published standards, and context-free trip generation rates.

I also found organizational culture clashes at my university. A strategic planning exercise revealed competing cultures among the university president, the academic senate, and operational divisions (Willson, 2006). Because of the importance of organizational culture, planning conflicts are not necessarily about plan outcomes; they are sometimes the vehicle over which organizational culture conflicts are fought.

Quinn (1988) characterizes organizations across two continua: (1) centralized versus decentralized, and (2) a focus on maintenance versus competition. Planning organizations land on many locations along these continua. Here are some organizational type scenarios associated with different planning jobs. Some of these distinctions were introduced in Chapters 4 and 5:

- *Environmental reviewer for a state transportation agency.* The work is done by a large, centralized organization whose mission is maintaining environmental review standards according to state and federal law. The planner performs well-defined roles in a hierarchical organization. The work emphasizes process, consistency, and defined metrics. Decisions go up and down the bureaucratic hierarchy. The planner is a specialist with a predictable workload.
- *GIS analyst for a multinational engineering and consulting firm.* As with a state agency, this is a complex organization with systems intended to produce profitability. Choices and strategy are made around financial targets delivered by central management. The planner's job is primarily technical, responding to assignments and clients, and meeting billable-hour requirements. The planner is a specialist and is rewarded for efficient work.
- *Land use planner for a small city.* The job encompasses current, long-range, and every other planning issue that arises because the department is composed of just a few people. The city manager or community development director emphasizes teamwork. The formation of group values and perspectives determines outcomes more than formal methods of planning or influencing. The planner is a generalist with varied tasks throughout the day.
- *Market analyst for a non-profit housing developer.* This job focuses on innovative ways of producing affordable housing. Good ideas are more important than organization protocols or deference to job titles. The organization is flexible but can be chaotic. The planner's work changes frequently depending on what is needed. Quick responses, independent thinking, and an ability to function in a dynamic environment are valued. The planner is an entrepreneurial generalist.

As described above, the planner's role is expected to respond to the characteristics of the organization. In some agencies, adherence to process is important, whereas others welcome a more chaotic, innovative culture. In larger organizations, there may be culture tensions *between* departments, as mentioned, or *within* departments. For example, planners processing development entitlements may adopt a procedural culture focused on consistent process, whereas economic development planners adopt an entrepreneurial approach.

In large organizations, the planners must move up the ladder to affect the organization's mission, but once they get there the impact can be great because resources and leverage are available to scale-up project and programs. On the other hand, small organizations offer more freedom at first but may have less impact because of a smaller influence. The point here is not to recommend one organizational setting over another one, but to emphasize the importance of understanding organizational culture in selecting jobs and figuring out how to work in such agencies. Planners should seek organizational cultures that are compatible, but also know that perfect alignment may be an unrealistic expectation.

Invisible Organizational Norming

The previous examples address how planners may understand organizational culture, as espoused and as practiced, but invisible organization norming is also important. Here is an example. Public sector administrators need to manage conflict among departments, between departments and governing boards, and between departments and the community. If a conflict between city departments plays out before the city council, it could undermine the credibility of the departments and make the administrator look bad. Administrators also want to reduce risk, because the financial and political consequences of missteps can be large. Adding to a cautious approach, staff proposing innovations are often asked by city council members, "where has this been done before?" They want a close-by example of a peer city finding success with the initiative. Lastly, administrators may suppress the articulation of dilemmas and conflicts because addressing them openly would undo tacit political and administrative agreements. They seek to avoid unmanageable conflict at the board or council level.

These three concerns may block consideration of innovative ideas. For idealist planners, it is frustrating to encounter limits to innovation. They want to make an impact, but they may be told to exclude an innovative or potentially controversial solution. The desire for conflict and risk reduction is an inherent part of organizational culture, as the managers set the tone regarding risk. It becomes "the way things are done." Of course, conflict and risk reduction are not written in an organization's mission statement—they are unarticulated but real organizational priorities. Arriving new to such an organization, it may take some time to discern these undercurrents.

An additional consideration is that public sector organizations may use indirect methods of controlling staff because access to traditional tools, such as firing, may be limited by union contracts and other policies and procedures. Such organizations may develop subtle methods of control, such as reassignment of work, shunning, non-responsiveness, gossiping, and scapegoating. Although this is a sign of a dysfunctional organization, some of this is present in every organization.

Because of all of these factors, the best answer doesn't always win the day. There is invariably more at play than that which can be seen, and the more idealist planners understand the informal, underlying culture, the better they can act strategically within those constraints.

Organizational Do's and Don'ts

The following ideas suggest how idealist planners may choose to act in an organization. Their application requires sensitivity to the norms of the organization. As mentioned, large consulting firms have detailed work processes, rules for bidding on work, and approval processes. Small non-profit organizations are less formal, with fewer levels of process. At first, it is wise to bend to the organizational norms, because organizations rarely change for an individual planner's vision, even though individuals can shape organizations long-term. This, of course, goes back to the importance of the job search—finding a job in an organization with norms that fit the planner. Here are suggested do's and don'ts.

Do:

- Be on time, follow the rules for lunches and breaks, and be willing to work extra hours (within reason). Arrive at work having had sufficient sleep, ready to be productive.
- Dress according to the norms of the organization. Keep your desk at a level of neatness that conforms with norms.
- Be attentive to opportunities to shine—a presentation to senior management, a lunch with a supervisor, or a role in a community meeting.
- Tailor language and communication styles to the workplace, considering the ages of workers in the organization and the expected level of formality. For example, try "good morning" instead of "hey."
- Take initiative in ways that supervisors support and that helps the team succeed. Although planners should promote themselves with personal initiative, that initiative should also serve the larger goals.
- Ask for help when you are stuck, but only after you have exhausted your own resources. Limit the number of times you ask your manager to the level she or he is comfortable with.

- Ask for feedback on work products outside of the formal framework of performance evaluations. Genuine interest in self-improvement makes managers happy and willing to mentor.
- Respect organizational hierarchy. Don't go behind a manager's back to pitch an idea to someone up the chain of command unless there is a really good reason, or that is accepted practice in the organization.
- Be careful about interacting with commissioners, board members, elected officials, and other decision-makers outside of public meetings and formal briefings. Decision-makers may want to quiz a staff planner for information they cannot get from higher-level managers. Their attention is flattering, but sharing information undermines a manager's trust, so avoid those situations, and always disclose and check in about what is appropriate.
- Take advantage of available services such as human resource training, continuing education, professional development conferences, and team-building exercises.
- Attend the holiday party even if the corny gift exchange is not much fun for you.
- Let your supervisor know if the work environment impedes your productivity, such as noise in a cubicle environment. Offer a reasonable solution to improve the office environment or work in alternative spaces when a task requires full concentration.

Don't:

- Tell what seems to be a minor, innocent lie for convenience or to avoid a difficult situation.
- Criticize the employer or your co-workers on social media.
- Talk about politics, religion, or other personal matters unless you are sure that those discussions are welcome and do not risk professional relationships.
- Call in sick when you're not sick. Don't post on social media a picture of you hiking on that day.
- Miss deadlines. If you do, don't make it worse by being evasive or unavailable about the missed deadline.
- Gossip about co-workers with friends and associates, even outside of the office. The planning profession is a relatively small world, and word gets around.
- Look at your cell phone in a meeting. That way, there will be no temptation to lose connection with those around you and better conversation with team members and managers present.

- Have an alcoholic drink or any other substance that affects your frame of mind at lunch, before an evening meeting, or at any other work-related event. Make exceptions to this rule only if the context and culture condones this.
- Refuse or resist mundane tasks. They need to be done, so be willing to help the organization accomplish its mission. Over time, more interesting tasks will come to you.
- Proceed with a task when you are not clear on its purpose, if your manager is available for consultation. If there is no consultation available, then proceed as best as possible.
- Ignore how your work habits or process affects your co-workers and the team. For example, your error could be compounded through many reports and require the team to work overtime to fix the document. Or worse, it could lead to a challenge that restarts an review process.

Working in Teams

Planning is a collaborative and team-oriented activity. It has its own specializations and draws on knowledge from other disciplines. Because planners link knowledge to action, they play a vital role in synthesis and evaluation. They move plans and decisions through internal review and approval processes as well as external ones that include community participation and appointed and elected officials. These job characteristics mean that planners spend much of their time working in teams, such as a cross-department project review team in a city, or a planner/architect/engineer/scientist team developing a master plan in consulting. This section suggests the basics of being a team member and introduces a framework for better understanding team dynamics.

The Basics

Teams rely on their members being of goodwill. That means bringing a positive, cooperative attitude toward the team task. Goodwill is not always present, though, especially if there are organizational or personal conflicts on the team. Acknowledging that reality, it is best to start each team activity assuming the best.

The qualities that make a good team member include:

- A willingness to show up, do one's part, and commit to the task and the team
- Reliability, in participation, completing tasks, and providing feedback

- A positive attitude toward other team members and a willingness to learn from them
- Honesty, straightforwardness, and forthrightness, tempered by tact and sensitivity
- Self-knowledge about ways of thinking and acting, especially under stress
- Attention to detail, including attending to the team process
- A problem-solving orientation
- Acceptance of hierarchy and team management necessary to complete the task
- Attention to team process and forthrightness in addressing team dynamics
- Good communication skills, especially in argumentation. This includes active listening to discern issues related to process, value issues, facts and evidence, and active listening.
- Appropriate flexibility; understanding that the goals, problem frame, and scope of activities will change as the effort proceeds
- Appreciation that team members bring different skills to the task and have different personalities, styles of learning, and acting

There are many teamwork challenges, of course, such as apathetic team members or those who seek to advance a narrow mission over the overall purpose. Teams are also affected by negative behavior, such as free riders who don't do their part or team members who are outwardly or passively aggressive. Planners should be realistic and aware of these possibilities, but start by applying the positive habits described above.

Personality Styles

Teamwork is enhanced if team members are aware of their personality styles of working and understand that other people have different ones. For example, one planner may favor brainstorming and freewheeling discussions whereas another is focused on the practicalities of delivering team products.

Many employers use the Myers–Briggs Type Indicator test in career coaching and team development (Murray, 1990). It asks a series of binary questions about a person's preferences in a variety of situations. The interpretation categorizes responses in terms of four dichotomous dimensions: extroversion/introversion, sensing/intuition, thinking/feeling, and judging/perceiving. These qualities then form 16 personality "types." Each type has strengths and weaknesses. No type is better than another; the goal is awareness of how people interact with their surroundings, how they see the world and process information, their decision-making and emotional reactions—especially under stress, and their approach to work. Ultimately, as evolving professionals, this information creates an opportunity to learn how to manage weaknesses and develop new strengths.

When I read the narrative associated with my Myers-Briggs type, I recognized my strengths and weaknesses, and I reflected on team settings where I have thrived and ones where I have been unhappy. In a given team, some people gravitate to leadership roles, whereas others are practical and fact-minded. Others may be focused on the social dynamics of the team, seeking to keep good relations among team members. Others may be "devil's advocate" types who challenge an early consensus to make sure that solutions are fully tested. Of course, the devil's advocate may annoy the person who is focused on bringing the group to conclusion. Good teams have a variety of team members, and they prosper if team members recognize and accept differences.

Myers-Briggs is just one of many tools that identify different personality "types" and characteristics. When planners reflect on their type, and understand other types, they make better decisions under stress and work more effectively with others. I should note that there is some debate about the scientific validity of these personality assessment tools. I recognize those criticisms, but they do not trouble me—no test with multiple-choice questions is going to fully understand me, much less define me. Rather, I look at them as providing insights for consideration and reflection that can make teamwork more effective and less stressful.

Although a wide variety of types exists among a planning team, this may be even more important in multidisciplinary teams. With an awareness of personality types, it may be easier to understand the approach of the engineer, the real estate developer, the scientist, and the attorney. It can be an insightful exercise to do as a team before getting to work.

Interpersonal Professional Conflict

Interpersonal conflict naturally arises in work settings. Let's say team Member A was to deliver a traffic analysis by a certain date. When that didn't happen, Team Member B confronts A and complains that the late report hurt the effort. Team member A reacts rudely, insulting Team Member Bs contributions to the team. These negative exchanges affect the whole team, as gossip magnifies the confrontation.

Usually, interpersonal conflict can be addressed and resolved, but the process of resolving it requires clear thinking on both sides. It is hardest, of course, to think clearly in a stressful moment. My first suggestion is that a planner should pause and not react to an affront immediately. Sleeping on it helps. Feelings about the conflict will suggest jumping right in. Feelings are rarely a reliable guide to behavior in the heat of the moment.

If planners manage those initial feelings, then they can think about the issue and possible responses in a more rational way. The planner can name the thing that happened, factually, without emotional interpretation. Was what happened a serious affront or was the other person just having a bad day? In this regard, it is useful to distinguish between a hurt and a wrong. Being hurt means someone disappointed me. This happens all the time—we are all clumsy in our interpersonal dealings. Being wronged is a true moral offense. This may justify rebuking the person who committed the wrong and asking them to make it right.

Handling conflict is a vital professional skill. In reflecting on a tough moment, planners should be precise. They can use the analogy of filing a "police report" on the incident (i.e., a summary of what was actually said, in what order, what happened next, and so on without any interpretation or emotional content). Parties to a conflict often have different views of what happened. It is useful to ask the other party what they remember happened. If a planner temporarily holds off the interpretation of motives, it could lead to a better understanding. This can reduce the urgency to act; it can slow things down. When stressed, people report mostly feelings and not many facts. Instead of asking "how do I feel?" a planner may consider asking "what is my duty?" By duty, I mean a responsibility or obligation to be a good person and to causes larger than personal self-interest.

If after reflection, a rebuke is appropriate, a planner should do it in a measured way, and even practice delivering it beforehand. The message should not tell the other person what they should do or how they should react. Also, there is no assurance that the person will accept the rebuke. The planners should state what they would like the other party to do to right the wrong but be open to taking "no" for an answer. The other party may accept the rebuke, counteract with an accusation, or refuse to make things right.

Rebuking another professional, face-to-face, is difficult. It is tempting to avoid it, or to do it by email or other social media, but I don't recommend that. When writing an email, looking at the words on the screen may make it seem like the message is the "perfect" rebuke, but that's far different from having a dialogue with another person. The planner should get on the phone, meet in person, or have a coffee together. The upside of this admittedly uncomfortable process is to diffuse dislike of the other person. In a way, it is not fair to be angry with a person and not say anything, because they can't defend themselves, understand what happened, or choose to make amends. Avoiding legitimate rebuke puts the other person in a "jail" of sorts, where the aggrieved party acts as prosecuting attorney, jury, judge, and jailer. That much power corrupts.

When It Is Time to Leave

Toxic and dysfunctional workplaces certainly exist in public, private, and non-profit sector planning. Some managers shame, yell, gossip, scapegoat, bully; others endorse staff to gang up on an employee. Some ostracize, withhold information, and make unreasonable work assignments. It may be that an organization has a negative management culture, and teamwork trouble can disable a planner's effectiveness. As this chapter suggests, planners should not act impulsively, but after doing due diligence about whether personal frustration is warranted, sometimes it is necessary to leave a job.

Wise mentors and other professionals can provide perspective about what level of manager, organization, or teamwork trouble rises above annoyance and justifies making a change. If the organization's mission is right and the work is right, putting up with bad management or interpersonal tensions may be worth it. But sometimes, problems undermine planners so much that their self-esteem suffers, hindering their growth and the search for a better job. It may also be that there is simply no time to plot the next move. Planners can feel trapped or see themselves as victims. If Sunday nights regularly bring an anxious feeling, then something is amiss.

It is usually better to get a new job while still employed than to quit and look for a job while unemployed. Human resources departments are usually curious about gaps in employment record. This section suggests coping strategies so that planners can hang in there until they find something better.

Idealist planners can outsmart a dysfunctional culture by pretending to be a "visiting scholar" in the field of workplace anthropology. They look at the goings-on as if it is a Shakespearean play. They note the role(s) they are assigned and the roles of others. They tweak their role slightly and see if it affects the chemistry. They think of themselves as actors in this play, not victims of it.

Dysfunctional workplaces can entice disgruntled planners into doing less than their best, but this can develop bad habits, impede growth, and undermine their credibility. By doing their best work every day, frustrated planners cultivate references and gain experience. They use the workplace to gain skills that help them on their way. In this way, such planners are *buying* something by putting up with bad management practices for specific reasons that serve them. This is a stronger place to be—the chooser—than the passive recipient of bad behavior. This can help avoid "victim" thinking.

Bad work environments can be more tolerable if frustrated planners realize that they are learning about what *not* to do when they are managers. They will remember how it felt when a supervisor made a critical comment about an employee within earshot. The world will certainly look different as a manager—the pressures that supervisors feel will be better understood—but attentive planners will select more appropriate management strategies.

It is hazardous to join an "anti-manager" gossip culture at the workplace. Work "gossip partners" can reinforce a sense of grievance. And, however friendly they are, colleagues may turn on a gossip partner. Planners shouldn't underestimate what others will do when their career advancement or self-identity is threatened. If the planner doesn't say it, others can't repeat it.

I recommend professionalism, containment, and stone-cold purposefulness. By staying until a better job is available, frustrated planners gain all they can from an organization that hasn't treated them properly. There *are* more team-like, manager-supported work environments out there. With this perspective, planners can go into the office, even on a Sunday, and feel like secret agents on a mission. It's temporary. It's for a greater purpose.

And Now to You: Cultivate Empathy

Communicative competency, emotional intelligence, and the ability to read organization and team context are among the most important factors in your career. Starting out, doing this and mastering technical skills can be a lot to take on, but you can improve these qualities over time. Whether it is dealing with superiors, understanding organizational culture, or dealing with teams, your investment will pay off. Learning how to prosper in the collaborative environment of planning will catapult your good ideas into implementation and advance your career.

Perhaps the simplest way to conclude this section is to recommend that you cultivate an ability to feel empathy. Empathy—the ability to understand how other people experience the world, from their point of view—is an antidote to excessive frustration and anger. Accepting that you and your fellow planners, decision-makers, and public stakeholders are flawed people, finding their way, can transform your initial reaction to sadness about the imperfect nature of the human condition. Empathy is a tool for understanding, action, and reconciliation. It goes hand in hand with generosity of spirit. None of this suggests that you should be a pushover who accepts wrong; on the contrary, empathy is a tool for making you more effective in working for the good.

Discussion/Reflection Questions for Chapter 10

1. Develop a list of ideal qualities for a manager. Find a discussion partner and compare notes. Is your list of desired qualities a reasonable expectation? What qualities are essential for you, and what qualities are preferred but not essential?

2. Reflect on the culture of an organization where you worked. Where did it fall on the centralized-versus-decentralized, and maintenance-versus-competition continua? Was the culture uniform or were there tensions across the organization? If you are working now, how can you take this awareness of the dynamics of organizational culture into your current job?

3. Take the *16Personalities* online personality type assessment. Review the write-up on your type and reflect on past teamwork experiences you have had. What insights do you have on those teamwork experiences? What worked well and what did not? Can you reach more understanding about the experience now that you have read about your type? Can you understand the actions of other team members better?

4. Consider an interpersonal conflict you have had in a professional work setting. Retroactively assess the roles of feelings and rational thought in how you dealt with it. In reflecting on it, were you realistic in your thinking? Were your needs and expectations reasonable for the situation? Did you act quickly based on feelings or only after reflection? If you could replay the interaction, is there anything you would change in what you did? If so, how can you apply that lesson to addressing future conflicts?

5. What is your core motivation in planning? Is it fairness and justice? Truth? Beauty? Love or benevolence for others? Thinking back on previous teamwork exercises, did the other team members have the same core motivation? If not, does that explain differences of opinion and recommendations for action?

References

Habermas, J. (1984). *The theory of communicative action: Reason and the rationalization of society.* Translated by T. McCarthy. Boston, MA: Beacon Books.

Healey, P. (1992). Planning through debate: The communicative turn in planning theory. *Town Planning Review* 63(2): pp. 143–162.

Murray, J. (1990). Review of Myers-Briggs type indicator. *Perceptual and Motor Skills* 70: pp. 1187–1202.

Schön, D. (1982). *The reflective practitioner.* New York, NY: Basic Books.

Quinn, W. (1988). *Beyond rational management: Mastering paradoxes and competing demands of high performance.* San Francisco: Jossey-Bass.

Tierney, W. G. (1988). Organizational culture and higher education: Defining the essentials. *Journal of Higher Education* 59(1): pp. 2–21.

Willson, R. (2006). The Dynamics of Organizational Culture and Academic Planning. *Planning for Higher Education.* April – June 2006, pp. 5–17.

Chapter 11

Working With Mentors

Dare to experience change
in the presence of another.

Many successful planners cite mentors who helped them along the way or are still involved in their careers. I say many, because other distinguished planners never had a mentor—they did it alone. Mentors aren't a prerequisite for success, but they can provide valuable help. I've collected planners' stories about mentors over the years, hearing about influential mentors who range from a strict high school English teacher, to a critical college professor, to a boss who stepped back so a staff planner could shine.

A mentor is often imagined as an older, wiser person who provides support and insight. This "mentor as sage" model is valid, but it can limit a planner's openness to the range of mentoring available. Mentors come in many forms and mentoring comes in many ways. Drawing from Kram (1985), mentors may have career functions, such as coaching, and psychosocial functions, such as role modeling. Johnson (2016, p. 29) further distinguishes mentoring relationships in terms of a transactional versus transformational approach, the strength of the working alliance, and the level of social support.

This chapter explains different kinds of mentoring, provides tips on recognizing and attracting mentors, and suggests how to navigate the mentee/mentor experience. Mentoring supports school and career choices, coaches for better job performance, and more broadly, helps identify the mentee's core purpose(s). Some mentors provide support and encouragement, whereas others offer challenges. The chapter concludes with a glimpse into the mentor's motivation and perspective.

Mentors can provide access to professional opportunities and networks, professional development opportunities, letters of recommendation, references, role models, challenges and accountability, substantive feedback, role modeling, emotional support, and/or a safe space for reflection. One mentor usually doesn't offer all of these things. Mentors may be teachers, friends, acquaintances, managers, employees, and colleagues. Some mentoring relationships occur over many decades, whereas others are one-time interactions. Certain interactions are explicit mentoring, others are informal, while still others are the byproduct of interactions that are not considered as mentoring.

To introduce the variety of messages mentors may give, Box 11.1 compiles messages I've received from mentors over the years—supportive, challenging, and perplexing.

Types of Mentoring

Mentor-mentee relationships take on many forms, but they are most effective when there is clarity about the type of mentoring that is occurring. Is the mentor offering action-oriented advice on how to address a work problem, or supporting self-knowledge through dialogue on values and life purpose? Is the mentor a professor or supervisor, or someone who has no role in evaluating the mentee's work? Does the mentor provide support and encouragement, or insightful criticism, or both? Is the learning one-way, mentor to mentee, or two-way, in which the mentor learns as well? This section maps the full range of opportunities.

Although formal mentoring experiences are arranged by schools, employers, and professional organizations, mentoring is also available in the normal flow of life. Idealist planners can gain insight from a broad range of people in everyday interactions. Mentors may be present without being acknowledged; in fact, the influence of unacknowledged mentors may be recognized only decades later. Furthermore, mentoring can be opportunistic and episodic, perhaps occurring in only one specific instance.

My experience suggests three main mentoring types, described as follows.

Box 11.1 What Mentors Tell You—A Collection Without Curation

I've received many messages from formal and informal mentors. These snippets of wisdom came over many decades. This compilation is broad, as it should be, because there are so many different situations. It provides a flavor of messages the mentee may receive:

- "People don't like you—in fact, I didn't like you when we first met."
- "Don't whine—work hard, compete."
- "Don't take things so seriously."
- "Have high standards and attention to detail as a professional. Be accurate. Don't take shortcuts."
- "I'm interested in you: what you know and what you think."
- "Be creative, brainstorm, have fun."
- "Be yourself."
- "You are welcome to join."
- "Don't take on other people's crap, have good boundaries."
- "Slow down, don't jump to conclusions, allow the process to unfold."
- "Keep the sword of battle in its sheath unless battle is truly called for."
- "Respect the dark side of human behavior—don't be naïve about how the world works."
- "Brand yourself—develop a message about your competence and knowledge."
- "Be mindful of your long-term reputation."
- "Don't 'leak' (get ahead of yourself, reveal too much, offer more than is asked)."

Type 1: Educational and Career Advice Mentoring

This is mentoring provided by college professors, supervisors, other planners, and professional organizations. This type of mentoring offers strategies for making decisions about planning schools, finding a planning specialty, gaining progressively responsible experience, landing jobs, re-launching a career, and so on. It includes being a sounding board and offering insights into planning practice issues, such as addressing technical planning challenges, interpersonal challenges, and/or imaging solutions. Mentors can be current professors or managers, or someone who has no power over the mentee. In the former, the power relationship should be acknowledged because the mentor is also evaluating the mentee.

Type 2: Mentoring-by-Doing

This "showing how" mentoring occurs by completing a task in collaboration with a mentor, similar to an apprenticeship. For professors, it includes conducting research with students or alumni, presenting at conferences, and/or submitting papers for publication. This demystifies the research process and professional protocols, allowing the mentee to assess his or her interests. For practitioners, mentoring-by-doing might be completing a professional task together in a way that the mentee learns about the processes and techniques the mentee uses to solve problems or run a public workshop. "Showing how" mentoring may include demonstrating technical skills, negotiating, fielding questions from politicians, or supervising employees. It may also address time management, client relations, community relations, or interdepartmental politics. Mentoring-by-doing can model how to say "no" or "yes," deal with rejection, failure or mistakes, and find a workable work-life balance. Seen this way, daily professional practice can provide mentoring if it is perceived as such. Idealist planners may also seek "showing how" mentors outside of their job, through programs offered by professional organizations or informally.

Type 3: Life-Coach Mentoring

The line between advice on a planning career and delving into a person's sense of identity is not well-marked. Previous chapters in this volume argue that planners should identify their core purpose and motivating values. This may be supported by mentoring discussions that are deeper than typical career choice advice. Life-coach mentoring is more holistic and personal. It is often organized around finding the right questions to ask and discussing ways of answering them. In it, the mentees may be guided to reflect on their core purpose, the meaning of their work, and processes for finding alignment between their core purpose and planning work. Issues of identity and self-worth may be addressed. In the process, mentees may encounter blocks to their growth or be made aware of blind spots in their thinking. This work is deeper and involves emotions. Because discussions may move personal issues, life-coach mentoring may create conflict or misunderstanding. Despite this possibility, it can be profoundly helpful in launching a career based on self-knowledge.

Box 11.2 provides an account of how a mentor may challenge the mentee in a way that promoted his growth. In this case, the writer's most influential mentor was the coach of his track team. As an aside, planners who have

Box 11.2 Follow Good Teachers
By Aiden Irish, Ph.D. Fellow, John Glenn College
of Public Affairs, Ohio State University

My approach to finding mentors came to me from an old family friend when I was young: "follow good teachers; I don't care if they teach ballet, take their class." Simple and to the point. Yet, the significance of this advice has deepened as I have grown, and reflecting on what it means necessitates some contemplation. Namely, what is a good teacher?

On this matter, my no-nonsense friend was making the point that good teachers, or mentors (I consider the two largely the same), are people from whom I have come away a different person. If I didn't, I didn't learn. This process is not easy. In fact, it has, at times, been downright painful. Each period of growth required reflecting on what I thought I knew and accepting the truth of challenges to that status quo. Good mentors have been the conduits for that self-reflection. Whether on policy opinions or my career trajectory, that succinct advice at the outset has encouraged me to seek out and follow people who challenge my positions.

With this attribute in mind, many people (myself included) do not necessarily like this kind of challenge. Thus, I find that "good teachers" are rarely the ones rated as "easy" on RateMyProfessor. My best teachers have come largely from the category of individuals who many of my compatriots designated as "too hard." Failing to realize this fact almost caused me to avoid one of my most important mentors.

During college, I steadfastly avoided a professor who was universally recognized in my department as "demanding" because I was afraid that I might not pass muster. Thankfully, this avoidance could not be maintained, and she became one of the most significant figures in encouraging my academic interests. Only during my second-to-last year did I start taking her classes. In retrospect, I regret avoiding her for so much of college. The simple lesson that I gleaned is to build connections with those people avoided by most. Among that crowd I have found teachers and mentors who unabashedly challenged my perspectives on the world. Nonetheless, challenge does not suggest lack of respect or kindness.

Without exception, my mentors have been kind, generous, and complimentary (when warranted). Yet, each has shared a willingness to not mince words for the sake of niceties, nor to avoid addressing my faults for the sake of my ego. A prime example comes from my cross country coach, my most lasting mentor. After a rather unorthodox and risky win that could have easily gone awry, I approached him expecting congratulations. Without slowing his walk, he remarked: "that was stupid; gutsy, but stupid." He recognized my effort but brought my attention to the expansive room for improvement. This is my favorite mentorship memory. It was respectful, yet unabashedly pointed. This characteristic—respectful yet unflinchingly willing to challenge me—remains my most trusted metric for seeking out "good teachers" in my life.

a background in sports, and therefore an experience of having a coach, often know how to benefit from mentors in their professional lives.

Box 11.3 illustrates a different mentor role—providing support and encouragement when a mentee is struggling over a decision. In this case, the mentor provides a point of view, but only after the mentee had done the work of thinking through the options. Mentors like this provide support and affirmation that can help the mentee move forward with confidence.

There are more forms of mentoring than the three types discussed above, and they are not mutually exclusive. I'm not proposing fixed categories but suggesting that the mentor and mentee be aware of the type of mentoring that is occurring, discuss it, and have mutual agreement about it.

To address the multiplicity of mentoring relationships, Table 11.1 provides a format to keep track of them. Mentees may use it to classify their mentors in terms of the roles they play. For each row, note the mentor, the time period, and the primary type (or types) of mentoring. Then enter the involvement in evaluation (managers and professors, versus people others), the tone of mentoring (support, critic, or both), and whether the mentoring relationship is formal (both parties have explicitly discussed the mentor/ mentee relationship) or informal (mentoring is implicit). The next column concerns whether the mentor helps at a specific point in time or is a long-term relationship. The last two columns have cells to note what the mentee has learned, personally and professionally. Updating the table every six

---

Box 11.3 The Life Coach Mentor
By Anonymous

A planner was facing a decision about a job offer and was having a tough time deciding. Although the opportunity was good, something was holding the planner back from saying yes. The planner wrote his mentor about the decision, processing his thinking by providing a list of "things I've given up on" and "things I care about." The mentor wrote back, saying:

> I've read your two lists . . . several times through since you sent them to me. They don't add up to [that job]. They add up to "planner's planner," "communicator of worthy ideas," "artist," "partner/parent," and always "colleague/friend." I guess I know something about your inner conflict: I have fought the demon of Worthlessness/Wretchedness all my life. It has been so good to know you, thus to know someone who has fought that same good fight, and fought it well. I tip my hat to you. I love you, as well."

Table 11.1 Classifying mentors

Mentor name, profession, and position	Start Date/ End Date	What type? (career; mentor-by-doing; life coach, other)	Involved in evaluation of work performance?	Primary style: supportive, critical, or both?	Formal or informal relationship?	Episodic or long-term?	What are you learning about yourself?	What are you learning about the planning profession?

months helps the mentees keep track of relationships and to plan for cultivation of new ones.

In the course of a career, planners may have many mentors of different types. The planner may have one person for career advice, a different person for mentoring-by-doing, and a third person who helps them deliberate on life issues. If *one* person is providing different types of mentoring, clarity is needed. For example, a mentor may query about personal issues when the mentee simply wants assistance in making a choice among job offers. Conversely, a mentee might share too much personal information with a mentor who expects a conversation about straightforward career planning. It is good practice for mentees to tell the mentor what type of mentoring they are seeking, and to understand what the mentor is comfortable providing. The last thing some mentors want to know is the mentee's personal angst, whereas others may be interested in it.

Table 11.1 can be used as a working document throughout a planner's career. It does not claim that all types should be represented. All of the mentors may be classified similarly, but that could suggest that a broader range of mentors should be cultivated. Planners can consider where they stand today—how many mentors of what types? What kind of mentoring would be most helpful? What kind of game plan would gain additional mentors?

How to Find Mentors

I am struck by how many of my students don't have a mentor. The pressures of performing in education and early career positions are great, so finding a mentor may seem like a luxury that falls to the bottom of the priority list.

Sometimes mentors find the mentee. As described in Box 2.4, my career was changed when a professor invited me to do research with him. I've heard other stories from students who had a mentor reach out to them, across many levels of the organization, and ask them to take on a special project. Box 4.3 is such a story. That planner asked her mentor, years later, how he selected her. He answered, "I asked around for the best project manager in the department, and people told me it was you." Until that point, the planner's direct supervisor had not told her that she was a good project manager. The process of vetting, therefore, can be unknown to the mentee.

It is common that the mentee approaches the mentor. The prospective mentee shouldn't ask the person to be a mentor on their first meeting. Rather, the mentee can engage with the prospective mentor over a series of interactions and then ask if the discussions could be more regular. The mentor has to know the prospective mentee well enough to make a decision. Once started, the mentor makes a significant time commitment to write letters of recommendation, act as a reference, or provide contacts. The best way to attract mentors is to cultivate them as a regular part of school, work, and professional organization activities.

The following are likely mentors:

- *Current and former professors.* Most professors find great satisfaction when a student or former student checks in with them and seeks their perspective. They've invested their time in the person and are interested in how things are working out. Knowing the prospective mentee over an extended period of time, they have a good sense of the mentee's strengths and weaknesses. Keep in mind that professors' ability to provide specific career advice depends on their level of planning practice involvement. They can also be effective "mentor-by-doing" and life coach mentors.

- *Current and former employers and supervisors.* Supervisors can be excellent mentors. They know the prospective mentee well, and will likely be able to offer good insights. Current employers may be motivated because they want to keep the mentee in the organization and promote their growth.

- *Experienced planners.* Experienced planners outside of the mentee's work environment can provide objective insights. The mentee can ask them for an informational interview at their workplace—a short meeting in which the mentee asks about the organization and explains goals and interests. Then, the mentee can follow up with thank-you notes and emails, and see if further interaction is possible. If the mentee has something to offer, such as knowledge of an innovative planning technique, framing an initial discussion about that is an enticement. Potential mentors may be seeking to attract talent to their organizations through these relationships, so always treat these interactions with seriousness and the appropriate degree of formality.

- *Wise people from all walks of life.* The dilemmas that planners face are not unique. Most everyone confronts questions about how to deal with workplace issues, when to compromise and when to fight for a cause, and how to make good decisions. As a result, the planner may find mentors in unrelated professions or outside the profession. Having a non-planner mentor provides a refreshing perspective.

- *Mentoring programs.* Many professional organizations, including the American Planning Association, the alumni association from the planner's school, and interested employers offer mentoring programs to create mentor/ mentee matches. Career development programs at universities can provide similar assistance.

In my experience, when mentoring accomplishes a certain task, such as helping the mentee apply to grad school or decide about a promotion, the mentor and mentee don't generally stay in touch. Yet some people naturally attract mentors to their corner, for a longer period. Extended mentoring and ongoing collaboration can provide benefits if both parties are interested. Longer-term mentor/mentee relationships are more likely if there is a measure of reciprocity—something in it for the mentor. In my case, I benefit from understanding challenging situations planners face over their careers, testing ideas, and learning, but that's because I wrote this book. Other mentors may find different satisfactions, such as learning about the latest GIS application or understanding how another generation sees the world. Long-term, mentors are attracted to mentee qualities of openness, curiosity, and responsiveness.

If there isn't an immediate connection with a particular mentor, the prospective mentee can attend professional conferences, request informational interviews, get involved in professional organizations, and keep looking—a strong mentor/mentee relationship can result from a very specific pairing of mentor and mentee qualities.

Mentee Do's and Don'ts

This section suggests do's and don'ts for mentees, but before getting to the list, one "do" is the most important: listen, comprehend, and ask.

Listening is a vital quality for learning and for life. Far more than hearing, it is taking things in, restating them to check for meaning, and a host of other active listening strategies. That's the comprehending part. Active listening, used in counselling, mediation, and conflict resolution, works like this: when a mentor introduces an idea, first listen without interrupting. Then, try saying it back to the mentor to check for understanding. This is different from agreeing—the mentee and the mentor might differ in opinions, beliefs, and philosophies. Seeking to deeply understand does not mean giving up a point of view. The first order of business is to understand the point being made. Then, asking questions makes the mentee an active participant in the process of communication and understanding. The mentee is not just taking knowledge from the mentor; they are co-creating the idea or thought together.

Some mentees parry things a mentor says with an already-developed point of view and position. This may stem from insecurity or trying to show their worth. They may feel that they have to show that they have things "worked out." The mentee shouldn't be a pushover or lack a point of view, but intransigence will alienate the mentor. A balance somewhere between being a sponge and a porcupine seems to work best.

Here are some mentee do's and don'ts:

In showing up to the mentee/mentor relationship, *do* the following:

- Be genuine, open to criticism, and willing to change. Discussions where the mentee seeks to "look good" are a waste of time.
- Frame good questions—not "what should I do?" but questions that expand your thinking and deliberation on the issue. Ask questions like: How did you do that? "How can I think more clearly about this situation?" "Do you see any blind spots in my thinking?" "Are there unanticipated benefits or risks in the course of action I am considering?" Ask open-ended questions that lead to good discussion.
- Discuss the type of mentoring (see Table 11.1) being sought. For example, when sharing a work product or personal statement, say whether support or criticism is desired, or both. Not all mentors appreciate being told what kind of reaction is sought, but the good ones want to be sensitive to the mentee's needs.
- Consider that there may be good things to learn from mentors who are unreliable, prickly, critical, and/or difficult. Some will respond sporadically or comment cryptically, whereas others appear not to be interested, even though they are. Not always, but sometimes, it is worth it to hang in there with a prickly porcupine.
- Disclose any learning disability that affects the way mentee/mentor interactions should occur, such as needing the mentor to slow down to allow note taking. It is the mentee's responsibility to communicate to the mentor about how they learn best.

In the practical realm of mentee/mentor interactions, *do* the following:

- Have good manners. Be timely in responding to a mentor. Be reliable. If engaged in a back-and-forth dialogue via email and you cannot reply within

24 hours, let the mentor know when a reply will be provided and stick to that. If a date for reply is missed, get in touch and explain what happened.

- Address difficult issues in person or using the next-best medium of communication. Because electronic media has replaced much face-to-face interaction, it may seem easier to email a mentor when there is a tough issue rather than talking in person, but asynchronous emails are a frustrating way to have a dialogue.

- Give the mentor sufficient notice and time to do the thing being asked, such as being a reference or writing a letter of recommendation.

- Apologize when a mistake or missed deadline has occurred. Don't leave the mentor in the dark, because then they don't know what non-responsiveness means—lost interest, a personal offense, or something bad has happened.

- Write handwritten thank-you notes when your mentor does something for you. There is a correlation between career success and writing thank-you notes. Thank-you notes may seem like a relic, but many mentors grew up in that age and so appreciate the practice.

Regarding the longer view of a relationship with a mentor, *do* the following:

- Think about, and ask, what does a mentor want from the mentor/mentee relationship? This question is most relevant to Type 2 and 3 mentoring. Are the mentors looking for a protégé to carry on their work? Someone to listen to their ideas and provide an objective, outside opinion? A future collaborator? Or are they primarily interested in the mentee's growth for its own sake, and that of the profession? How do the mentor's goals fit with the mentee's?

- Keep in touch after launching the next step of your career. Apart from the mentor's motivation of advancing individual planners and the profession, many mentors enjoy "riding along" with the mentee's career progress. Life takes on such urgency at the beginning of a career that it is easy to put off keeping in touch. Someday the mentee will be a mentor, so act with the consideration that you would want.

Here are three *don'ts* in the interpersonal realm:

- Be passive. Instead, prepare for mentoring sessions. Ask questions and follow up on suggestions and recommendations.

- Treat mentors like peers. Instead, treat them with a level of deference appropriate to their experience and wisdom. Don't say "we'll have to agree to disagree." Don't rely on peers for mentoring advice, even if they seem more relatable and sympathetic.

- Ask for feedback and then refuse to consider it. Don't be excessively defended.
- Be dramatic. The idealist planner's life *is* dramatic, with numerous life and career decisions to be made, but the mentors are older, have been through this period, perhaps have children the age of the mentee, and so are unlikely to be impressed with the drama.
- Don't depart from a mentoring relationship without communicating the decision and saying a proper thank you and goodbye. Be courteous and show gratitude.
- Don't tell mentors how busy you are. They probably have more on their plate.

Regarding using mentors as references and other protocols, ***don't***:

- Use the mentor's name as a reference without asking, unless there is a prior agreement about listing the person for all applications. Even if they have authorized the use of their name without permission, let them know each time as a courtesy.
- Don't submit a recommendation pretending to be the mentor.
- Don't take more credit on the resume than is true (e.g., claiming to be first author on a paper when you were the second author).

Don't fight your mentor more than fits the situation:

- Adopt the position, "that's what I'm like" if the mentor points out a path to personal growth, or a weakness or challenge that should be addressed. Give the point due consideration.
- Resent your mentor. Because mentoring relationships are voluntary, this may be difficult to imagine. But if a mentor points to a path that is uncomfortable, the mentees should assess their feelings and own them. The mentees may resent having some things drawn to their attention.

Boundaries in Mentor/Mentee Relationships

The professional and personal development of the mentor and mentee are more intertwined in "mentoring-by-doing" and life-coach mentoring. Career exploration, research, or work supervision relationships may lead to a more personal relationship. The mentor may seek to guide a mentee's personal development work, such as developing qualities of character. Conversations may turn to internal motivations. In this regard, the mentees should establish appropriate boundaries—the mentee should let the mentor know if that not desired. The relationship benefits from clarity about the level of privacy desired and any off-limits topics. This can be awkward, because mentees may be flattered by the attention, and there is a natural deference to title, experience, and age. It is best for the mentee to be honest. True mentors want nothing else but that which benefits the mentee.

Mentees will outgrow mentors. Sometimes, a message is right for one period in life but not another. Once a mentor helps a mentee reach a certain plateau, the mentee may want to take the next step on alone. It is also possible that the mentee may wish to take a pause for growth and experiences, only to reconnect at a later time. Being kind to mentors outgrown by keeping in touch is a good practice. Remember, the mentor has put the mentee before his or her own gain.

Finally, watch out for the occasional mentors who want to steal the mentee's work or use them without helping you. More benignly, they may seek to bring the mentee into their "production" machine—either in a research lab in academia or in practice—where they put their interest in using mentee's skills ahead of the mentee's growth.

And Now to You: A Mentoring Game Plan

As you can see, mentoring is varied and inclusive, but there is one type of interaction that is *not* mentoring. That's when a mentor tells the mentee what to do. At its best, mentoring gives you perspectives and tools to figure out things for yourself. It should help you define goals, think clearly, and solve problems. Mentors may suggest better thinking processes, but they should not take your experience from you.

Mentoring is a selfless act for the empowerment of another. Real learning comes from honesty, if mentor and mentee are open to learning. Mentoring reaches its potential when you own your decisions and career path.

Your career will be on a good path if you develop a plan for acquiring and benefiting from mentors. When faced with a challenging work decision or a job choice, it is relieving to have a person with whom you can honestly share your views and thought process. Use Table 11.1 as an ongoing working document to have a clear strategy for mentoring, but don't forget serendipity—the reasons for connections between mentors and mentees can be mysterious. Be open to mentoring from a wide a range of sources, and someday, be a mentor yourself.

Discussion/Reflection Questions for Chapter 11

1. Reflect on previous mentors, from school, sports, work, or religious institutions. What qualities of a mentor worked the best for you? How does the mentoring process work the best?
2. Imagine yourself a few decades down the road. Would you seek to mentor young planners? If yes, why would you do it? If no, why not? What would be the downsides?
3. Conduct a review of your "good manners" practices. Develop a "to-do" list: write previous mentors, create systems to remind you to say thank you, offer assistance to those who have helped you, etc.
4. Fill out Table 11.1 for your current experience. Make a six-month plan to address any gaps in your mentoring network.

References

Johnson, W. 2016. *On being a mentor: A guide for higher education faculty.* New York: Routledge.

Kram, K. 1985. *Mentoring at work: Developmental relationships in organizational life.* Glenview IL: Scott Foresman.

Chapter 12

Conclusion

Your Idealist Story

Here I am.
Who am I?

Our fireside chat is almost over, but a few embers are still glowing. The take-away? Think about *what* you are doing *while* you are doing it. Be a reflective planner. That's pretty much it.

Having started with the notion of idealism, I finish with a new appreciation of how planning requires both idealism and realism. You may lean more toward one aspect than the other, but we all encounter this tension in practice. Effective, inspiring planners prosper in it.

Miguel Vasquez's career path (see Figure 6.1) reminds us that we are in the process of writing the story of our careers. Pivotal moments, important mentors, and key decisions shape the story arc. I ask you to consider that story as you live it. The nature of planning—the idealism, the drama of politics, and the breadth of activities—means that there is no standard career. Every planner's career is a page-turner. You plan in community with reformers through the ages, whose commitment to the good lives on long beyond their own contribution. They are with you.

Admittedly, the day-to-day challenges of professional practice crowd out time for reflection. Starting out, practical matters such as salary, job location, and life obligations often drive career decisions. But when you look back at the end of your career, it *will* form a story, whether it's deliberate or happenstance. Reflecting on your planning career while doing it is the best way to match your passion and talents with the world's needs.

The work environment is too dynamic for a career plan blueprint—and you are too dynamic as a person—so consider Lew Hopkins's metaphor of planning as paddling a canoe in a moving stream (Hopkins, 2012). Actively navigate the stream rather than letting the current carry you where it will. Canoers assertively seek the smooth, deep water in the flow—and you should, too.

If you are looking for your first planning job, find the best fit you can, but by all means get started. If you are already working in planning, reflect on your job as a way of considering future steps. We planners should plan for our careers as well as for our clients and constituents.

Your Career Narrative

An idealist planning career relates to Joseph Campbell's idea of the "hero's journey," a process by which a person is called to a higher purpose, faces challenges along the way, receives help, has low points and crises, undergoes transformation, and then returns with new powers and perspective (Campbell, 2008). Some idealist planners see a hero's journey in their work. The journey is their own growth and their effectiveness in bringing repair and flourishing to the world. The calls to higher purpose are varied—environmental sustainability, affordable housing, equitable transit services, poverty alleviation, social justice, restorative design, and so on. The dangers are many—disillusionment or the prospect that a solution makes matters worse. This desire for the good plays out in the journey, as idealist planners experience success and setbacks.

In your career, job opportunities, mentors, purposeful action, chance, coincidences, and collaborations will offer opportunities to grow. The guest box writers throughout the book provide personal insights into this varied and somewhat mysterious process. Embrace it.

I find comfort in realizing that I am on a journey with like-minded planners. We set out on a road on which the path is unclear. I know that others have gone before me, faced challenges, and like me, didn't have the whole thing figured out. Knowing I am not alone, I accept setbacks and challenges. I am part of a community of planners. This realization helps shift any trepidation to respect for the journey as its own process.

You may object to this individualistic characterization of planning. We work in organizations that serve the collective, not individual planners' visions.

Planners comply with laws, city manager's and council's directives, and client and community wishes. No one wants "hero" planners *imposing* their vision on the community. So then, shouldn't you "remove" yourself—adapt your personal vision, avoid talking back, and play the prescribed role in your organization? Shouldn't you sublimate your own agenda?

I say no. You can have a personal agenda in a way that respects the organization and community in which you work. Planners are reformers, after all. Every planning context offers room for personal authenticity. Of course, this does not mean you always get what you want, when you want it. It doesn't mean that all options are on the table. It means showing up as a grounded person in the politically constrained world of planning. You don't control the outcomes, but you control yourself and your interpretation of things and your actions. Being authentic means being awake, relational, capable, and accepting of the world. This is the critical dimension of realism. As, of course, it is necessary to bring planning expertise and effective strategy along with your value agenda.

A caution about having a hero story is the potential for an accompanying "shadow" story—implicit, behind the scenes, less-lofty motivations. For example, counseling professionals may have an underlying desire to control others. Economists may have an aversion to the realm of feelings and messy human interactions. Activists may seek to be above reproach—safe—so no one can call them out. The less-pretty list of shadow motivations goes on and on: avoiding vulnerability, being special, feeling security and control, and avoiding moral dilemmas, complexity, and contradictions.

I suggest asking yourself if there is a "shadow" career story that goes along with your "official" one. Examine your internal motivations. Don't question your mission, but ground it as you work as a change agent. Acknowledging a shadow story, even if just to yourself, can check excess pride that might interfere with the work. It doesn't mean that your agenda changes, just your attitude towards it. Recognizing complex motivations will make you more empathetic and ultimately more effective.

Translating Reflection to Practice

It's one thing to be a reflective planner, but of course, you must demonstrate planning competency. Here, I present my takeaway messages about practice, based on a 40-year planning career (I started early):

- Build your practice around Paul Niebanck's notion of the planning enterprise: consciousness, comprehensiveness, collaboration, civility, and commitment to change (Niebanck, 1988).

- Think about the planning *process* while developing planning solutions.
- Don't be disrespectful of "this is the way we've always done it," but don't accept that as your model.
- Build professional credibility with attention to detail, accuracy, clarity, and timeliness.

For communication practices, I suggest the following:

- Become an expert listener and interpreter; learn how to understand the "story." No matter how compelling the numbers, analysis, and visuals, planning ideas should make sense as a narrative. Data require interpretation to have meaning.
- Learn how to see a situation through the other person's eyes—the community member, the elected official, the developer, the environmentalist, the student, and the homeless person. But don't be naïve about economic self-interest, xenophobia, and hatred.
- Don't demonize those with whom you disagree. First, learn about their perspectives and understand the facts and values that underpin them. Then disagree if it is appropriate. Use clearly articulated values and evidence to back your position. If their facts and values are incoherent, then fight that nihilism productively.
- Recognize that some planning differences stem from prioritizing different values, such as freedom versus collectivism. Learn how to disagree and rebuke in a friendly way. Be cautious about declaring evil, but fight it aggressively if you encounter it.
- Be boringly reliable.

For values and your conception of the public interest(s), consider:

- Your practice is embedded in politics: be realistic about politics but not beholden to it.
- Avoid planning dogma—it is the answer to yesterday's questions. Instead, cultivate an active imagination that sees planning problems anew. Be willing to be wrong.
- Maintain an internal dialogue about the public interest(s). Test your thoughts in dialogues with other planners, other professionals, the public, and elected officials.
- Maintain an internal dialogue about the ethics of your professional behavior. Discuss your interpretations with others. Allow that you may misstep. Take corrective actions and make amends if you do.

- Learn about whatever is "other" to you—political affiliation, class, race, ethnicity, country of origin, religious affiliation, gender identity, or sexual orientation. Pursue a vision of an inclusive society and work to bring people together while respecting difference.

For your emotional health, integrity, character, and career longevity, contemplate the following:

- Guard against being seduced by your powers—personal, political, technical, rhetorical, or otherwise.
- Accept that you won't get everything at once, but don't use that as an excuse for not trying. Be prepared to be broken-hearted when a vision is not realized, but don't dwell there too long. Some negative planning experiences offer lessons for growth.
- Understand that you could make things worse, unintentionally. Let that knowledge sober you up.
- Know that behaving ethically does not "cost" you in the long run, because your reputation is invaluable. Once lost, you cannot get it back.
- Find ways to heal the wounds you may endure if you really try, and continue to really, really try. Have a reasonable sense of your rights—avoid extremes of exaggerated rights and being a pushover. A riled-up person tends to forget what's important in the heat of the moment.
- Don't be a lone wolf—seek mentors, advisors, collaborators, and helpers.
- Take satisfaction that the planning profession offers the privilege to make the world a better place while making a living.
- Celebrate the planning profession with other planners.

This Is It

A reflective planning practice will help you navigate planning's idealism/realism tension and achieve authenticity as a change agent. There's no right place to land, just the right place for you. Accept your gifts and the obligations that come with them. You are headed toward the truth of your being—never accomplished, but a worthwhile journey, in some ways, the only journey.

A planning career is like building a ship while at sea—things are provisional. Seek to reduce the gap between the person within and the planner without. There is a heaviness to living in estrangement from true purpose, but once purpose is found, there is joy in aligning your work with it. Speak the truth to yourself as much as you can.

Planning is a continual, growth-inducing enterprise. It is not a problem to be solved but rather an encounter with humanity. Allow for imperfection in human affairs; don't chase away paradox. Stare down the frustrations inherent in planning in a liberal democracy with grit and grace. There is no other way. The first step is to do your duty, in hopes of realizing the satisfactions of improving the world. Live for something higher, something whose realization may not occur on your watch.

Of course planning is hard, but why shouldn't it be? Everybody's work is hard. Ditch diggers know their work is hard. Telemarketers experience soul-crushing rejection. Don't wait for inspiration or validation. An instant impact is rare, but lasting impacts are common. Change doesn't come fast and easy. Put the plough in the ground, and commence.

If you protect an inner compass of conscience, you will have insight that helps distinguish wrong from right. Everything matters—small actions can be the basis for big changes, positive and negative. It's not so much that "everything happens for a reason" but everything happens for reasons.

Engage idealism and realism in your planning work. This space is unstable, provisional, and the way to approach the truth of the matter. The extremes of fundamentalism and nihilism offer no opening for dialogue and transformation. A fundamentalist planner aligns with his or her tribe and will hear nothing else, whereas a nihilist planner avoids engagement.

A planner using a principled adaptability style navigates the space between idealism and realism as a relational act, through internal reflection and in dialogue with others. Idealism is emotional, as is engagement. In noting how emotions in planning have been ignored by scholars, Baum (2015) wrote that some plan with "half a mind," referring to the Enlightenment tradition of rational thinking without recognition of emotions. Although the principled adaptability planning style does not place emotions in a central position, it resonates with Baum's call to plan with a full mind—in my conception, idealism and realism.

"Idealism and realism" is an oxymoron. The concealed point is engagement, which carries the possibility of transformation. That engagement is a position of faith.

References

Baum, H. (2015). Planning with half a mind: Why planners resist emotion. *Planning Theory & Practice*: 16(4): pp. 1–19.

Campbell, J. (2008). *The hero with a thousand faces*. Third Edition. Novato, CA: New World Library.

Hopkins, L. (2012). *The logic of making plans*. New York, NY: Island Press.

Niebanck, P. (1988). Planning education: Unleashing the future. *Journal of the American Planning Association* 54(4): pp. 432–442. doi:10.1080/01944368808976670

Appendix A

Research on Generational Differences

Popular media reports suggest significant differences between generational groups such as Millennials, Generation X, and Baby Boomers. Having taught over many decades, I notice that current students define themselves strongly as individuals or as aligned with small affinity groups. Many resist being externally defined and feel judgment in being called Millennials or other generational labels. Although self-definition is a sign of emotional health, some of my students have taken this to a level to which they have anxiety about planning jobs in which they are a "cog in the wheel" of a large bureaucratic system.

The challenge in making personal observation as above is that I do not have pure objectivity about what I and my fellow planning students were like when we were in school. I'm not sure that we were much different. So for these questions, it is best to rely on empirical studies of generational differences. The research on generational groups reveals the following:

- Popular accounts of differences do not necessarily match up with empirical research: an age group may be characterized one way in popular media, whereas attitudinal surveys reveal different characteristics (Deal, Altman, and Rogelberg, 2010).

- There are differences between one generation's attitude about *another* generation and that other generation's own perceptions. For example, Generation X'ers who prefer to work independently may misinterpret and/or criticize Millennial planners' preference for group work as a desire for excess meetings (Myers and Sadaghiani, 2010).

- Studies must control for the age of respondent (e.g., Boomers at age 25 compared to Millennials at age 25). In addition, *circumstances* may affect attitudes separately from generational characteristics. For example, greater Millennial satisfaction with work, as reported in some studies, may stem from an appreciation for having a job because of the difficult economic times of the Great Recession (Kowske, Rasch, and Wiley, 2010).

Acknowledging the limitations discussed above, the literature associates the following characteristics with the current generation of young people:

- Career paths—they seek flexibility, work/life balance, a desire to be recognized, and are impatient for important roles (Smith and Nichols, 2015; Kuron, Lyons, Schweitzer, and Ng, 2015; Hershatter and Epstein, 2010; Myers and Sadaghiani, 2010).

- Communication at work—they prefer frequent, open, team-oriented, and less hierarchical patterns of interaction (Myers and Sadaghiani, 2010; Smith and Nichols, 2015; Hershatter and Epstein, 2010).

- Social perspective—they are aware of cultural diversity and seek close relationships (Myers and Sadaghiani, 2010; Smith and Nichols, 2015; Hershatter and Epstein, 2010).

- Personal qualities—they are confident, empathetic, and interested in public service (Deal, Altman, and Rogelberg, 2010; Myers and Sadaghiani, 2010; Smith and Nichols, 2015; Hershatter and Epstein, 2010).

Although these qualities have been found among the Millennial generation, a number of research studies suggest that the generations are more similar than different, or that the differences are modest when proper controls are applied (Kowske, Rasch, and Wiley, 2010; Smith and Nichols, 2015; Deal, Altman, and Rogelberg, 2010; De Hauw and De Vos, 2010).

References

Deal, J., D. Altman, and S. Rogelberg. (2010). Millennials at work: What we know and what we need to do (if anything). *Journal of Business and Psychology* 25(2): pp. 191–199.

De Hauw, S. and A. De Vos. (2010). Millennials' career perspective and psychological contract expectations: Does the recession lead to lowered expectations? *Journal of Business and Psychology* 25(2): pp. 293–302.

Hershatter, A. and M. Epstein. (2010). Millennials and the world of work: An organization and management perspective. *Journal of Business and Psychology* 25(2): pp. 211–223.

Kowske, B., R. Rasch, and J. Wiley. (2010). Millennials' (lack of) attitude problem: An empirical examination of generational effects on work attitudes. *Journal of Business and Psychology* 25(2): pp. 265–279.

Kuron, L., S. Lyons, L. Schweitzer, and E. Ng. (2015). Millennials' work values: Differences across the school to work transition. *Personnel Review* 44(6): pp. 991–1009.

Myers, K. and K. Sadaghiani. (2010). Millennials in the workplace: A communication perspective on Millennials' organizational relationships and performance. *Journal of Business and Psychology* 25(2): pp. 225–238.

Smith, T. and T. Nichols. (2015). Understanding the millennial generation. *The Journal of Business Diversity*, 15(1): p. 39.

Appendix B

Methods of Reflection

Reflection provides the path to wisdom—I think.

I say "I think" because some argue that it is action, not reflection, that stimulates growth. In this view, excessive navel gazing and continual internal dialogues are ways of avoiding decisions and action. When I say reflection, then, I don't mean reflection instead of action, but reflection-in-action. In other words, don't ask the world to stop, don't disengage, but do consider what you are doing while you are doing it.

Reflection is the cornerstone of recommendations provided throughout the book, yet it does not come naturally. Early in your education and career, pressing day-to-day issues crowd it out. I didn't reflect much when I was young. Recognizing this reality, I suggest methods of reflection that can be easily integrated into your life. Seek a reflection method that works for you, because nothing discourages it more than trying to force yourself to do it. A regular process of reflection is a great way to make career choices.

Journal and Write

I'll start with my favorite. Create a password-protected file on your computer and use it to write about successes, failures, hopes, anxieties, the meaning of things, concerns, and tough decisions that you face. Write letters that you never intend to send. Make lists, or write in a stream-of-consciousness style. Put it in verse if that opens you up to discovery and insight.

Store the journal in the Cloud so you can access it from your computer, tablet, or cell phone. Make notes when they come to you. Alternatively, go "old school" and rediscover cursive handwriting in a hard-copy journal. You may be surprised that your voice is different when handwriting than typing, and it may be different when printing or writing in cursive. If you are right-handed, try writing with your left hand. The point is to play around to allow free expression.

Write when you need to. Don't censor yourself. It is natural to reflect in a way that makes the writer look good, but that is truly a waste of time. If you write as if someone else is reading your journal, you will be writing press releases for an idealized version of yourself. Be honest. Write the truth even if you don't look good in the story.

What you write about is up to you. Sometimes, I rant about people I'm mad at, but this isn't often. More frequently I write about experiences and my interpretations of them. I express feelings, thoughts, and vague urgings. I write about upcoming decisions. If I am thinking too much about something, writing gets it out of my head, puts it on paper, and allows me to understand it more objectively. Writing allows different versions of "me" to speak. Don't write about the person you already know—the person you present to the world; write to find the person you are seeking to be.

Journaling is only one form of reflective writing. A planner can write poetry, short stories, or plays. There is surely a local writing group, or one online, that provides a community engaged in the same activity. Avoid types of writing that are so daunting that they produce writer's block or that lead you to think that you need a big chunk of time to write "properly." The important thing in journaling is to get the flow going. Just start. The book *The Artist's Way* (Cameron, 2002) suggests writing for 20 minutes each morning before doing anything else. This helps you to connect to what you dreamed about and gets things started before your rational editor wakes up and starts censoring.

Reflective writing and poetry are popular right now, so you will be the cool person in the office if you take this path. Once you have a writing practice, you may find that reading back over old journal entries helps put things in perspective. Sometimes it is useful to flip to a random page and just start reading. This can help you see what has changed in you and what in you still holds true.

Talk and Listen

There is an art to conducting a reflective conversation. It takes a conversation partner who understands the purpose of the conversation and who is willing to participate. Dialogue is a better word for it. A dialogue is a process of going deeper in conversation to get to the heart of the matter—to discover something, aided by an attentive partner. A dialogue is different from catching up, gossiping, or discussing the prospects for your favorite sports team. It isn't a debate in that there is no winning point, and it isn't venting your feelings. All of these types of conversations have their place, but dialogue will help you understand yourself.

A dialogue has prerequisites:

- A dialogue partner whom you trust, who will keep confidences if that is appropriate.
- A pre-dialogue discussion in which you explain what you are seeking. For example, if you need emotional support and sympathy, make your need clear. You may find healing in sharing and receiving support. That healing may help you reflect, but it's not the same as a dialogue seeking new insights, criticism, or helping you solve a specific problem.
- A place that is suitable for a long conversation and the appropriate time to have the dialogue.

The role of the dialogue partner is to listen without judgment, refrain from offering advice, and ask questions when something doesn't seem right. A dialogue partner may notice a blind spot—something you are avoiding. The dialogue partner is a guide in the conversation, not an advisor or amateur therapist.

Your role as the person initiating the dialogue is to tell the dialogue partner the general topic or issue of concern. You should be flexible about the conversation moving in different directions. And of course, offer to be a reflective listener if the dialogue partner has an issue to discuss.

Dialogue partners can include close friends, mentors, family members or family friends, or anyone who can sustain a deep and extended conversation.

Diagnose Your Ability and Interests

There are many types of personality assessment and career preference tools for reflecting on your life and career choices. These tools don't tell you what to do—it is always your choice. They categorize you, which could be inappropriate if it limits your thinking, but they are worth considering. Look at them as tools that help *you* think and reflect. Use them to compare what you know and what others say about you.

Many employers use the Myers-Briggs test in career coaching and team development, as discussed in Chapter 10. It asks a series of binary questions about your preferences in a variety of situations. As noted, the interpretation categorizes your responses in terms of four dichotomous dimensions: extroversion/introversion, sensing/intuition, thinking/feeling, and judging/perceiving. These qualities then form 16 personality "types."

My "type" understands the thoughts and motivations of others well, which is a good quality but isn't the best way to be a manager. I can have a tough time drawing limits and making decisions for the good of the larger group. Of course, such an insight does not mean I shouldn't be a manager—I've done it successfully. Rather, it suggests that I need to recognize that my empathy might not serve the performance of the organization.

The other great benefit of understanding "types" is the way it supports the planner in transitioning from an entry-level planner to a planning manager. Understanding types, you will be more adept at the interactions with your staff. You will know that a communication and management approach that works for one person will not work for another. The more you can shape your management and communication style to the individuals who report to you and to whom you report, the more effective you will be. This study of types will also increase your effectiveness in responding to elected and appointed bodies.

Myers-Briggs is just one of many tools that identify different personality "types" and characteristics. There are many options. Reflecting on your type and understanding that others have different types can help you make decisions and work more effectively with others.

Physical Activity That Produces Reflection

Reflection happens in many ways. An insight may come to you during a long walk in the woods or after raking leaves for a few hours. Moving your body, being in nature, and feeling genuine physical fatigue can disable the scripts running in your head—the ones that tell you who you are. Physical exertion allows other parts of you to make themselves known. Sometimes our bodies know things that our brains do not perceive.

Contemplative physical activity, such as yoga, can unlock reflective ability, but if weightlifting is your thing, that works too. The point is that there is a mind/body connection, and attending to your body helps your mind work better.

My bias is to physical activity outdoors without any entertainment. You may get the greatest benefit from experiencing yourself removed from your music, podcast, or audio book. Being alone is helpful. Physical strain reduces your ability to control your thoughts, and so you may go on a wild ride of fantasy, petty resentments, or issues morphing into other issues. Being bored allows for breakthroughs. Physical exertion breaks down barriers—after musing about many issues, sometimes the truth of a matter comes to you.

Another outlet is improvisation. If you're shy, learning to express yourself can be beneficial personally and professionally. Try an improvisation class or an acting for non-actors class where you can try on different roles and personalities and gain experience dealing with unfamiliar circumstances. Learning to conceal your emotions or expressing them in a powerful way may come in handy when dealing with difficult people, making presentations to large groups, or answering questions of executive management and elected officials. In addition to learning about self-expression, acting skills improve confidence, public speaking, resourcefulness, and success.

I don't fish, but those who do say it causes them to slow down and be attentive to world around them. Under these conditions, you can reflect.

Meditate

Meditation can be practiced in multiple ways. Some approaches seek to quiet the mind by distracting it with a mantra, which is a repeated word or phrase, gently replacing thoughts that come up by directing attention to the mantra. In this quieted mind, there is space for the murmurs of the soul to be perceived. This does not mean that answers should be expected from meditation, but new realizations or priorities might emerge. This quiet mind activity is *not* a replacement for rational thought; rather, it provides rich raw material for rational consideration.

Another meditation approach is analytical. Rather than replace thoughts with a mantra, give them deep consideration. Let's say feelings of anger arise about a colleague who hasn't fulfilled his work responsibilities. You can review the facts of the case, consider if you correctly perceive the situation, identify your needs, and try to see the issue through the other person's eyes. After such deliberation, you may decide the problem was just two people having a bad day, or you may decide to rebuke the person. In either case, you will do so having calmly and rationally considered the facts as you understand them, and considered how your values affect your deliberation.

I don't find any method of meditation to be superior. It depends on the inclination and makeup of the individual. If meditation appeals to you, try different methods until you find the right one.

Make Art

Art-making includes a wide range of activities from building a birdhouse to jamming on a guitar to creating an impromptu play with friends. For urban planners, a pop-up urbanism project may appeal, such as creating a parklet. Art-making trips up the part of the brain that is keeping a lid on things. Some people resist art-making because they judge the quality of the product. Rather, art-making can be seen as a process, as a means to achieving a goal of releasing deeper insights. They key is to not worry about whether the art is any good.

Here are some ideas for art-making for those who think they lack artistic talent. These projects avoid art where there is pressure to comply with conventional standards of representation and quality:

- *Make a collage.* Gather materials from a variety of sources, cut and tear them into interesting shapes, and glue them to a surface. This avoids tricky art materials and the intimidation of creating something that is representational. Making a collage of found objects in nature is another option, and it doesn't require special skills. Collage is fun and can be done with a group.
- *Write a group poem.* Assemble a group in a circle and send a piece of paper around. The first person writes a line to kick off the poem, folds the paper to hide the line that was written, and hands it off to another person to write another line. Because the next person does not know the previous line, all seriousness is eliminated. Go around the circle a few times and then unfold the paper so all the lines are visible. Read the poem out loud and enjoy the amusing non-sequiturs and sneaky insights that emerge. This process usually opens doors to reflection and insight.
- *Make something out of clay.* Wet clay in your hands brings you in contact with your ancestors, who fully lived in the tactile world. Making an object is an elemental task—feeling the material in your hands slows down your brain. Allow thoughts to bubble up as you create.

- *Organize a drumming circle.* A drumming circle requires someone to create and keep a steady beat around which others craft their rhythms. It works best when it goes on for long enough for the participants' hands and minds to relax and feel the beat. Fancy drums aren't needed—upside-down pails, water bottles filled with rice, and anything that makes a clicking noise can work. Assemble five to ten people and have a go at it for an hour or so. See what comes up at the end of the session.

- *Start a garden.* This isn't normally considered art-making, but if you have ever walked by (or made) a beautiful garden, you may know of the reflective benefits. Deeply observing growing plants and flowers over time, and getting your hands in the dirt, allows reflection.

- *Knit.* I've never knitted, but I've watched others do it and know that the focus on needles and yarn calms the mind and allows a concentration and stillness. Join a knitting club.

- *Create a play using handmade sock dolls.* Sock dolls are quick and easy to make using waste materials and supplies around the house. They are great props for role-playing job interviews and telling stories about your planning experiences.

These examples are only that: examples. Find the art-making practice that works for you, not to have the best garden or knitted sweater, but to give yourself time to reflect.

Join a Group on a Similar Journey

Forming a close community around a shared interest provides reflection opportunities. Playing soccer with a group of friends allows your core self to emerge so that you can see it and others can reflect back to you about it. On the team, for example, the way you respond to situations provide important information. Do you take fouls and the quality of refereeing seriously? If so, justice may be your touchstone. Or, if you find yourself in stitches, laughing after a silly and unsuccessful kick, then play and freedom are important to you. Or you may find meaning in the idea of team—a community in which the individual is subservient to something larger. Understanding that each team member has a different experience can hone your empathy.

Your core self can emerge when a familiar group helps you feel a level of trust, so you let down the guard of your everyday persona. Group acceptance lets you be yourself. You may not be aware of this self, but your teammates may give you insights. Ask them what they see. It doesn't have to be sports. Any kind of group will do—a bridge club, a painting group, or a hiking club.

When you are young, making new friends is easier as you enter school, move to a city for a job, or change jobs in the same community. The friend groups you make may last your whole life. I shared a house in college with four guys—three of us have kept in touch for over 40 years and get together every year. Our silly, wisecracking, and immature selves are instantly rekindled to cathartic effect. Even though it's hard to imagine 40 years into the future, the friends you make now may stay with you for your whole life. They will be sounding boards for you as you reflect on challenges and opportunities over your lifetime.

If you don't have friend groups, become a joiner. Expand your circle so that you can make long-term friends. If you "brand" yourself too narrowly, you may choose one affinity group and stick with that group. Having affiliations with multiple groups allows a broader basis for experiences and reflection. Insights about yourself and your purpose emerge when you are with a familiar group. If you are attentive to them, they won't get filed away as you return to your so-called normal life.

What to Do With Reflection

Use reflection to frame questions that might require more traditional career research, such as testing job prospects in your planning interest. Use it to identify issues associated with decisions that you are facing. Use it when you are in a jam—you don't know what to do but can't rely just on factual information. Use it to frame questions that you will explore later. Use it to find out who you are.

Reflection doesn't come naturally. You live in the here-and-now, and may not see a need to belabor personal feelings and intuitions. If that's you, give it a try, as a lark. Keep your role as the decider about whatever comes up. That way, you won't feel hostage to those thoughts and feelings.

It is true that reflection and vulnerability go hand in hand. Reflection takes self-confidence—that the version of you is strong enough to deal with it. Reflection undermines the "established" version of you. You may realize that you want to make an inconvenient choice, such as taking a lower-paying job, or embarrassingly, realize you aren't working in the right field. Allow enough vulnerability so that reflection guides you to the best path, personally and professionally.

Exercises for Appendix B

1. Keep a detailed log of how you use your time for a day or two. Categorize the uses of your time and see if there is something you can change to provide more time for reflection.
2. When possible, turn off your phone for one hour and assess the impact. See how that changes how you think and what you think about.
3. Brainstorm 10 reflection methods that you might try. Do one a week for the next 10 weeks.
4. Search the Internet for a fun class that you've always wanted to try, and take it.
5. Write a "morning page" (undirected free writing) every morning for two weeks.
6. Develop a simple strategy for capturing insights that may come to you throughout the day—a note typed in your phone, a voice recording, or a handwritten journal you carry everywhere. Set aside time to compile and summarize the notes.

Reference

Cameron, J. (2002). *The artist's way: A spiritual path to higher creativity.* New York, NY: Tarcher/Putnam.

Index